CAN AMERICA SURVIVE?

UPDATED EDITION

Can America
SURVIVE?

UPDATED EDITION

STARTLING REVELATIONS
AND PROMISES OF HOPE

JOHN HAGEE

HOWARD BOOKS
A DIVISION OF SIMON & SCHUSTER, INC.
New York • Nashville • London • Toronto • Sydney

Howard Books
A Division of Simon & Schuster, Inc.
1230 Avenue of the Americas
New York, NY 10020

Can America Survive? © 2010, 2011 by Pastor John Hagee

First Howard Books trade paperback edition March 2011

HOWARD and colophon are trademarks of Simon & Schuster, Inc.

For information about special discounts for bulk purchases,
please contact Simon & Schuster Special Sales at 1-866-506-1949
or business@simonandschuster.com

The Simon & Schuster Speakers Bureau can bring authors to your live event.
For more information or to book an event, contact the Simon & Schuster Speakers
Bureau at 1-866-248-3049 or visit our website at www.simonspeakers.com.

Designed by Joseph Rutt

Manufactured in the United States of America

10   9   8   7   6   5   4   3   2   1

The Library of Congress has cataloged the hardcover edition as follows:
Hagee, John.
   Can America survive? Startling revelations and promises of hope / John Hagee.
     p.   cm.
   Includes bibliographical references.
     1. United States—Foreign relations—2009–   2. United States—Foreign relations—
Middle East.   3. Middle East—Foreign relations—United States.   4. Bible—
Prophecies.   5. Christianity—United States.   6. Jerusalem in the Bible.   7. End of the
world—Biblical teaching.   8. Israel (Christian theology)—Biblical teaching.   I. Title.
   E907.H34   2010
   261.70973—dc22   2010012409

ISBN 978-1-4391-8985-6
ISBN 978-1-4391-9056-2 (pbk)
ISBN 978-1-4391-8993-1 (ebook)

Dedicated to the brave and heroic men and women in the United States military who have fought and died to birth and preserve freedom from 1776 until today. May God help us not to throw their valiant sacrifice to the wind by a federal government out of control!

Contents

PART FOUR
THE FINAL DAYS

PART FIVE
HOPE FOR A TROUBLED NATION

PART ONE

A Nuclear Iran

ONE

Anatomy of Disaster!

Where were you the day John F. Kennedy was shot in Dallas, Texas? If you were alive on planet Earth, you know exactly where you were and what you were doing when Walter Cronkite took off his thick black glasses and announced to America, "John F. Kennedy, president of the United States, died at 1:00 p.m. Central Standard Time."

He paused and looked again at the studio clock. "Some thirty-eight minutes ago." The seasoned newscaster momentarily lost his composure, winced, and cleared his throat before resuming with the observation that Vice President Lyndon Johnson would take the oath of office to become the thirty-sixth president of the United States.

The heart of America was broken!

We had been swept up in the dream that was Camelot. We wept as a nation when Jackie walked into the Capitol Rotunda with Caroline and kissed the flag-draped coffin of JFK. His cortege of matched, prancing black horses pulled the caisson past the White House and the Capitol for the final time while John-John saluted his father and our president with a final farewell. It was a tragic and heartbreaking moment in history America will never forget! There is no greater agony of the soul than to live in the wonder of what might have been.

Where were you on 9/11?

What did you feel when you watched radical Islamic terrorists fly hijacked commercial airlines as missiles of death into the Twin Towers in New York City?

What did you feel when you saw fellow Americans jumping to their horrific and gruesome deaths from hundreds of feet in the air in a futile attempt to escape the blazing inferno?

Every living soul was someone's beloved father or mother, someone's loving husband or wife, someone's cherished son or daughter that would never come home again. Their families would forever after gather on special days of celebration—Thanksgiving, Christmas, birthdays, and anniversaries—and look with pain and heartache at their pictures with tearful eyes knowing that the nightmare of 9/11 would never end in their lifetime.

What did you feel as you watched the Twin Towers implode, floor after floor, and in a handful of thundering seconds see concrete, steel, and the lives of three thousand fellow Americans crushed together into an eternal monument of pain and suffering.

Brave New York City firefighters dashed into the blazing inferno and gave their lives trying to save the lives of others. "Greater love has no one than this, than to lay down one's life for his friends" (John 15:13 NKJV).

They gave their all without hesitation. They died and will forever remain American heroes. We make a living by what we get out of life, but we make a life by what we give. No man was ever honored by what he received. Honor is the reward for what he gave. The New York City firefighters gave their all!

Do you remember American citizens running in terror down the streets of New York City, screaming as a massive mushroom cloud of dust from the Twin Towers filled the air and turned a golden day into darkest night? For the first time since the British burned the White House in 1813, we had been attacked in the continental United States—the land of the free and the home of the brave.

The American illusion of being untouchable by foreign military powers was shattered in a day by the agents of radical Islam. America would never be the same!

It couldn't happen . . . but it did happen!

THE PERFECT STORM

On April 12, 1912, the *Titanic* raced through the icy waters of the Atlantic trying to set a new transatlantic speed record. This mountain of steel and mechanical genius had been pronounced "the unsinkable ship"!

Minutes before the *Titanic* struck the iceberg, some of the richest and most powerful people in the world danced the night away, unaware that disaster was imminent and that the Angel of Death was aboard. They would have gladly traded their power and their fortunes for a crude lifeboat, but none was available for the more than 1,500 souls who drowned in the frigid waters of the Atlantic on this night of unspeakable disaster.

The demons of denial pushed the agony and horror off the celebrated ship. Even after striking the iceberg and with the ship sinking by the head and taking on tons of water, Mr. J. Bruce Ismay, president of the company that owned the *Titanic,* pledged to his powerful passengers: "Not to worry, all is well. This ship is unsinkable and it's clear as far as the eye can see."

That message was so desired by the masses that twenty-four hours after the *Titanic* was at the bottom of the ocean, twenty-four hours after 1,522 souls had slipped into eternity, the headlines in the New York papers screamed: "All Saved from Titanic After Collision."

Telegrams were received reading, "All Titanic Passengers Are Safe!" Another telegram read, "The Virginian Is Towing Titanic into Halifax." There was a total and complete denial of reality.

It couldn't happen . . . but it did happen!

The unthinkable horror became reality.

The unbelievable nightmare was a fact!

How did it happen?

Why did it happen?

It happened because a perfect storm of human error driven by the winds of complacency and overconfidence birthed an unspeakable disaster.

First, the well-known fact that there were not enough lifeboats— because the *Titanic* was said to be "unsinkable," which proved to be absolutely false—led to the deaths of many souls.

Second, there was no one to receive the distress signal from the *Titanic* as it was sinking because all ships closed their telegraph systems at midnight. This maritime law was promptly changed after the *Titanic* disaster so that all ships at sea would have an operator on duty twenty-four hours a day.

Third, had there been a ship nearby, the *Titanic* had no red flares that were the international maritime signal for "emergency" or "need help."

The *Titanic* had only white phosphorus flares used for many things, but never danger.

Think of it!

If they had had but one red flare, the ship *California,* which was less than ten miles away, might have seen it. It could have come quickly to the rescue and not one life would have been lost. One red flare could have saved 1,522 lives!

Fourth, there were no binoculars available to the watchmen in the crow's nest staring into the frigid and clear night looking for any sign of danger. When the watchmen spotted the massive iceberg by natural sight, it was too late.

With one pair of binoculars, they could have seen the iceberg in plenty of time to turn the ship away from danger and the certain death lurking beneath the icy water. One set of binoculars could have saved 1,522 lives.

Last, it was customary for all ships to measure the water temperature when in this part of the ocean. Water in the 30-degree range meant icebergs were near. They read water temperature by dropping a canvas bag overboard by rope and reading the seawater with a thermometer. The temperature of the seawater was then entered into the logbook for the captain of the ship to read.

In Senate hearings, it was discovered that the rope that let the canvas bag overboard was too short to reach the water in the ocean. It was too short because this was the largest ship in the world. The crew made a small but deadly miscalculation.

The seaman in charge of taking the temperature of the seawater filled the canvas bag with drinking water taken from the ship. When the captain read the temperature report in the log, there was absolutely no concern of danger.

Think of it!

Fifteen hundred and twenty-two of the most powerful people on the earth could have been saved if the rope had been long enough.

Why do I belabor this point?

Because America, believed to be the most powerful and "unsinkable" nation on the face of the earth, is now racing across the stage of history in a similar perfect storm—this one driven by the winds of political correctness, economic meltdowns leading to the death of the dollar, the rejection of Israel, the maniacal nuclear ambitions of the theocratic dictatorship in Iran, the ten prophetic signs that we are the terminal generation now being fulfilled in Bible prophecy for the first time in world history, and the very real fact that in the near future planet Earth is going to experience, on a specific day, global ecological disaster in which one-third of humanity will die.

The concepts are not mine, but those of St. John on the Isle of Patmos in the book of Revelation.

> *So the four angels, who had been prepared for the hour and day and month and year, were released to kill a third of mankind.*
> *—Revelation 9:15 NKJV*

Think it can't happen?
Think again!
St. John the Revelator confirms to his readers in all generations that follow him until the end of days . . .

> *"These words* are *faithful and true . . . Blessed* is *he who keeps the words of the prophecy of this book."*
> *—Revelation 22:6–7 NKJV*

America and Western civilization have made and are making a series of serious blunders that are now pushing America in the twenty-first century toward the edge of the abyss. It is far more than a banking crisis!

It is far more than just a credit crunch!

It is a perfect storm that has been brewing for centuries that is about to explode in all its fury affecting the lives of every person on planet Earth.

IN THE THROES OF DEATH AND BIRTH

In America, we are watching the *death* of capitalism and the *birth* of European socialism; because of our titanic debt, we are watching the *death* of the dollar. The *birth* of nuclear warfare in the Middle East with a nuclear Iran will change the world forever!

We are watching the *birth* of a shadow government of Czars that are not answerable to Congress and therefore escape the protections of the Constitution of the United States. This is not a government of "We the

People." We are watching the *birth* of a New World Order where nations surrender their sovereignty and follow a Global Czar that will be the world's new Caesar. The Bible calls him the Antichrist.

With geopolitical and financial danger signals in abundance the word of absolute denial we get from Washington is "All is well, America is the unsinkable nation, entertain yourselves by shuffling deck chairs on the *Titanic* while the band plays on."

Think it can't happen?

Think again!

Consider the following facts: Our recent credit crisis revealed that the Federal Reserve, which no one in America controls, has loaned $2 trillion in the span of two months but would not tell us to whom they loaned the money. Who asked for it? Who authorized the loan? *You*, the taxpayers of America, will most certainly pay for it.

America has ceased to be a producer nation and has become a consumer nation. Think what that could mean in a time of war for our national defense when we have to get what we need to defend ourselves from a nation or nations hostile to the United States.

We have intentionally dumbed down our schools, ignored our history, and no longer teach our students the founding principles of America. Students graduate who cannot read, write, or speak intelligently. A significant percentage do not graduate from high school, thus forever joining the legions of the unemployed and poverty-stricken who will be slaves of the state for life!

America lives under the iron fist of judicial tyranny. Federal judges who are not elected by the people rule over the will of the people after they go to the polls and vote. We do not have a government "of the people, by the people, and for the people." Why can't we have the right to vote federal judges off the bench?

The prophet Isaiah writes:

"Woe to those who decree unrighteous decrees, Who write misfortune,
Which *they have prescribed.*

—*Isaiah 10:1 NKJV*

Abortion is an unrighteous decree!

Roe v. Wade has made it possible for 40 million babies to be murdered in the wombs of their mothers. Mother Teresa said, "The nation that kills its unborn has lost its soul." I agree!

Think about it!

Forty million souls is a river of blood that cries out to God for justice.

Then the LORD said to Cain . . . "What have you done? The voice of your brother's blood cries out to Me from the ground."
—Genesis 4:9–10 NKJV

A CNN poll found that 61 percent of Americans oppose taxpayer funding of abortion. But we know from comments of top White House officials that the president himself will intervene behind the scenes to make sure that ObamaCare subsidizes abortion on demand. (The poll also found that 63 percent of Americans think that abortion should be illegal in most cases.)[1] Let me tell you why Social Security is broken and will remain broken. *Abortion!*

The Baby Boomers are retiring and there is no "next generation" to pay the tab for Social Security. They have been killed under the banner of the "right to choose."

This infamous law that celebrates *death* over life will be one of the principal causes for the *death of the dollar*! Why? Because capitalism thrives on supply and demand! If there is no demand for a product, the economic engines of America stop!

Fact! There will be no demand from 40 million Americans for new homes, new cars, or college educations. Why? They have been murdered through abortion!

Our universities and colleges are now filled with students recruited from foreign countries. They have no love or loyalty to America. They come from the global community with the "One World" view. They could not care less if America surrenders its sovereignty to the United Nations, and they are here by the millions. Is the big picture coming together?

We mainstreamed ACORN, a Marxist organization, which corrupted the political process of fair and open elections. Even after being caught on film educating prostitutes and their pimps on how to dodge taxation from the IRS and how to run a brothel with underage children, some

U.S. congressmen defended this toxic and corrupt organization. Why did they have such a vested interest in the preservation of Acorn?

Why did it take so long for someone in Congress to call for a full investigation by the FBI?

If there is no confidence in the political process through which we elect our leaders, there can be no confidence in government.

A NATION OF CONSUMERS

Long before America was founded, the Greeks decided that a democracy could never work. Their logic was that once the citizens discovered they could vote themselves money from the public treasury, their numbers and demands would grow until they outnumbered the financial producers in any democracy, bringing bankruptcy to the state. We are at that point in America! The welfare state has far more voters than those who pay taxes to pay for the demands of the welfare legions.

Washington's present solution is to tax those who are working day and night and to give it to people who are social parasites, who are able to work but refuse to do so. It's a numbers con game where the producers cannot reverse the burden of extreme taxation because the consumers are demanding more . . . more . . . more, and Congress, desiring to be reelected, gives them more. What happens when the producers stop producing? What happens when Washington runs out of other people's money to spend?

Consider the fact that there are about 8 million people in New York City, more or less. The vast majority of all taxes for New York City are paid by fewer than 45,000 people. The New York *Post* reports that almost 2 million New Yorkers fled the state over the past decade. They're leaving for new jobs, lower taxes, and better opportunities. Simply put, the state is in a self-inflicted economic death spiral that won't be solved by resorting to Albany's usual tricks.

Anyone who can read a newspaper knows that California is swimming in an ocean of debt.

We have reached a point in our national economy where the consumers outvote the producers and a change from the socialistic concept will not be possible. Remember: The government that's big enough to give you everything is big enough to take everything from you. You cannot tax your way to wealth. Socialism has failed in Europe and will fail miserably in the United States.

We are facing a nuclear war in the Middle East as Iran threatens to "wipe Israel off the map" and then release a sophisticated series of terrorist attacks against America via sleeper cells which are already here.

Our president has been much tougher on Israel than he has been on either Iran or North Korea, which is launching missiles at will, or Russia, which has bluffed America into backing away from the European missile shield, and Venezuela, whose leader Hugo Chavez never misses an opportunity to demonize America.

A CLEAR AND INCONVENIENT TRUTH

Why are we so tough toward our "only friend in the Middle East," while apologizing for America's strength before nations sworn to our destruction?

On November 18, 2009, America read this glaring headline: "Obama Calls Israeli Settlement Building in East Jerusalem 'Dangerous.' "

President Obama called it "dangerous" that Israel plans to add nine hundred new apartments to an existing Jewish settlement in East Jerusalem, an area Palestinians hoped to claim as their capital absent a peace agreement with Israel.

Prime Minister Benjamin Netanyahu said that building permits were permitted for construction in Gilo for what would be upscale dwellings in the lower-middle-class neighborhood.

The U.S. administration has roundly criticized the decision to expand the neighborhood, a point of bitter contention for Palestinians who wish to make East Jerusalem, as well as other sites holy to Jews, Muslims, and Christians, part of its capital in the future.[2]

There is a clear and inconvenient truth about Israel that America and Europe need to remember. That truth is: Israel is a sovereign nation and not a vassal state of the United States. It does not need the approval of the White House or the U.S. State Department to build in its capital city. This land was given to Israel by covenant from God Almighty to Abraham 3,500 years ago and that covenant stands *today*!

The president of the United States does not have the authority to tell the Jewish people they cannot live in East Jerusalem, their own capital, and/or in Judea and Samaria, where Jews have lived for millennia.

GOVERNMENT-CONTROLLED HEALTH CARE—IMPENDING DISASTER

Our health care system is broken, and the government wants complete control over your medical future. Just for good order, let's review the U.S. government track record for managing mega-corporations. Remember that health care is going to control 20 percent of America's income. This is HUGE!

- Medicare . . . BROKE!

- Medicaid . . . BROKE!

- Social Security . . . BROKE!

- Amtrak . . . BROKE!

- Health care . . . you guess!

Dr. Jeffery Flier's op-ed article in the *Wall Street Journal* diagnosed the Democrats' health care "reform" legislation. Here are some key excerpts:

As the controversy heads toward a conclusion in Washington, it appears that the people who favor the legislation are engaged in collective denial . . . In discussions with dozens of health-care leaders and economists, I find near unanimity of opinion that . . . the final legislation . . . will markedly accelerate national health-care spending rather than restrain it. Likewise, nearly all agree that the legislation would do little or nothing to improve quality . . . Worse, the legislation would undermine any potential for real innovation . . . by overregulating the health-care system . . . there are important lessons to be learned from recent experience with reform in Massachusetts. Here, insurance mandates similar to those proposed in the Federal legislation increased total spending.[3]

In case you're wondering, Dr. Flier is not on the payroll of some right-wing think tank; he's the dean of Harvard Medical School.

If the government gets control of the health care system, you can expect long delays for medical treatment. I get calls on a regular basis from friends in Canada, where socialized medicine reigns, asking for my help to get them into American medical facilities.

When you have a deadly cancer attacking your body and you can't get into a hospital for months, it's a death sentence.

Recently, the *Wall Street Journal*'s website posted two columns that exposed the glaring contradictions of the health care policy proposed before Congress.

In the first column, Peter Suderman notes that in our federalist system of government the states have been called "laboratories of democracy" free to try "novel social and economic experiments without risk to the rest of the country." Several states have already experimented with key elements of the proposed health care policy, and the results are not good.

The second column by Peter Suderman, entitled "Obama's War on Specialists," was an analysis of how the proposed health care plan will impact any American suffering from heart disease, cancer, or any ailment requiring a specialist. Here is what it said:

> Democrats are systematically attacking specific medical fields like cardiology and oncology . . . trying to engineer a "cheaper" system so that government can afford to buy health care for all . . . even if the price is fewer and less innovative ways of extending and improving lives . . . The increase in specialists has tracked advances over 50 years in medical science and technology. Democrats look at these advancements and see only the cost, not the benefits.
>
> Markets are supposed to determine the composition of the workforce, not a command medical economy run out of Washington . . . Americans might take a different view of health care "reform" if they understood that it means snuffing out the best medicine.

This is a very important point that cannot be ignored. In 2009, the director of the Congressional Budget Office told Congress, "In explaining why health costs rose over the past several decades, most analysts agree that *the most important factor* has been the emergence, adoption and widespread diffusion of new medical technologies and services"[4] (emphasis added). Do we want to save money by going back to 1970s technology, by denying MRIs, mammograms for women until they are fifty, and life-saving drugs like the socialized "command medical economies" in Europe?

The *Washington Times* recently pointed out a study by the University of Pennsylvania which shows that for the eight most common types of cancer, Americans have dramatically higher survival rates than Europeans. The study indicated, "For all malignancies, the five-year survival rate for men is 66.3 percent in America. In Europe, it is only 47.3 percent. The rate is 63 percent for women in America, but only 55 percent for European women." The lives these statistics represent are yours and mine!

It's *your life* that's on the line in the health care "reform" being presently considered in Washington, DC.

OUR MILITARY IS BREAKING DOWN!

Our military is breaking down! We are fighting two wars, Iraq and Afghanistan, and our economic engines are sputtering. General Stanley McChrystal has asked the president for 40,000 more troops in Afghanistan and as of this date, none has been sent.

In November 2009, U.S. Army Major Nidal Hasan murdered thirteen soldiers in cold blood at Fort Hood while shouting "Allahu Akbar" and firing his semi-automatic weapon, injuring thirty more. Military suicides and stress disorders are running off the chart.

Was Major Nidal Hasan a psycho under too much stress or was he a radical Islamo-fascist who was only practicing his faith? In chapter 2, I'll give you fourteen facts concerning this situation and let you decide.

What is the solution?

Could it be that too few are being required to do too much for too long?

The rights and privileges of veterans are being revoked, and the care of our military personnel is being conducted in rat-infested facilities that are substandard in third world countries. This is not the way to treat our heroes. This is not the mark of greatness.

General McChrystal, who was appointed by President Obama, is credited with capturing Saddam Hussein and killing the leader of al-Qaeda in Iraq, Abu Musab al-Zarqawi. The general told CBS reporter David Martin that he had talked to the president one time in seventy days.

This revelation comes amid the explosive publication of a classified report written by the general that said the war in Afghanistan *"will likely result in failure"* if more troops are not added next year.

Former U.S. ambassador to the United Nations John R. Bolton said the lack of communication with the general was indicative of Mr. Obama's misplaced priorities.[5]

THOUSANDS OF AMERICAN FARMERS ARE OUT OF WORK

A portrait of our food supply can be seen on national television with Sean Hannity of Fox News talking to thousands of American farmers who are out of work and cannot produce on their farms because the federal government has turned off the water to save a two-inch minnow that feeds the salmon in Washington State.

Think about it!

Farms in California that are usually lush and green with vegetables now look like a dry and barren desert. Farmers who want to work can't work because environmental extremists see a two-inch minnow as having more value than human life.

Everyone who eats has an interest in agriculture! Reduced farming will lead to food shortages, food shortages will lead to food fights, rioting, and martial law.

WAKE UP, AMERICA!

Wake up, America! This is not going to happen . . . it is happening right now.

Through tax-and-cap and a plethora of other methods to increase your taxation, people will stop working, work less, or lie to the IRS about their taxes to survive. You can't spend your way to wealth, and taxation shuts down the economic engines of any family or nation.

Simply stated, America's present economic crisis was caused by widespread greed in government and on Wall Street. That corruption has not been corrected and cannot be legislated out of existence. Our economic future is very uncertain!

Could the reason why America's financial masterminds are announcing that the financial crisis is over be because they are standing on the crow's nest staring into the future without binoculars? Lurking just ahead of America and the world, a radical Islamic terrorist attack that could make 9/11 pale by comparison or an attack on several American cities simultaneously that will shake the economic foundations of the nation.

THE NIGHTMARE OF RADICAL ISLAMIC TERROR

Recently, the FBI arrested radical Islamic terrorists making bombs for Denver, Dallas, and New York. Congratulations to the FBI for its fantastic efforts to keep us safe.

The worst nightmare for the intelligence community has become reality: American Muslims going abroad to be trained in the art of terror to return home and kill us as a tribute to their theology of death. Or homegrown radical Muslims like Major Hasan.

Think the unthinkable!

In the near future a nuclear Iran, whose passion is to utterly destroy America and Israel, will have the power to do the "unthinkable."

The *New York Times* reports:

> The Israelis have argued that there will be little or no warning time before Iran completes building an actual weapon, especially if Iran has hidden facilities. Israeli officials cite two secret programs in Iran, Project 110 and Project 111, the code names for what are believed to be the warhead design programs run by Mohsen Fakrizadeh.
>
> Israeli officials say privately that the Obama administration is deluding itself in thinking that diplomacy will persuade Iran to give up its nuclear program. Even inside the White House, some officials think Mr. Obama's diplomatic effort will prove fruitless.[6]

The only thing that can prevent the imminent nuclear attack on America, Europe, and Israel is to prevent Iran from becoming a nuclear nation. The best way to win a nuclear war is to make sure it never starts.

America's government does not presently have the will to face down Iran with the military option. Can it be that Europe and America will stand down and let one of the smallest nations on Earth, Israel, attempt mission impossible to save themselves from a nuclear holocaust and give Western civilization a very brief time to solve the problem?

Think the unthinkable! Think about a day in the near future when you may see a screaming headline on your newspaper: "Nuclear Bombs Crush Seven American Cities!"

Millions dead . . . chaos reigns.

Think it can't happen? Think again!

Paul L. Williams, a former consultant to the FBI on terrorism, claims these seven cities as being New York, Miami, Houston, Las Vegas, Los Angeles, Chicago, and Washington, DC. He warns that the attacks are planned to occur simultaneously at the seven cities.

Paul Williams indicates "that there is empirical proof that al-Qaeda possesses nukes. British agents posing as recruits infiltrated al-Qaeda training camps in Afghanistan in 2000. In another instance, an al-Qaeda operative was arrested at Ramallah with a tactical nuke strapped to his back."[7]

If you are having trouble believing that teams of terrorists maintaining a nuclear weapon in the United States wouldn't be detected, think about this. Williams reports that there isn't just one team, but at least seven. They are working with mosques and Islamic centers. In the United States, a federal judge will not provide any FBI or law enforcement agent with a warrant to search a mosque or an Islamic center for any reason since such places are listed as "houses of worship."[8]

Intelligence experts believe Iran has developed the technology to unleash an electromagnetic pulse (EMP) designed to be used against America in a time of war.

Here's what the EMP does. This electromagnetic blanket does not kill people . . . it kills electrons. In short, it stops every form of electricity instantly and for months, maybe years. Here's how it could be used against America in warfare.

A fake satellite crossing over America at the height of 280 miles suddenly explodes over the Great Plains of the United States, releasing several pounds of enriched plutonium, blanketing the United States of America with gamma rays. Instantly, in a fraction of a second, all electrical power is cut off, and cut off for months.

No lights or refrigerators will work in your home. Every ounce of food you have will rot in your freezer. Your car won't work because it starts with electricity. Trucks won't work, meaning transportation bringing you everything you use will stop. All machinery will stop. The radio and television stations will go off the air. Planes that are in flight will crash because their electronic systems will fail. The missile systems will fail to function. We will cease to be a superpower in a fraction of a second.

The president will not be able to communicate with his military people in the field because the phones will not work. America's refineries will shut down. There will be no gas and no oil. The gas at the service station won't be available because those pumps get the gas out of the ground with electricity. Computers won't work, which means city, state, and government offices will be shut down. There will be a nationwide food and gas shortage within a few days.

You say this can't happen?

The enemies of democracy are planning it right now! It's not new. It's been talked about for decades. Only now, rogue states have the ability to put this weapon to use, and it will happen unless they are stopped by force.

Can Iran do it?

Our government says yes. Iran is presently ruled by a theocratic dictatorship under Ahmadinejad who would be more than willing to use those weapons to destroy America and Israel.

The *Congressional Report* reads: "Even primitive scud missiles could be used for this purpose (electronic blankets). And top U.S. intelligence officials reminded members of Congress that there is a glut of these missiles on the world market. They are currently being bought and sold for about $100,000 apiece." [9]

Think about that!

This great, magnificent, "unsinkable" nation so technically oriented has created an obvious Achilles' heel: electricity. With one $100,000 missile fired from a used submarine two hundred miles offshore and a few pounds of enriched plutonium exploding over the United States, every form of electricity would stop instantly and for months. In one second, we would be living in the nineteenth century. Military experts believe that Iran would launch this electronic blanket as the opening shot of a nuclear war.

9/11 proved that radical Islam has the will to kill us. When Iran gets nuclear weapons they will have the power to kill us. Headlines that you could read in the near future will be a global game changer: IRAN HAS NUCLEAR WEAPONS.

Think it can't happen?

It probably already has!

In the following chapter some very creditable people believe it has . . . everyone except America.

TWO

Iran Is Ready for War!

The intelligence coverage of Iran's nuclear readiness varies greatly. One reason for the extreme variation is that if American intelligence admits there is a problem, they must take positive action to solve the problem.

Punting the "nuclear crisis" down field is comforting to the general population who are absorbed by *Desperate Housewives* and *Dancing with the Stars,* comforting to politicians running for office who have mastered the art of almost saying something while standing boldly on both sides of every issue on the evening news.

It's very much like the owner of the *Titanic* cheerfully admonishing his deluded silk-stocking millionaires with "all is well" as the nose of the ship was sinking into the frigid waters of the Atlantic, the eternal resting place of more than fifteen hundred souls.

This "see no evil" political skill was demonstrated recently by the U.S. intelligence community in the Senate Foreign Relations Committee hearings as reported by the *Washington Times*.

Nicholas Burns, former Undersecretary of State for Political Affairs said: "There is no question [Iran is] seeking a nuclear weapons capability. No one doubts that."

No one?

Actually, America's spy agencies belittle the Iranian threat. On March 12, 2009, the CIA released a report to Congress that concluded: "We do not know whether Iran currently intends to develop nuclear weapons."

Their report was a rework of the controversial conclusions made in the December 2007 National Intelligence Estimate to wit that Iran had stopped its nuclear weapons program in 2003 and kept it frozen. The U.S. spy agencies reached this dubious conclusion while apparently knowing about the secret nuclear site near Qom. Why the discrepancy?

HOW THE CIA GOT IT WRONG?

The following shocking report comes from Edward J. Epstein of the *Wall Street Journal* concerning the unspeakable bungling by the CIA: "In a stunning departure from a decade of assessments, the 2007 National Intelligence Estimate on Iran declared: 'We judge with high confidence that in the fall of 2003, Tehran halted its nuclear weapons program.'" [1]

Unfortunately, as the Obama administration has now acknowledged, the NIE's conclusion was dead wrong, costing us precious time in dealing with a serious threat. What caused such a disastrous mistake?

As James Risen, the *New York Times* national security reporter, explains in his book *State of War*, in 2004 a CIA communications officer accidentally included data in a satellite transmission to an agent in Iran that could be used to identify "virtually every spy the CIA had in Iran." [2]

This disastrous error was compounded because the recipient of the transmission turned out to be a double agent controlled by the Iranian security service.

This allowed the Iranian security service to control the information these agents provided the CIA, which may have been vulnerable to receiving misleading secret intelligence that Iran had abandoned its nuclear ambitions.

HOW EFFECTIVE ARE SANCTIONS?

The following report comes from Representative Elton Gallegly (R-CA) who is a senior member of both the House Foreign Affairs and Intelligence Committees as told to the the *Jewish Journal*. [3]

Now that the president has signed into law additional sanctions aimed at stopping Iran's nuclear weapons program, will the sanctions work?

One key to that question is whether the president allows all the sanctions in the new law to take effect or if he will use the considerable waiver authority of the White House before giving the green light to Congress for the sanction bill's final passage in June.

The new law depends heavily on the willingness of the White House to fully implement it. There is considerable doubt about this since no U.S. administration has fully implemented the previous sanctions on Iran in place since 1996.

The other key ingredient to the success of the new sanctions is timing. Several, including Central Intelligence Director Leon Panetta, have said that sanctions, no matter how strong, may be too late. If that is the case, the United States needs a backup plan in place if Tehran is undeterred. Tehran's goal is not just to "wipe Israel from the map" but to directly threaten U.S. security and interests.

RUSSIA HELPS IRAN FUEL
FIRST NUCLEAR POWER PLANT

On August 21, 2010, history will record the infamous marriage between Russia and Iran as nuclear partners wedded for the purpose of dominance in the Middle East.

On this day of infamy, Russia supplied fuel to the nuclear power plant located in the southern city of Bushehr. Both Russia and Iran insist that Iran's nuclear program is for peaceful purposes, though many in the international community are deeply suspicious.

"From that moment the Bushehr plant will be officially considered a nuclear energy installation."[4]

Russia has been building the nuclear project at Bushehr for fifteen years at the cost of 1 billion dollars. Sergei Kiriyenko, the director of Russia's Nuclear Agency, Rosatom, was present for the August 21 ceremony that was also "attended by the Iranian vice president Ali Akbar Salehi, who also heads the Atomic Energy Organization of Iran."[5]

Iran, under United Nations sanctions because of concern that it is concealing a nuclear weapons program, is the first Middle East country to produce atomic energy.

"As long as there's an Iran problem, the West will need Russia," said Rajab Safarov, head of the Center for Contemporary Iranian Studies in Moscow, "and Russia will feel like an important geo-political player."[6]

"Just keeping up tensions in the region is beneficial to Russia because tensions keep up the price of crude oil and block Iranian gas from the world market," said Mikhail Krochemkin, director of East European Gas Analysis, a Malvern, Pennsylvania, based industry consultant.[7]

ENRICHMENT CONCERN

The United States has repeatedly stated they recognized Iran's right to produce nonmilitary nuclear power. Iran is the world's fourth largest producer of crude oil in the world; why do they need nuclear power for civilian purposes?

If their purpose for producing nuclear power was completely for civilian use, why did they hide their nuclear ambitions from the UN's International Atomic Energy Agency?

Russia is playing both ends against the middle with Iran. They are both the carrot and the stick. Russia supported a fourth round of UN sanctions against Iran (the stick) and then fueled their nuclear facility at Bushehr (the carrot).

Russia has offered Iran the delivery of the very sophisticated and powerful S-300 antiaircraft missiles, which would make an Israeli attack on Iran's nuclear facilities a virtual mission impossible.

"Russia shouldn't overplay its hand because Iran is a potential arms buyer and could meddle in the mainly Muslim North Caucasus Region," said Ruslan Pukhov, director of the Center for Analysis of Strategies and Technologies in Moscow. "Russia may have lost 4.5 billion dollars in future contracts because of the delay in delivering the S-300 missiles according to Pukhov."[8]

Fyodor Lukyanov, editor of the Moscow-based journal *Russia in Global Affairs,* said, "If Russia had refused to finish Bushehr it would have ruined relations (between Russia and Iran). The question is if relations between Russia and Iran will develop into the future?"[9]

The answer to this critical geopolitical question is YES!

According to the writings of the Prophet Ezekiel, found in chapter 38, Russia and Iran will join forces in the future to lead an Islamic military juggernaut that will invade the nation of Israel. This Russian-Iranian Islamic coalition will also be joined by Libya, Ethiopia, and Turkey.

The result?

The Islamic coalition will be wiped out by the hand of Jehovah God. It will take the State of Israel seven months to bury the dead of the invading army. It will take seven years for Israel to burn the weapons of war brought into the land of covenant by the invaders.

God's purpose in this Gog-Magog War?

"So the house of Israel shall know that I am the LORD their God from that day forward. . . . Then they shall know that I am the LORD their God, who sent them into captivity among the nations, but also brought them back to their land . . . and left none of them captive any longer. And I will not hide My face from them anymore; for I shall have poured out My Spirit on the house of Israel," says the Lord God.

—Ezekiel 39:22, 28–29 NKJV

How close are we to this monstrous war in the Middle East? Read the following headline:

ISRAEL HAS UNTIL WEEK'S END
TO STRIKE IRAN NUCLEAR FACILITY

Former U.S. Ambassador to the United Nations, John Bolton, made the above startling statement as reported by Fox News. This statement was made when Russia pledged to load nuclear fuel into the Bushehr reactor. The logic is that when the nuclear fuel makes contact with the rods, any explosion caused by a military preemptive strike would trigger massive and harmful radiation throughout the Middle East.

Israel obviously did not attack!

But will they . . . and when?

Ambassador Bolton continued by saying: "What this reactor does is give Iran a second route to nuclear weapons in addition to enriched uranium. It's a very, very huge victory for Iran. Iran will have achieved something that no other opponent of Israel, no other enemy of the United States or in the Middle East has, and that is a functioning nuclear reactor." [10]

Iranian leaders dared Israel to take military action against the nuclear reactor. Iran's defense minister, Ahmad Vahidi, was quoted in the Iranian media as saying Israel would be taking a huge risk if they attacked Iran in the future: "We may lose a power plant, but the whole existence of the Zionist regime will be jeopardized." [11]

THERE'S A CLEAR AND PRESENT DANGER

Ambassador John Bolton addressed a live audience of five thousand plus people over national television at the annual "Night to Honor Israel" at Cornerstone Church in San Antonio, Texas. The following are comments and excerpts taken entirely from Bolton's speech, which was warmly and enthusiastically received by the pro-Israel audience. He addressed the crisis the world faces in the Middle East saying:

Today we're in a "very difficult position." This phrase is often used to apply to the Middle East . . . and Israel finds itself in a very difficult position. What saddens me at the moment is that one of the reasons it's a difficult position is because of the political administration in power in Washington today. This effort that's underway for the last twenty months, I am very concerned is not an effort to bring peace to the Middle East; it's an effort to impose peace on the Middle East.

When you find yourself in a negotiation with two sides, one of which is reasonable and one of which is not, the temptation is always to pressure the reasonable side. That's exactly what's happening today. This is not an idle concern or one that really rests entirely on Israel. I'm worried about this peace initiative for what it's doing to the United States . . . because it will fail!

Diplomacy can only bridge differences that are bridgeable. And indeed of a peace negotiation, you have to have two sides that are capable of negotiating on behalf of their respected principles, and then carrying out the commitments that they make. That is not the case, I'm sad to say, on the Palestinian side.

So eventually, these peace negotiations will break down. That will leave the United States in a worse position in the Middle East and around the world because everyone will understand that we have committed enormous amounts of energy and American prestige to an effort that will fail. It will leave the United States in a worse position after it happens.

And let's be very careful here; the Security Council is being asked to recognize a Palestinian state within the 1967 borders or to have the Palestinian Authority call on the United States to recognize a Palestinian State within the 1967 borders.

This is a fundamentally dangerous threat to the continued legitimacy of the state of Israel. Why is that? Because it is fundamental to the definition of a state that it has recognizable borders. You can't recognize an entity that doesn't control territory. That's basic to customary international law. So to say that the Security Council and the United States would recognize a Palestinian State within the '67 borders means that every inch of Israel's territory beyond the '67 borders is illegitimate and has to be given back to the new Palestinian State.

Let's be very clear! If and when these negotiations between Israel and the Palestinians break down, the momentum will inevitably turn to this question of recognition. And I think and urge all of you to be clear that the American people will not accept the imposition of a Palestinian State on Israel.

NOW, THIS IS A VERY CLEAR AND PRESENT DANGER. But it is not the most important risk to Israel today. Our government's concentration on the Israel-Palestinian balance reflects a fundamental misunderstanding of where the real danger in the Middle East is. It is the conventional wisdom in Europe that everything in the Middle East will get better if only you could impose peace on Israel. This is 100 percent wrong! It is like looking through the wrong end of a telescope.

Addressing the role of Iran as the world's central banker of international terrorism, Ambassador Bolton said:

It's an equal opportunity funder of terrorism, Sunni or Shia, it doesn't make any difference. Iran funds Hamas in the Gaza Strip. It funds Hezbollah in Lebanon. It funds terrorists, who are killing Americans and other NATO forces in Iraq. It funds its once sworn enemy, the Taliban in Afghanistan who is also devoted to the deaths of our young men and women over there. It will fund anybody, in short, that advances its interest.

And yet, it is this government [speaking of Iran's theocratic dictatorship], this terrorist-supporting government that our president wants to extend an open hand to. It's no wonder they laugh at us in Tehran. [The audience exploded with applause.]

I think we need to understand it is never American strength that's provocative. What's provocative is America's weakness, and we are being very provocative today.

THERE IS A WAR PLAN IN PLACE FOR IRAN

Retired Air Force Lt. General Thomas McInerney, a former fighter pilot, described in detail how a military attack on Iran could wipe out their nuclear power:

> A pentagon strike against Iran would rely heavily on the B-2 bomber and cruise missiles to try to destroy the regime's ability to make nuclear weapons, analysts say, after the top U.S. military officer said a war plan is in place.
>
> The missiles, fired from surface ships, submarines, and B-52 bombers, would take out air defenses and nuclear related facilities. The B-2s would drop tons of bombs, including ground penetrators, onto fortified and buried sites where Tehran is suspected of enriching uranium to fuel the weapons and working on warheads.
>
> It would be primarily an air attack with covert work to start a "velvet revolution" so that Iranian people can take back their country.[12]

The question now is this: Does the U.S. military in the Obama administration have the will to attack Iran now that the Russians have fueled the nuclear plant at Bushehr, risking radiation over the Middle East? This attack would also destroy any chance the Obama administration would have to bring peace in the Middle East between Israel and the Palestinians.

Will America wait until Iran gives nuclear suitcase bombs to radical Islamic terrorists who are already in America waiting for the nuclear jihad to begin?

Think it can't happen?

Think again!

UN SECRET REPORT SAYS IRAN HAS THE ABILITY TO MAKE A NUCLEAR BOMB NOW!

Senior staff members of the UN nuclear agency have concluded in a confidential analysis that Iran has acquired "sufficient information to be able to design and produce a workable" atomic bomb. The report's conclusions, described by senior European officials, go well beyond the public positions taken by several governments, including the United States.

According to the information gathered from rogue nuclear experts around the world, Iran has done extensive research and testing on how to fashion the components of a weapon.

The report, titled "Possible Military Dimensions of Iran's Nuclear Program," draws a picture of a program begun in 2002, run by Iran's Ministry of Defense, "Aimed at the development of a nuclear payload to be delivered by using the Shahab 3 missile system," which can strike the Middle East and parts of Europe."[13]

HOW MANY SECRET NUCLEAR FACILITIES DOES IRAN HAVE?

Recently, the chief of Iran's Atomic Energy Organization, Ali Akbar Selehi, told Iranian State Television that he was working out a timetable for the inspection of the just revealed secret nuclear site outside of Qom.

Then Selehi said he was preparing a letter for international inspectors "about the location of the facility *and others.*" That got everyone's attention.[14]

Some intelligence officials and inspectors have suspected that Tehran maintained a network of secret nuclear sites, projects, and personnel that paralleled the nuclear program that Iran declared. Said in another way, they have as many *secret* facilities as they have facilities that are *known*.

BRITISH INTELLIGENCE

Britain's Secret Intelligence Service (SIS) says that Iran has been secretly designing a nuclear warhead "since late 2004 or early 2005," an assessment that suggests Tehran has embarked on the final steps toward acquiring nuclear weapons capability.

Britain has always privately expressed skepticism about the U.S. assessment on Iran but is only now firmly asserting that the weapons program started in 2004–2005.[15]

Here is the "$64,000 question" that no one is asking: If Iran produced this nuclear energy for peaceful purposes, as they claim, why did they have to do it in secret? Clearly, their purpose is to fulfill the promise of

President Ahmadinejad of Iran to the Islamic world: "to wipe Israel off the map." Iran is ready for war!

It is important to remember that the Iranians are a very intelligent and persistent people. They are Persians and are insulted if you refer to them as Arabs. The Persians invented the game of chess that requires contestants to always conceptualize future moves—not to be fascinated by where you are at the moment on the chessboard, but how to cleverly maneuver your forces to entrap your opponent into submission. Iran has been manipulating Washington, DC, and Europe on their political chessboard with great finesse. Stated bluntly, Iran has been playing the West like a harp.

Rather than face the wrath of the UN Security Council that claims it is determined to call a halt to Iran's illicit nuclear program, Ahmadinejad has bought Iran more time without making any serious nuclear concessions. During the six years that Iran has been negotiating with the West over its nuclear program, it has taken the politics of delay and procrastination to an entirely new level.

Keep the talks going, keep those centrifuges spinning, and stay on schedule with their nuclear weapons program. From the outset of the West's attempts to negotiate a nuclear deal with Iran, the Iranians have promised much and delivered little. They have repeatedly promised to freeze their enrichment activities at Natanz, only to resume enrichment once they realized there was nothing the West could do to stop them.[16]

IRAN: A BRUTAL THEOCRATIC DICTATORSHIP

The Iranian people now find themselves under the iron fist of a theocratic dictatorship. This is a corrupt, fanatical, ruthless, and unprincipled regime which is detested by the masses as seen in the riots following the last presidential election.

Tens of thousands of Iranians took to the streets to cry out for freedom and democracy. Some were beaten, others were shot dead while the world watched on global television without a word of encouragement coming from America.

It is urgent that Americans understand the brutality and cunning of this theocratic dictatorship. How brutal are they?

During the Iran-Iraq War, the Ayatollah Khomeini imported 500,000 small plastic keys from Taiwan. The trinkets were meant to be inspirational. After Iraq invaded in September 1980, it had quickly become clear that Iran's forces were no match for Saddam Hussein's professional, well-armed military. To compensate for their disadvantage, Khomeini sent Iranian children, some as young as twelve years old, to the front lines. There, they marched in formation across mine fields towards the enemy, clearing a path with their bodies. Before every mission, one of the Taiwanese keys would be hung around each child's neck. It was supposed to open the gates to paradise for them.

At one point, however, the earthly gore became a matter of concern. "In the past," wrote the semi-official Iranian daily *Ettela'at* as the war raged on, "we had child-volunteers: 14-, 15-, and 16-year-olds. They went out into the mine fields. Their eyes saw nothing. Their ears heard nothing. And then, a few moments later, one saw clouds of dust. When the dust had settled again, there was nothing more to be seen of them. Somewhere, widely scattered in the landscape, there lay scraps of burnt flesh and pieces of bone." Such scenes would henceforth be avoided, *Ettela'at* assured its readers. "Before entering the mine fields, the children [now] wrapped themselves in blankets and they roll on the ground, so that their body parts stay together after the explosion of the mines and one can carry them to the graves." [17]

At the height of the Iran-Iraq War, the child volunteers of Iran were part of a Revolutionary Guards' mobilization force, known as the Basij. They reached a total strength of 400,000 children. [18]

The willingness of the Iranians to fight and die when the cause is hopeless is demonstrated in this Iran-Iraq War. The war could have been over after its first two years, when Iran recovered the territories it lost from the initial assault that had been launched by the armies of Saddam Hussein in 1980.

However, Iran kept the war going for another six long years, despite losing hundreds of thousands of its people and facing repeated chemical attacks upon its troops. Iran's absolute fanaticism could not be deterred. The Islamic Republic continued to fight on even as Tehran itself absorbed hundreds of Iraqi missile attacks toward the war's end.

At the time of the Islamic Revolution, Dr. Hadi Modaressi provided some insight into this military behavior that would become a trademark of Tehran's policies in the coming years: "We welcome military aggression against us because it strengthens the Revolution and rallies the masses around it."[19]

The Western mind cannot grasp the fanaticism of this radical Islamic culture of death. Consider the following comparison between Hitler's Nazis and the Islamo-fascists led by Ahmadinejad of Iran.

HITLER'S NAZISM AND AHMADINEJAD'S RADICAL ISLAM

Who was Adolf Hitler, and what was his agenda?

In 1933 Winston Churchill gave a modern-day prophecy warning of Germany's anti-Semitic leanings; "There is a danger of the odious conditions now ruling in Germany being extended by conquests to Poland, another persecution and pogrom of Jews being begun in this new area."[20] Churchill's prediction came to pass within ten years. Who was this German leader, and how did he come to office?

Adolf Hitler was born in Austria on April 20, 1889. Hitler's hatred of the Jewish people was greatly influenced by the works of Dr. Karl Lueger, the anti-Semitic mayor of Vienna; Adolf Stoecker, a leading anti-Semite of the nineteenth century; and by philosopher Eugen Duhring and journalist Wilhelm Marr, who expounded biologically founded anti-Semitism.[21]

At the age of thirty, Hitler produced his first anti-Semitic writing when he was asked to answer the question, *Why did Germany lose World War I?* In his hateful response, Hitler established three crucial points; first, the Jews were the reason for losing the war, second, Jewish identity should be established by race not religion, and third, the approach to the Jews should be that of "rational anti-Semitism," which espoused the "removal of the Jews altogether."[22]

Through his virulent hatred, Hitler authored the book *Mein Kampf,* meaning "My Struggle," during his short imprisonment for attempting to overthrow the Bavarian government. In his book, Hitler blamed the Jews for everything he hated and claimed that the Jewish people were slowly taking over the country, even though they accounted for about 1 percent of the population. Through propaganda and violence Hitler's influence rapidly grew, and by 1932 he became the leader of the Nazi party, the largest party in the state with nearly 13 million votes. After continuing to spew anti-Semitic lies and terrifying his opponents through the brutal acts of violence of his Brownshirts, also known as storm troopers, Hitler became Germany's dictator shortly after the 1933 election, even though the Nazi party did not win the majority vote. Hitler coerced himself into power.[23]

Hitler was now in position to carry out his Final Solution; the systematic elimination of the Jewish people from the face of the earth! Hitler was true to his vision, by the end of his life; Hitler was responsible for the death of over 6 million Jews.

Who is Mahmoud Ahmadinejad, and what is his agenda?

Ahmadinejad was born on October 8, 1956, in Iran. He was raised in Tehran where he attended the university and became politically active. Influenced by professors, writers, and dissidents looking to overthrow the Shah's regime, he secretly produced and distributed an anti-Shah propaganda magazine called *Jiq va Dad,* which means "Scream and Shout." The young student nonconformist was suspected of planning and participating in several terrorists activities prior to being appointed mayor of Teheran, including taking hostages at the U.S. embassy in Teheran in 1979.

While serving as mayor, Ahmadinejad repealed reforms established by earlier moderate rulers and imposed cultural restrictions favored by Iran's more radical religious leaders. With the help of his charismatic personality and persuasive political skill coupled with the endorsement of the religious faction that included the Supreme Commander, the Ayatollah Khomeini, Ahmadinejad became the president of Iran in 2005.

Ahmadinejad has made no qualms about his hatred of Western society, going so far as calling for a baby boom to almost double the country's population to 120 million for the express purpose of threatening the West. He also emphatically deems that the United States perpetrated the horrors of September 1, 2001, on the Twin Towers in New York. He stated to the United Nations General Assembly that the "crises facing capitalism and the Western-dominated world order will record that a failing dominator used the attacks as a pretext for occupying two countries, Afghanistan and Iraq." Ahmadinejad further stated that the United States proceeded to use the events of 9/11 to "prolong a dying world order of domination."[24]

More radical is Ahmadinejad's hard stance on the development of nuclear weapons and the destruction of the State of Israel. A fervent Holocaust denier, Ahmadinejad calls the atrocities committed against the Jewish people "a myth." He is broadly known for his anti-Israel rants, including those he has delivered to the United Nations Assembly. His most infamous statement is that Israel should be "wiped off the face of the map," which he delivered in Teheran at the World Without Zionism Conference. During his visit in Lebanon in October of 2010, Iran's president was quoted as saying, "The entire world should know that the Zionists will disappear. Today the Zionist occupiers have no choice but to surrender to reality and return to their homes and countries of origin."[25]

Like Hitler, Ahmadinejad has instituted strict measures to control free speech and suppress any opposition to his regime through harassment and imprisonment. And like Hitler, Ahmadinejad is now in position to carry out his "Final Solution," the systematic elimination of the Jewish people from the face of the earth via a nuclear holocaust.

Much has been written of the Nazi-Islamic alliance which concludes that during the 1930s Muslims of all nationalities were sympathetic to Hitler and Nazism. Mutually, Hitler and Himmler had respect for Islam. Hitler said that it would have been better if Germany had possessed the "Mohammedan religion rather than the 'meekness and flabbiness' of Christianity."[26]

At the same time, Nazi-like movements began to spring up in the Arab world. There were the "Nazi Scouts" of Arab youth in British-mandated Palestine, which were based on the Hitler Youth, the "Green Shirts" of Egypt, and the Syrian Social Nationalist Party. Even the Muslim Brotherhood of Egypt was influenced by the Nazis in its political ideology, and many fleeing Nazis were warmly welcomed in Arab countries after World War II.

Nazi ideology also had an effect on Iran. In 1935, Persia was renamed Iran (Land of the Aryans).[27] There was also an Iranian Nazi party known as SUMKA or the National Socialist Political Party of Iran whose own Nazi-like symbol has a striking resemblance to the Nazi Swastika.[28]

The Grand Mufti of Jerusalem, Haj Amin al-Husseini, went to Germany in 1941 to meet with *Adolf Hitler* in an effort to persuade him to expand the Nazis' anti-Jewish program to the Arab world. Hitler believed the Arabs were Germany's natural friends because they had mutual enemies—the Jews. The Mufti offered Hitler his "thanks for the sympathy which he had always shown for the Arab and especially Palestinian cause, and to which he had given clear expression in his public speeches."[29]

Germany stood in active opposition to the Jewish national home in Palestine and would furnish aid to the Arabs involved in the same struggle. "Germany's objective . . . solely the destruction of the Jewish element residing in the Arab sphere. . . . The Mufti was the most authoritative spokesman for the Arab world during that time in history."[30]

In 1945, Yugoslavia sought to indict the Mufti as a war criminal for his role in recruiting twenty thousand Muslim volunteers for the *Nazi* SS, who slaughtered the Jews in Croatia and Hungary.[31]

NAZISM, RADICAL ISLAM, AND ANTI-SEMITISM

After WWII, Europe was covered in the blood of 6 million Jews who were systematically slaughtered by Adolf Hitler through Nazism and the Final Solution. The world today is facing a blood bath that will far exceed that of the over 60 million people who died in WWII—this time at the hand of another militant leader: Mahmoud Ahamadinejad. Through radical Islam and nuclear warfare (if he carries out his threats), the world as we know it will come to an end.

Nazism: *Sought to dominate the world with an exclusive Aryan rule.*
Hitler claimed, "The struggle for world domination will be fought entirely between us, between Germans and Jews. All else is facade and illusion. Behind England stands Israel, and behind France, and behind the United States. Even when we have driven the Jew out of Germany, he remains our world enemy."[32]

Radical Islam: *Seeks the total Islamization of the world.*
Numerous passages in the Qur'an show that Mohammed imagined Islamic world domination: "He it is who sent his messenger . . . that he may cause it [Islam] to prevail over all religions." [33] M. M. Ali, renowned translator of the Qur'an in English, designates these three passages as "the prophecy of the ultimate triumph of Islam in the whole world." [34]

Nazism: *Hitler's hatred of the Jews was mirrored by the Nazi party*
The Nazi party believed that all Jews were racially the same and greatly inferior to the Aryan race. This radical viewpoint was further fueled by writings such as Hitler's *Mein Kampf.*

Radical Islam: *The radical form of Islam cries for jihad, which means "my inner struggle."*
The Qur'an specifically refers to "striving in the way of Allah." Radical Islamists believe that all non-Islamists are infidels and should be eliminated. Section 7 of the Hamas Covenant states that "The messenger [Mohammed] said, 'The Muslims will fight the Jews and the Muslims will kill them, until the Jew hides behind the stones and the trees, and then the stones and the trees will say, 'Oh, Muslim, Abd Allah, there is a Jew who is hiding, come and kill him.'" Another quote in the Qur'an concerning the Jews: "The Jews are a nation of liars. . . . The Jews are a treacherous, lying, and evil people." [35]

Nazism: *Sought to annihilate the Jews.*
Hitler believed: "By warding off the Jews, I am fighting for the Lord's work." He arrogantly spewed on another occasion, "Today I will once more be a prophet! If the international Jewish financiers inside and outside of Europe should again succeed in plunging the nations into a world war, the result will not be the bolshevization of the earth and thus the victory of Jewry, but the annihilation of the Jewish race throughout Europe." [36]

Radical Islam: *Ahmadinejad promises to "wipe Israel off the face of the earth."*
Iran's maniacal leader stated in 2008 that "The Zionist [Israeli] regime is dying. The criminals assume that by holding celebrations . . . they can

save the sinister Zionist regime from death and annihilation."[37] Sheikh Muhsin Abu Ita stated on the Al-Aqsa channel that "the annihilation of the Jews is a wonderful blessing." Dr. Ahmed Bahar, acting speaker of the Palestinian parliament stated that "the Jews are cancer, and they and the Americans should be destroyed to the last person."[38] Another radical cleric was quoted as saying that all non-Muslims were "filthy" and encouraged Muslims to take part in a jihad against the infidels.[39]

Nazism: *Created a propaganda tsunami against the Jews.*
Joseph Goebbels spearheaded the Ministry of Propaganda. He was a "master manipulator who threw gasoline on the fires of anti-Semitism." The main objective of the Germany's well-oiled propaganda machine was to portray the Jews as subhuman. He depicted the Jews as "race defilers," "vermin," and as the "official enemy of the state." Goebbels succeeded in his diabolical mission through every means possible, including feature films; bogus radio programs and newsreels; and false documentaries, newspaper articles, and periodicals. The Nazi propaganda machine fabricated textbooks as well as children's story books.[40] Once that goal was accomplished, it was easier to condone the Führer's Final Solution.

German children's textbooks taught that Hitler was a Nordic warrior and that Jews could not be trusted. Children's books depicted evil caricatures of Jews and taught the bigotry of racial biology. The following is a verse in a German children's book in 1939: "The Devil is the father of the Jew. When God created the world, He invented the races: the Indians, the Negroes, the Chinese, and also the wicked creature called the Jew."[41] Eventually Jewish teachers and students were removed from German schools. German youth were taught to hate Jews; the Hitler Youth group grew to nearly 9 million strong and assisted the Nazi's in indoctrinating Germany's young in military training and radical racist ideology against the Jewish people.[42]

Radical Islam: *Continues active propaganda against the Jews.*
Today's world is drowning in a sea of lies, half lies, and damaging misinformation about the free world, the Jews, and Israel. In a recent article in the *Jerusalem Post,* writer Fern Oppenheim states, "Children's TV shows, textbooks, etc., teach young Palestinians that Israelis have no historical ties to the land, that Jews are evil, that terrorism is justified, etc., the

children targeted are being brainwashed to believe what they are being taught. Unlike adults, they are not yet able to assess the quality of information being fed to them. They become the unwitting vessels of the poison being served."[43] In his article, "Saudi Arabia's Dubious Denials of Involvement in International Terrorism," Dore Gold, former Israeli Ambassador to the United Nations, describes a "kindergarten graduation involving some 1,600 Palestinian pre-schoolers, where children wore uniforms and carried mock rifles. There was a reenactment of lynching Israelis and other terrorist attacks. One five-year-old girl dipped her finger in what was supposed to be Jewish blood and displayed it before cameras. The photo was posted on the Al-Jamiya Al-Islamiya website that sponsored the event."[44] Both Nazism and Radical Islam seek to influence the minds of the future.

Does the Bible recognize this evil against the Jews? Yes. David gives the prophecy of this continue hatred against the Jewish state:

> *Do not keep silent, O God! Do not hold Your peace, and do not be still, O God! For behold, Your enemies make a tumult; and those who hate You have lifted up their head. They have taken crafty counsel against Your people, and consulted together against Your sheltered ones. They have said, "Come, and let us cut them off from being a nation, That the name of Israel may be remembered no more." For they have consulted together with one consent; they form a confederacy against You.*
>
> *—Psalm 83:1–5 NKJV*

God showed David that Israel's enemies will surround her and conspire against her for her demise; He also showed Isaiah that He will defend Israel against her enemies:

> *"You whom I have taken from the ends of the earth, and called from its farthest regions, and said to you, 'You are My servant, I have chosen you and have not cast you away: Fear not, for I am with you; be not dismayed, for I am your God. I will strengthen you, yes, I will help you, I will uphold you with My righteous right hand.' Behold all those who were incensed against you shall be ashamed and disgraced; they shall be as nothing, and those who strive with you shall perish.*

You shall seek them and not find them—those who contended with
you. Those who war against you shall be as nothing, as a nonexistent
thing. For I, the LORD your God, will hold your right hand, saying to
you, 'Fear not, I will help you.'"

—*Isaiah 41:9–13 NKJV*

Radical Islam has now brought jihad to America.

This is a war they fully intend to win, a war many of America's political leaders refuse to recognize even exists.

On December 25, 2009, a Nigerian man on a flight from Amsterdam to Detroit attempted to ignite an explosive device hidden in his underwear. The explosive device that failed to detonate was a mixture of powder and liquid that did not alert security personnel in the airport. The alleged bomber was Umar Farouk Abdulmutallab.[45]

On May 2, 2010, in New York City, authorities discovered a bomb in a smoking vehicle parked in Times Square. They arrested Faisal Shahzad, a Pakistani who recently became a naturalized U.S. citizen, and charged him with attempted use of a weapon of mass destruction and several other federal charges.[46]

Further evidence that radical Islam has declared war against America is evidenced in the Fox News report as given by Sean Hannity on February 17, 2009.

The Fox News report showed a frightening film of U.S. terrorism training camps operating on American soil. "Islamic terrorist camps are operating right here in America in our backyards. The group, Muslims of America, or Jamaat ul-Fuqra, as they're called in Pakistan, have established over thirty-five communities across the United States.

The group claims to be peaceful, but a video revealed that they call themselves "The Soldiers of Allah," featuring Sheikh Mubarak Ali Gilani, the mastermind and the leader of the group here in America.

The video goes on to teach Islamic followers tactics in guerrilla warfare, including scaling mountains, subduing enemies, murdering guards, hijacking cars, kidnapping, weapons training, and setting off explosives.

Gilani is a Pakistani national best known for being the person that journalist Daniel Pearl was on the way to meet in 2002 when he was abducted and eventually gruesomely beheaded.[47]

The Islamic Army is not coming to America; they are here! They live in your neighborhood and are waiting for orders to attack a slumbering America.

Muslim TV Mogul Is Accused of Beheading His Wife

This shocking story was carried by the *Buffalo News* stating that the founder of American-Islamic TV station is accused of beheading his wife.

> The gruesome death of Orchard Park resident Aasiya Zubair Hassan, who was found decapitated, and the arrest of her estranged husband are drawing widespread attention, as speculation roils about the role that the couple's religion may have played.
>
> Muzzammil Hassan, 44, was arrested . . . and charged with second-degree murder after telling police his wife was dead at the office of their television station in the Village of Orchard Park. . . .
>
> "This was apparently a terroristic version of honor killing, a murder rooted in cultural notions about women's subordination to men," said Marcia Pappas, New York State president of the National Organization for Women. . . .
>
> While domestic violence affects all cultures, Muslim women find it harder to break the silence about it because of the stigma, she said.
>
> "Too many Muslim men are using their religious beliefs to justify violence against women," she said. . . .
>
> A teacher of family law and Islam at the University at Buffalo Law School, [Nadia] Shahram said that "fanatical" Muslims believe "honor killing" is justified for bringing dishonor on a family.[48]

Honor Killing in a Parking Lot

A young Iraqi woman—Noor Faleh Almaleki—whose father, by his own admission, hit her with his car because she became too Westernized, died from her injuries after lying in a coma for nearly two weeks. Police say her father ran down her and her boyfriend's mother with his Jeep as the women were walking across the parking lot in the west Phoenix suburb of Peoria.

The father fled the scene for the United Kingdom, which denied him entrance and sent him back to Atlanta, where he was arrested. County Prosecutor Stephanie Low told a judge that Almaleki admitted to committing the crime.

"By his own admission, this was an intentional act and the reason was that his daughter had brought shame on him and his family," Low said. "This was an attempt at honor killing." [49]

Police said the Almalekis moved to Peoria from Iraq in the mid-1990s. Evidently, after living in America for more than a decade, the theology of death did not surrender to the love of life.

JIHAD: A CLEAR AND PRESENT DANGER TO THE WEST

While sitting on the platform waiting for my time to deliver the keynote address at the Night to Honor Israel event, I heard this astonishing testimony from David, a person I have known for years as a man of truth, honor, and integrity.

David and his wife were on a vacation in an Arab country when they heard the call to prayer echoing across the city from the Islamic mosque nearby. Their guide was a young Arab man who was the portrait of poise and sophistication. He was immaculately dressed, he spoke the English language flawlessly, and was totally confident as a consummate professional.

With the echoes of the call to prayer reverberating between the buildings, David asked his young Arab guide, "Are you Muslim?"

"Absolutely," was the immediate and polite response.

"My wife and I are Christians. If the spiritual leader now making the call to prayer were to ask you to kill Christians, would you?" David asked.

Without hesitation the educated, poised, and sophisticated young Arab guide said, "Yes!" Why? Because his interpretation of his faith demands that he hate Christians, Jews, and anyone else who will not proclaim, "There is no God but Allah."

Another case in point is Abdurahman Alamoudi, once a prominent figure in the American Muslim community, who had been invited to the White House on numerous occasions, who was also an admitted supporter of Hamas and Hezbollah. Speaking before the Islamic Association for Palestine's 1996 convention in Illinois, Alamoudi predicted that Muslims would one day take over America, saying:

> I have no doubt in my mind, Muslims sooner or later will be the moral leadership of America. It depends on me and you, either we do it now or we do it after a hundred years, but this country will become a Muslim country. And I [think] if we are outside this country we can say, "Oh, Allah destroy America," but once we are here, our mission in this country is to change it.[50]

ISLAMIC POPULATION BOMB

Few Americans consider the power and influence Muslims demand as a result of the Islamic population bomb. A Muslim man is permitted to marry up to four wives at a time and birth control is not typically on his mind.

The most famous Muslim in the world today is Osama bin Laden, who is one of fifty-three children.[51] He himself has twenty-seven children.[52] Look at those numbers. If you look at Osama bin Laden and his father, they have produced eighty children. How many parents do you know in America, Christians or Jews, who have produced that many children in such a brief period of time?

The Islamic population bomb is what is tipping the scales in Europe. Once the Muslims become the majority, they will start demanding more rights in government. They will demand more representation.

The Civil War in Lebanon happened when the Muslims became the majority with the influx of Palestinians out of Jordan when King Hussein kicked Yasser Arafat out of Jordan in the Black September conflict. Yasser Arafat and the PLO joined forces with the Muslims in Lebanon and declared war on the Christians. The strategy of militant Muslims in conquering a new country is to concentrate their numbers in a specific region and take it over via population explosion. That's why they view their war with America as a fifty-year war that they fully intend to win.

9/11: THE TERROR BEGINS IN AMERICA

On 9/11 Islamic terrorists flew hijacked commercial airliners into the Twin Towers of New York City killing three thousand wonderful American people. They went to work that day not knowing it would be their last day on the earth. They went to work to provide for their wives, children, husbands, and families. They died horribly—some jumping to their deaths to escape the flames.

I guarantee that Khalid Sheikh Mohammad and the four thugs who helped plan this murderous deed will have high-profile criminal attorneys lining up for the "honor" of defending these murderers against the United States. This trial will give global terrorism a platform to praise and deify the crimes of these mass killers, inspiring millions of young Muslims to match or surpass their acts of murder.

It sends the signal to all terrorists to stop fighting in Iraq or Afghanistan and come to America where you will be given a high-profile ACLU lawyer at no cost to defend you. You will be covered on national and global television for months and become a hero to all terrorists. Bring the fight to the streets of America. Be charged in America, tried in America and, who knows, you might be acquitted in a jury trial. Remember: They turned O. J. Simpson loose.

Holding these trials in civilian courts for war criminals is an act of massive irresponsibility in government. Why? Because our CIA, under oath, is going to have to testify and give classified information and secret data in an open court that will be a treasure trove for radical Islam.

America will be put on trial, and the practices that kept us safe after 9/11 will be exposed, condemned, exploited by radical Islam, and Americans will die in the future because those protections for our citizens will be removed. How positively stupid!

Here are some bipartisan reactions to the news:

- Senator John Cornyn (R-TX): "These terrorists planned and executed the mass murder of thousands of innocent Americans. Treating them like common criminals is unconscionable."[53]

- Rep. Peter King (R-NY): "This, I think, will go down as one of the worst decisions any president has ever made."[54]

- Tim Brown, a former New York City firefighter: "The only thing they're going to do is give them a stage to mock us . . . and this makes me sick to my stomach."[55]

- Senator Joseph Lieberman (ID-CT): "The terrorists who planned, participated in, and aided the September 11, 2001, attacks are war criminals, not common criminals. Not only are these individuals not common criminals but war criminals, they are also not American citizens entitled to all the Constitutional rights American citizens have in our federal courts. The individuals accused of committing these heinous, cowardly acts . . . should therefore be tried by military commission rather than in civilian courts in the United States."[56]

MUSLIM'S WEBSITE CALLS FOR GOD TO "KILL THE JEWS!"

A New York bicycle cabbie, who last year used his website to mock the beheading of journalist Daniel Pearl, posted a prayer calling for the murder of Jews and exhorting Muslims to "throw liquid drain cleaner in their faces." And there's nothing authorities can do about it.

Yousef al-Khattab, who runs RevolutionMuslim.com and pedals a pedicab in New York City, insists the words he has posted on his website are a prayer and not a threat and that his hatred is protected by the First Amendment.

"If it was a threat, I'd be in jail," the forty-one-year-old al-Khattab said on his website from his home in Queens. "I'm asking my God, that's what it is. Every supporter of Israel is an enemy combatant, and the immune system is not anti-Semitic for resisting disease." Al-Khattab called on Allah to carry out "wrath on the Jewish occupiers of Palestine and their supporters."

"Please throw liquid drain cleaner in their faces," he wrote, "burn their flammable sukkos while they sleep . . . Oh God, answer my prayer." ("Sukkos" refers to the Jewish holiday during which the Jews build and eat their meals in outdoor huts known as "sukkahs," which represents the huts the Jews lived in during their exodus from Egypt.)

Judge Andrew Napolitano, senior legal analyst for Fox News, said the posting is "absolutely protected by the First Amendment."[57]

The posting reflects the "prayer of every true Muslim," al-Khattab

said. Every true Muslim would say the same thing. The pedicab operator for the past three years is married with four children and said he has
driven plenty of Jewish passengers without incident.

"I've never killed one . . . I suffer from mental Tourette's [syndrome]. I
say what's on my mind. We have freedom of speech." [58]

Al-Khattab stated that his mission is "preserving Islamic culture" and
seeking support of the "beloved Sheik Abdullah Faisal, whose preaching
the religion of Islam and serving as a spiritual guide." [59]

Sheik Faisal was convicted in the United Kingdom in 2003 for spreading messages of racial hatred and urging his followers to kill Jews and
Westerners. In sermon recordings played at his trial, Sheik Faisal called
on young, impressionable Muslims to use chemical weapons to "exterminate unbelievers" and to "cut the throat of the Kaffars [nonbelievers]
with a machete." [60]

JIHAD AT FORT HOOD

Every American should be outraged about the murderous rampage
against U.S. soldiers in Fort Hood, Texas, by jihadist Major Nidal M.
Hasan, who killed fourteen and wounded thirty. I am aware that pres-
ently only thirteen counts of murder are being charged against Major
Hasan, but one of his victims was pregnant and that baby, in the eyes of
God, is a living soul. He killed fourteen people!

Can you believe it?

America has been fighting radical Islamists around the world for eight
years, and one of the greatest tragedies in U.S. military history happened
on a U.S. military base at the hands of an Islamic terrorist who was a
U.S. Army officer.

Major Hasan's attack was the third incident this year in which U.S.
military installations were targeted by radicals. The sleeper cells buried
in the U.S. military are watching how the government handles Hasan's
case with kid gloves. It's an invitation for future deaths of America's military personnel.

In September, two North Carolina men were charged for conspiring
to kill U.S. personnel at Quantico, home of the Marine officer training
school and the FBI Academy.

In June of 2009, Abdul Hakim Mujahid Muhammad, an American

Muslim convert fired at two soldiers outside a recruiting center in Little Rock, Arkansas, killing one and injuring the other.

Here are the facts concerning Major Hasan. You decide if he was an Islamic radical carrying out the principles of his faith.

1. Several months before the tragedy, Major Hasan defended Muslim suicide bombers on his webpage and compared such acts to the sacrifice a U.S. soldier makes when he falls on a grenade to save his fellow soldiers.[61]

2. Colonel Terry Lee, who worked with the killer, said Major Hasan said, "Muslims shouldn't be fighting Muslims." In June 2009, when a Muslim convert assassinated a U.S. soldier at a recruiting station in Little Rock, Arkansas, Colonel Lee said that Major Hasan seemed happy about the event and that he was confronted by other officers.[62]

3. No one seemed to notice the significance of the attire Major Hasan was wearing the morning of his premeditated murders. It was captured on a store surveillance video where he bought coffee and put on national television. Hasan was wearing the *shalwar-kameez,* the traditional attire worn by Pashtuns on both sides of the Pakistan-Afghan border. Hasan was dressed for war.[63]

4. Major Hasan passed out Qur'ans on the morning of the shooting.[64]

5. Survivors in the facility where Hasan went on his murderous attack reported that he yelled, "Allahu Akbar [Allah is great]" before he opened fire. This is the same phrase the jihadists used on 9/11 and which has been repeated by our enemy in every Islamic attack on America.[65]

6. Lieutenant Colonel Val Finnell, Hasan's classmate at the Uniformed Services University of Health Sciences in Bethesda, Maryland, told Fox News: "There were definitely clear indications that Hasan's loyalties were not with America. Hasan told his classmates and professors, 'I'm a Muslim first and I hold the Sharia, the Islamic law, before the United States Constitution.' "

   Major Hasan is an officer in the U.S. military who took an oath to defend the Constitution of the United States against all enemies both foreign and domestic.

His remarks are words of outright sedition. Why didn't the professors and officers in Bethesda confront him? Lieutenant Colonel Val Finnell states: "They were too concerned about being politically correct."

7. Lieutenant Colonel Finnell recalled one time when his classmates were giving presentations in an environmental health care class on topics like soil and water contamination and the effects of mold. When it was Major Hasan's turn, he got up in front of the class and began to speak about his topic: "Is the war on terror a war on Islam?" Hasan's anti-American vitriol continued for two years as he worked toward his degree in public health funded by the taxpayers of America.

8. Senator Joe Lieberman has announced his intention to lead a congressional investigation into the Fort Hood murders, saying there were "strong warning signs" that Hasan was an "Islamic extremist. The U.S. army has to have zero tolerance. He should have been gone," said Lieberman, who is chairman of the Senate Committee on Homeland Security and Governmental Affairs.

9. Hasan attended a mosque in northern Virginia that two 9/11 hijackers also attended.

10. The thirteen men and women who died and the dozens who were wounded at Fort Hood richly deserve to receive the honor of the Purple Heart. Again, political correctness may prevent that from happening. Here's why: Congressman Frank Wolf (R-VA) is calling on President Obama to award the heroes at Fort Hood with the Purple Heart. There's just one problem: In order to award the Purple Heart, the Secretary of the Army must acknowledge that what occurred at Fort Hood was not a random attack, but an act of terrorism.

In 1973 the army modified the requirements to present an individual with the Purple Heart. It may be awarded "as a result of an international terrorist attack against the United States or a foreign nation friendly to the United States, recognized as such an attack by the Secretary of the Army."

I am hopeful that our president will not allow political correctness to get in the way of awarding these men and women the proper recognition for their service to the United States. What happened at Fort Hood *was* a terrorist attack. There is overwhelming evidence that Major Hasan was a radical Islamist who carried out the attacks because of his ideological beliefs. The families of the victims at Fort Hood deserve better than political correctness. They deserve the truth![66]

11. We now know that Major Hasan sent between ten and twenty messages to Amwar al-Awlaki, an Islamo-fascist cleric known for his exhortations for Muslims to rise up and kill infidels. Counterterrorism officials intercepted the communications but concluded—are you ready for this?—that the emails were probably part of a research project on posttraumatic stress disorder that the psychiatrist had been conducting at the Walter Reed Medical Center.

Amazing!

Amwar al-Awlaki is an expert on jihadist methodologies in cutting the throat of a nonbeliever and what an appropriate ritual beheading requires. He's not a normal resource for posttraumatic stress disorder.

No matter how "innocent" the emails seemed, our "intelligence" community alarm bells should have gone off when an army major sent messages to a murderous monster.

After the Fort Hood rampage, al-Awlaki praised Major Hasan on his webpage. He wrote, "Nidal Hasan is a hero. He is a man of conscience who could not bear living the contradiction of being a Muslim and serving in an army that is fighting against his own people. Any decent Muslim cannot live, understanding properly his duties towards his Creator and his fellow Muslims, and yet serve as a U.S. soldier."[67]

Think about this!

Perhaps our homeland security people are so traumatized by the constant left-wing attack accusing them of violating Constitutional rights that they have been rendered ineffective. CIA officers have been threatened with prosecutions, and phone companies may be sued out of business for cooperating with the Bush administration on wiretaps in the aftermath of the 9/11 attacks. Some of our counterterrorism officials may be so worried about ending up in jail if they are too aggressive that they have become paralyzed by political correctness.

This is exactly why there is serious concern across the nation as millions of Americans are now thinking the unthinkable: Can America survive?

12. Major Hasan once gave a lecture to other doctors at Walter Reed Army Medical Center in Washington in which he said nonbelievers should be beheaded and have boiling oil poured down their throats.

Colleagues had expected a discussion on a medical issue but were instead given an extremist interpretation of the Qur'an, which Hasan appeared to believe.

One army doctor who knew him said a fear of appearing discriminatory against a Muslim soldier had stopped fellow officers from filing formal complaints.[68]

When military officers who lead our army are completely intimidated by political correctness to do nothing, can America survive?

13. *The Washington Post* reports that Major Hasan delivered a one-hour, fifty-picture PowerPoint presentation titled "The Koranic World View as It Relates to Muslims in the U.S. Military."

The last bullet point simply read: "We love death more then [sic] you love life."

This is the hard-core doctrine of radical Islam. The death of a martyr is the only absolute guarantee you gain entrance into heaven with virgins waiting your arrival.

If the radical Muslims are willing to die by the millions for what they believe without hesitation, can an American nation paralyzed by political correctness possibly hope to defeat them? Can America survive?[69]

14. A photograph taken November 6, 2009, in Killeen, Texas, shows a business card that Major Nidal Hasan gave his neighbors a day before going on a shooting spree at the Fort Hood army base. The business card had the initials SoA, the abbreviation for "Soldier of Allah," ABC News reported.

15. After hearing the shocking story of Major Nidal Hasan, Fox News contributor Monica Crowley stated, "Political correctness is turning out to be the death of this country." Amen, Monica!

These are the facts. You decide! Was Major Nidal Hasan an Islamic terrorist practicing his faith chapter and verse? Or was he a traumatized psychiatrist?

While America remains a neophyte to the tactics of terrorism, the nation of Israel has been at war with terrorists who intend to destroy the Jewish nation. This war began on May 15, 1948, the day Israel declared statehood.

Israel is the front lines in the war between a democracy and the Islamic theocratic dictatorship. Unless the world community acts immediately and aggressively to deter Iran through sanctions and diplomacy, Israel will have only two options remaining. The first is a vigorous military preemptive strike against Iran, setting their nuclear ambitions back for several years, or living every day of their lives under the very real threat of a nuclear holocaust.

A confidential source from Israel came to my office and gave me in detail what he believes to be Iran's plan of attack on Israel and America!

It's *bold*!

It's *believable* . . . and it's in the following chapter, "Iran's Plan of Attack!" Can America survive?

THREE

Iran's Plan of Attack

Insider information has shaped the destiny of nations and the financial fortunes of empires. Noah built the Ark based on insider information that a great flood was coming that would destroy all living flesh on the earth.

The three wise men came all the way from the east to visit Jesus at the time of his birth when people next door didn't know who he was much less his global spiritual significance.

Mayer Rothschild bought the wealth of Europe for a fraction of its value in a matter of hours because the carrier pigeons coming to him from the battle front where Wellington and Napoleon were battling for the control of Europe produced insider information that was much faster and more accurate than messages by horseback that the stock traders in London were using. Rothschild knew that Wellington had won at Waterloo hours before other stock traders in London heard the truth. In that handful of hours, he became the richest man in Europe. The Rothschild family ruled Europe financially for centuries because on one particular day one man had insider information no one else had.

Each nation's intelligence agencies are created and designed to give that nation inside information that no one else has, information that may mean the difference between a smashing victory and disastrous defeat. Any nation without an aggressive and sophisticated intelligence agency will soon become an historical footnote.

For several years I have had a special source in Israel whose confidential insider information over the years has proven extremely accurate. Months ago, this source flew from Jerusalem to San Antonio to give me what he believes to be Iran's plan of attack against Jerusalem, Saudi Arabia, and America. The source never tells me in advance that he's coming; he just appears without notice, gives the message, and leaves.

He entered my office, we warmly greeted each other, then he sat across the desk from me. There is never a waste of time or words. The message is given and he leaves.

"What can you tell me about the present crisis in the Middle East?" I asked.

He responded without hesitation: "I believe that it's the absolute intention of President Ahmadinejad to attack Jerusalem with a nuclear missile, to attack Saudi Arabia's oil fields with conventional missiles, thereby crushing the American economy in a day. This attack will all be done in one day at the same hour!"

As he spoke, I thought about America's addiction to foreign oil. Thanks to radical environmentalists, we have not built an oil refinery in this nation since 1976, and although we have plenty of oil, we refuse to drill for it. OPEC must be laughing its head off at the stupidity of our national energy policy.

If Iran attacked the Saudi oil fields or blocked the Strait of Hormuz, America's delicate economy would shatter.

"How soon do you think Iran will have the ability to make and deliver a nuclear warhead?" I quizzed him.

"I can only tell you what everyone knows . . . we are running out of time . . . and the time factor is now critical as Iran has become the master of diplomacy, which is deception by design with the West."

"Why would Ahmadinejad attack fellow followers of Islam in Saudi Arabia?"

"Because he believes they are an apostate branch of Islam, and there are strong doctrinal differences about who the true descendants of Muhammad happen to be."

"When do you think this might happen?"

"Only God knows the day and hour, but we are down to two options: The first is a military preemptive strike against Iran's nuclear facilities before they get the Russian missiles to protect those sites. The second option is for the world to get ready to live with a nuclear Iran because dialogue and sanctions will not stop Ahmadinejad. If he gets his hands on nuclear weapons, he will use them to initiate a nuclear holocaust, and he will use them against America. Remember, he believes that if he can create a global chaos, his messiah will suddenly and mysteriously appear to lead the world into global Sharia."

"What will Israel do if the missiles start falling on Israel?" I probed.

"We will do exactly what we have done for centuries. As Jews, we will do everything in our power to protect ourselves, and then we will get ready to defend our actions against the world press that will accuse us of overreacting." He smiled, rose from his seat, and thanked me for my friendship as we embraced, then he left the office.

DECEPTION BY DESIGN

All war is based on deception.
—Sun Tzu

Iran's chief nuclear negotiator was Hassan Rowhani from 2003 to 2005. He represented Iran in the key negotiations that resulted in a temporary suspension of its uranium enrichment activities in 2003.

This did not prevent Rowhani from making a staggering disclosure in a speech delivered in a closed-door meeting in Tehran when he bragged that he had cleverly outmaneuvered—and essentially deceived—the Western powers, led by the European Union, with whom he had negotiated. Rowhani stated bluntly: "When we were negotiating with the Europeans in Tehran, we were installing [nuclear] equipment in parts of the facility in Isfahan."[1]

Isfahan is known by Western intelligence agencies to be exactly where the Iranians had erected a facility for completing the second important stage in the production of fuel for their clandestine nuclear weapons program.[2]

Rowhani was proud of Iran's technological success in completing this second critical stage of uranium fuel production. He boasted that as a result of what his deceptive diplomacy had accomplished, "the world would face a fait accompli" [an accomplished fact] which "would change the entire equation."[3]

In another interview Rowhani detailed the real magnitude of Iran's success by relying on the diplomatic process with Europe: "The day we started the process, there was no such thing as the Isfahan project."[4]

In fact, during the period of Rowhani's talk with the Europeans, Iran began actually converting thirty-seven tons of yellowcake into UF_6 which was enough by Western assessment to build five atomic bombs.[5]

Iran was so completely successful in deceiving the West despite Western diplomatic efforts that Britain's *Daily Telegraph* reporting on Rowhani's speech on April 3, 2006, ran a headline that tersely captured the significance of what Rowhani had said: "How We Duped the West, by Iran's Nuclear Negotiator."[6]

Rowhani also boasted of successfully driving a wedge between the United States and the Europeans. "From the outset, the Americans kept telling the Europeans, 'The Iranians are lying and deceiving you and they have not told you everything.' " Rowhani then sarcastically noted: "The Europeans used to respond, 'We trust them.' "[7]

Then there was the admission of Abdollah Ramezanadeh, the government's spokesman under President Khatami, who looked back on this entire period of time and summarized Iranian negotiating strategy in very blunt terms: "We had an overt policy, which was one of negotiation and confidence building, and a covert policy, which was a continuation of the [nuclear building] activities."[8]

Iran's use of diplomacy that was deception by design was bluntly admitted before dozens of network television camera by former deputy foreign minister Mohammad-Javad Larijani, who stated: "Diplomacy must be used to lessen pressure on Iran for its nuclear program."[9]

Foreign Minister Larijani added that diplomacy, for him, was a "tool for allowing us to reach our goals."[10]

For Iran, nuclear talks were a "contest of the wills" for Tehran and not an opportunity to reach some kind of "common ground" that American politicians constantly try to achieve. Iran's diplomatic duplicity— saying one thing at the negotiating table while doing the exact opposite— was not something of which to be ashamed, but was rather considered a source of national pride.

What the admission of Iran's chief nuclear negotiator, Hassan Rowhani, clearly demonstrated was that Europe's efforts at diplomatic engagement with Iran concerning its nuclear program were a complete failure. America's present diplomatic engagement with the Islamic Republic is going nowhere. It's more of what we have seen for the past thirty years: diplomatic deception designed to give Iran time to achieve its maniacal dream of nuclear power to dominate the Middle East and the world.

The clock is running out!

The ship is sailing toward the iceberg full speed ahead. The perfect storm in the Middle East has arrived.

Just after the Islamic Revolution in Iran in 1979, Aytollah Khomeini came to power and made the following statement, which is a shocking revelation of the mind-set of radical Islam:

> We do not worship Iran, we worship Allah. For patriotism is another name for paganism. I say let this land burn. I say let this land go up in smoke, provided Islam emerges triumphant in the rest of the world.[11]

Iran's radical Islamic leadership does not fear war; they welcome it as evidenced by the statement of Dr. Hadi Modaressi, a leading religious leader who was close to Khomeini:

> We welcome military aggression against us because it strengthens the revolution and rallies the masses around it.[12]

President Ahmadinejad believes that creating a global chaos with nuclear weapons would only hasten the reappearance of the Hidden Imam from the ninth century, a Messianic figure known in the Shiite religious tradition as the Mahdi. War will accelerate the arrival of this Shiite version of the "end of days."[13]

Ahmadinejad himself linked the spread of chaos to the arrival of a new era of divine revelation. In a meeting with foreign diplomats in New York City on September 15, 2005, Ahmadinejad asked the diplomats: "Do you know why we should wish for chaos at any price?" He then answered his own rhetorical question: "Because after chaos, we can see the greatness of Allah."[14]

Even more dramatic, Ahmadinejad pressed the issue that the return of the Hidden Imam was not an event in the distant future. He stated: "Those who are not versed [in the doctrine of Mahdism] believe the return of the Hidden Imam will only occur in a very long time, but according to the divine promise [his return] is imminent."[15]

Most Americans feel that to announce a massive attack against Iran for using nuclear weapons would prevent a rational people from pursuing nuclear weapons.

Not so!

The prospect of thousands of Iranian civilians lying dead in the street would fulfill the radical Islamic obsession with martyrdom and death. Remember the last PowerPoint slide on Major Hasan's presentation was "We love death more than you love life."

The cold, naked truth is this: Iran has thumbed its nose at Europe and America through a diplomacy of planned deception designed to give Iran time to do the unthinkable.

There will be a nuclear war in the Middle East unless prevented by military force. Does Israel have a partner for peace in the Middle East? Unless the world community acts aggressively and immediately through sanctions and diplomacy, Israel will be down to two options: a military preemptive strike or life under the constant threat of a theocratic dictator with nuclear power.

The world is watching and waiting!

Time is running out!

The iceberg is just ahead!

Iran has begun war games to practice the defense of its nuclear sites. There is the sound of diplomats shuffling deck chairs in the background as the music plays on.

HOW IRANIAN NUKES WOULD
RESHAPE THE MIDDLE EAST

An Iranian nuclear program would rearrange the political, economic, and cultural furniture in the Middle East. When Iran gets the bomb, other regional powers will be forced to pursue nuclear programs or bow to the demands of Iran, which will become the bully of the Middle East.

Inevitably, in a region as volatile as this, there could be a few small-scale nuclear catastrophes. History proves that the radical Islamists are not shy about killing their own people. Remember that Saddam Hussein gassed the Kurds and slaughtered the Shiites, Hafez Assad massacred the Sunnis of Hama, and mass graves throughout the region testify to the willingness of Arab leaders to kill their own people. Nuclear weaponry under their control is merely an upgrade in repressive technology to force their will on anyone who opposes them.

An Iranian bomb is concrete evidence that Iran's strategy of "resistance" to America is a winning one. This will change the region's political culture from radical to many times more radical. An Iranian bomb sends a message to the rest of the terrorists in the Middle East that they should feel free to make a run at open terrorism in America. There is no military solution to terrorism!

If the Americans are folding by giving known war criminals like 9/11 mastermind Khalid Sheikh Mohammed an ACLU lawyer and prime-time television coverage for years without the threat of nuclear retaliation, how much more quickly and completely will America fold when Iran has the bomb.

How much more daring will they be in controlling the oil in the Persian Gulf while yanking the chain around America's neck forged by our addiction to foreign oil? Be certain Russia is in the corner clapping in thunderous applause for Iran.

WHY RUSSIA IS NOT AFRAID OF AN IRANIAN BOMB

Years ago after Prime Minister Benjamin Netanyahu had completed his first term in office as Israel's bold and aggressive leader, we sat together in my office chatting moments before we were to go out and have the "Night to Honor Israel" at Cornerstone Church, which was telecast to the nations of the world.

The prime minister and I were discussing how reluctant American intelligence was to admit that years ago, in the 1990s, Russian scientists were helping Iran build its nuclear facilities and medium-range missiles that had the ability to reach Jerusalem, London, and the East Coast of America.

I asked the prime minister: "How did you convince our government that Russia was in fact helping Iran?"

"I took the time and effort to get photographic proof and hand delivered the photos to Washington, DC, so there could be no denying that Russia was and remains an ally with Iran."

The conversation ended and we left the office for the auditorium packed with five thousand dedicated, pro-Israel Christians who believe

that Israel has the right to exist, the right to defend itself against all enemies, and the right to control and to build anywhere within the city of
Jerusalem.

Why is Russia so committed to Iran?

Russia's tactical and strategic interests cannot be ignored. Iran is an
existential threat to Israel and Saudi Arabia. Iran traditionally opposes
radical Sunni Islamic movements such as the Taliban and Wahabiyya,
which have become a serious threat to the Russians in their Northern
Caucasus area, especially Dagestan. These common enemies unite Russia
and Iran.

Russia and Iran will be committed partners until the end of time. According to the prophet Ezekiel, they will unite their forces and invade
Israel at some time in the future.

The end result is that God, according to the prophet Ezekiel, will
crush the Russian-Islamic army in much the same manner as He destroyed Pharaoh and for the same reason—they attacked the Jewish
people! Russia and Iran will be annihilated by the hand of God as He
defends the "apple of his eye"—Israel.

At the present time, Iran's most powerful military force, the Revolutionary Guard, says Tehran will "blow up the heart of Israel" if the Jewish state or the United States attacked Iran." [16]

THE ATTACK ON AMERICA HAS BEGUN!

Do you remember 9/11? Every terrorist who hijacked American commercial airliners and used them as missiles of death were radical Muslims.
You can be sure they were quoting the Qur'an, anticipating the appearance of seventy virgins as they crashed into the Twin Towers and killed
some three thousand Americans. The 9/11 terrorist attack proved that
radical Islam has the will to kill us en masse, they just lack the power.
When Iran has the nuclear power, America's security will be in constant
and deadly peril.

Paul L. Williams, a former consultant to the FBI on terrorism, indicates that seven cities in America have been targeted by radical Islamic
terrorist organizations who are here and who are highly organized and
sophisticated enough to execute an attack on seven cities simultaneously.

Those cities are New York, Miami, Houston, Las Vegas, Los Angeles, Chicago, and Washington, DC.

A recent headline in *USA Today* was a wake-up call for all Americans. It proved the radical Islamic passion to kill us has not passed nor abated.

The *USA Today* headlines scream "Alleged Terror Threat Seen as 'Most Serious' Since 9/11." [17]

This breaking story was the worst nightmare for the American intelligence community. Najibullah Zazi, an American homegrown terrorist living in the United States, flew from Newark, New Jersey, to Pakistan for terrorist training.

Zazi attracted the FBI's attention with his August 28, 2008, visit to Peshawar, a global crossroads for terrorist groups. After five months of training in the al-Qaeda terrorist camp in Pakistan, Zazi returned to America and morphed from an anonymous Denver airport shuttle driver to the central figure in a national terrorism probe "committed" to attacking the United States by detonating bombs against targets here.

Federal officials warned that sports stadiums, entertainment venues, and other places could be targets of terrorist strikes.

"This is the most serious threat . . . I've seen since 9/11," says Tom Fuentes, a former FBI official who once directed the bureau's operations in Baghdad. "You had a person here who received explosives and weapons training, and he was apparently trying to assemble a team to carry out the operation." [18]

Georgetown University professor Bruce Hoffman, who has examined terrorism issues for three decades said, "For anyone who doubted whether al-Qaeda was still in the picture, this should answer that question." [19]

In addition to the Zazi case, federal prosecutors are charging Jordanian immigrant Hosam Smadi with plotting to blow up a Dallas skyscraper. Zazi may have been in the country legally, but Smadi was not. He was here on an expired visitor's visa. His case highlights the troubling fact that, as the *New York Times* put it, "Eight years after the September 11 terrorist attacks . . . the United States still has no reliable system for verifying that foreign visitors have left the country."

Once again, the outrageous deficiencies of our immigration system are proving to present tremendous national security risks.

PRESIDENT REASSURES MUSLIM WORLD

When President Obama gave his first TV interview as the President of the United States, he chose to do so on an Arab-language satellite network. In his remarks, the President made two assertions that give us an insight to his worldview.

First, the President said he felt his "job" was to communicate "to the Muslim world . . . that the Americans are not your enemy." Why does the President feel he must reassure Muslims that "Americans" are not their enemies?

It was the United States that was attacked on 9/11 by jihadists acting in the name of Islam. America's response to that cowardly act was to send our military not to subjugate Muslims but to liberate millions of them in Iraq and Afghanistan from the rule of tyrants and thugs.

People of both countries were able to vote for the first time in their lives. In Afghanistan today, in those areas where the United States is in control, Muslim girls are permitted to go to school. Where radical Islamists are in control, acid is thrown in the faces of girls who try to go to school, and their classrooms are blown up.

After the 9/11 attack, America went out of its way to ensure that mosques in the United States were safe from any kind of backlash. Throughout the Muslim world, Christians and Jews continue to be persecuted. Jews are not permitted to enter Saudi Arabia lest the soil be contaminated by the soles of their feet. Saudi Arabia has what Hitler was trying to achieve: a Jew-free country. In spite of all the good America has done, the President feels a need to tell the Muslims that we are not their enemy.

The President told his Muslim audience that he had another task. Here is how he put it: "And my job is to communicate to the American people that the Muslim world is filled with extraordinary people who simply want to live their lives and see their children live better lives."

Here's the problem!

Those Muslims who simply want to enjoy peace and quiet are not the problem. It is the Muslims who nurture groups like al-Qaeda, the Taliban, Hamas, Hezbollah, Islamic Jihad, and countless other religious fanatics who matter most. From London to Madrid, Manhattan to Mumbai, Beslan to Buenos Aires, it is those Islamists who have intentionally inflicted death and destruction on helpless civilians in the name of Allah. If only 10 percent of the "Muslim world" supports these murderers, then our enemies number 150 million.

Unfortunately, there is ample evidence that the number is much, much larger. Add to that the vicious Jew-hatred that appears to infect the populations of "moderate" Muslim countries, like Indonesia and Jordan, and the magnitude of our problem becomes obvious.

If I had the opportunity to speak personally to our president, I would make the following statement:

> Mr. President, you are our duly elected leader and the leader of the free world. As the spiritual leader of a congregation of some twenty thousand people and many thousands of people across the nation and around the world on global television daily, I have asked my national and international congregation to pray for you, to pray for the members of your family, and to pray for the members of Congress on a daily basis.
>
> Mr. President, your read on Israel is pushing Israel toward a military preemptive strike on Iran's nuclear facilities. That strike could be successful or it could fail. Whatever the result, the price of oil will skyrocket, there will be another war in the Middle East, perhaps nuclear, and American troops will be caught in the middle in Afghanistan. The fragile American economy would crash, and the world as we know it will end.
>
> Mr. President, Iran is beyond the reach of eloquence. We have been talking to Iran thirty years and have absolutely nothing to show for it. The truth is, our "negotiations" have advanced Iran's goals above all else. With each day that passes, Ahmadinejad's regime gets closer to the day when it will be able to transform the Middle East and the world by proudly declaring itself a nuclear power.
>
> We know Iran has lied to us about its "secret" nuclear facilities.
>
> We know it is willing to murder its own citizens in the streets on global television who cry out for freedom when a presidential election has been stolen.
>
> We know Iran is directly responsible for the murder of U.S. troops in Iraq and Afghanistan.

We know Iran's leaders are Shiite radicals who believe an Islamic messiah is coming soon to destroy the infidels (anyone who does not accept Islam) and Iran has a special role to play in forcing their messiah to appear by creating great global chaos.

We know that Ahmadinejad denies the Holocaust, while promising his followers that the day is coming when Israel will be "wiped off the map" and America will no longer exist.

Most important, we know it is an abdication of a superpower's responsibility to outsource matters of war and peace to another state: Israel.

We know you have given the driver's seat to Prime Minister Benjamin Netanyahu, whom I know personally. He has been in my home and my office on several occasions and I have been in his. He is a man of boundless courage and will defend Israel with every weapon at his disposal. His words are recorded for the world to read, as captured in the headlines of *The Atlantic* . . .

"STOP IRAN—OR I WILL!"

Mr. President, would it be possible for the two democracies, America and Israel, to join forces to defeat the radical theocratic dictatorship that threatens world peace?

Will we wait until global terrorists, encouraged and emboldened by the trial of KSM in New York City, pour into this country to make bombs or deliver nuclear suitcase bombs via Iran that could kill millions of Americans per blast?

What would it be like if a suitcase nuclear bomb exploded in your city? Discover the truth in the following chapter: "The Day After the Bomb."

Think it can't happen?

Think again!

PART TWO

The Fall of America

FOUR

The Day After the Bomb

I stood on the shores of Normandy Beach where almost ten thousand hopeful, handsome young American soldiers stormed those beaches on June 6, 1944, and sacrificed their all for life, liberty, and the pursuit of happiness.

Those who perished died a horrific death! Standing there, I saw them in the theater of my mind climbing out of more than five thousand ships that covered the English Channel as far as the eye could see. This battle theater stretched for seventy miles, the largest amphibious military operation in the history of warfare. It was the Longest Day and the last day for thousands of America's finest heroes.

They scrambled over the sides of their respective ships on cargo nets into the flat-bottom Higgins boats bound for the shore and the deadly fire of the demons of the Third Reich.

As the small boats plowed their way through the churning tide of the English Channel, thousands of those youthful troops were looking into their last sunrise. Those who had spiritual roots were praying the Lord's Prayer aloud; others were kissing the cross that had been given to them by some praying mother thousands of miles away.

The boats struck the sands of the shore, the front ramp lowered, and many stepped into eternity as German machine gun fire killed them to the last man before they got out of the boat. Survivors leaped over the sides of the boat in full battle gear, while others had a few more moments of precious life as they ran up the beach only to face the unspeakable terror of a beach covered with machine gun crossfire, mortar blasts, and barbed wire strung through long rows of steel crossbars to prevent their progress. The steel crossbars were designed to sink any boat whose captain was foolish enough to attempt a landing at high tide.

The first waves of Americans to reach Omaha Beach were slaughtered. They stained the beaches and shoreline of Normandy with the most precious gift one human being can give another—their life's blood. "Greater love has no one than this, than to lay down one's life for his friends" (John 15:13 NKJV).

They died on those beaches screaming in agony, calling out to God, pleading for a medic to come. Finally, when no one came and death was tugging at their sleeves, they turned to the ultimate source of love and comfort all men know—they cried out in their agony for their mothers.

With a gifted guide giving me every gory and heartbreaking detail of the vicious and historic battle between America's freedom-loving sons and Hitler's Nazis, we climbed the bluffs to the cliffs where Hitler's massive artillery, shrouded in thick concrete walls, blasted their rain of terror and death upon America's sons on that historic day.

Between the monster cannons—which could shoot for miles into the ocean, sinking approaching ships—were concrete fortifications for Nazi machine guns that could fire 1,200 rounds per minute, creating a lethal crossfire with three machine guns in each "nest" of weapons.

I stood in one of those machine gun concrete bunkers staring out at Normandy Beach and marveled that any living soul could make it from the boats, through the barbed-wire barriers with crossed steel beams, to climb the bluffs, to fight against impossible odds for the sacred cause of life, liberty, and freedom.

Finally, I left the scene of battle for the cemetery and saw the endless rows of marble white crosses and Stars of David planted in the rich green grass, row upon row upon row as far as the eye could see.

Every cross was some mother's precious son, some child's daddy that would never come home, some wife's husband, someone's brother, some father's son. These people would forever sit at the dinner table looking at a photo of their missing loved one and at his empty chair.

I walked between the rows of fallen heroes, reading their names and observing their dates of birth. Most were between the ages of eighteen and twenty years. They had everything to live for, and they willingly laid down their lives on the altar of sacrifice so that the next generation might live in freedom. Freedom isn't free!

I sat down on a marble bench and stared at the ocean of human sacrifice before me in Normandy, and in the theater of my mind, I was transported to another battlefield. It was not on foreign soil!

It was a battlefield in the streets of America between the trained terrorists of radical Islam and America. It was a battle for survival and, unlike WWII and Normandy, America was stumbling in a politically correct fog, not even aware that the do-or-die battle had begun.

People in our government refuse to use the word *terrorist,* and our national leadership is bowing to the leaders of foreign countries who are funding the war to destroy us. War criminals are being tried under civilian law in New York City, giving the radical Islamic terrorists a global platform to preach their "kill for Allah" theology and vomit their anti-American and anti-Israeli venom to the four winds of the earth.

There are now about seven thousand headstones in the cemetery in this battle for America with radical Islam. Four thousand in Iraq and Afghanistan and three thousand in New York, victims of 9/11, murdered by radical Muslims quoting the Qur'an as they flew their missiles of death into the Twin Towers.

Tragically and unbelievably, thirteen more brave warriors have fallen at Fort Hood at the hand of a radical Muslim, and our leaders are saying we shouldn't race to judgment on the U.S. Army Major Hasan, who slaughtered and wounded our troops.

How many thousands more will fall before our leaders snap out of this politically correct fog and admit we are at war? Will they wait until a series of nuclear dirty bombs set off at one time in seven cities send millions of Americans to their deaths?

Think it can't happen?

Think again!

Radical terrorists have been slipping across our open borders for years to form sleeper cells across the nation. They have been recruited from our colleges and universities to be trained in the terrorist boot camps of Pakistan in the art of making bombs, shooting automatic weapons, becoming masters of murder and mayhem, all to return home and kill innocent Americans at some appointed date in the future to please their Islamo-fascist masters.

History in the future may call it "The Fifty-Year War" between America and radical Islam, but its final battles will be fought in the streets and cities of this nation. The jihad against America began on 9/11 . . . and it will not end until America defeats radical Islam or the flag of Islam flies over the White House.

THE DAY OF THE BOMB

What will it be like for *you* in your city the day terrorists set off a nuclear 10-kiloton uranium fission nuclear bomb without warning at or about ground level? What difference will it make?

A ground-burst nuclear weapon would spread blast damage and fire over a smaller area than an airburst nuclear bomb released from a high-rise office building. A nuclear bomb released from a high-rise office building would have far greater radioactive fallout and would kill more people than the initial blast. On the day of the bomb, the way the wind is blowing would determine who lives and who dies!

The nuclear express is coming!

President Ahmadinejad of Iran has faithfully promised all Islamic terrorist groups that he will share his nuclear power with them to conquer the infidels.

Ahmadinejad's friendship with fellow dictator Hugo Chavez of Venezuela would make it a piece of cake to send dirty bombs via ship to Venezuela, then to cross them into America by walking them across the Rio Grande with the legions who cross on a regular basis without detection.

The Islamic terrorist cells that have the ability to make and set off nuclear dirty bombs are not coming—they are already here. They are trained! They are ready! They are willing! *You* and your family are the targets!

A former consultant to the FBI on terrorism, Paul L. Williams, indicates that there is empirical proof that al-Qaeda possesses nukes. British agents posing as recruits infiltrated al-Qaeda training camps. In another instance, an al-Qaeda operative was arrested at Ramallah with a tactical nuke strapped to his back.

If you are having trouble believing that teams of terrorists maintaining a nuclear weapon in the United States wouldn't be detected, think the unthinkable!

Williams reports that there isn't just one team, but at least seven.[1] They are working within mosques and Islamic centers, and in the United

States a federal judge will not provide the FBI or law enforcement agents with a warrant to search a mosque or an Islamic center for any reason since such places are listed as "houses of worship."[2]

Williams also states that seven cities in America have been targeted by terrorists as prime targets. Those cities are identified as New York, Miami, Houston, Las Vegas, Los Angeles, Chicago, and Washington, DC. The attacks are designed to occur simultaneously in these seven cities.

Before you breathe a sigh of relief and say "I don't live in one of those major cities," do you remember Oklahoma City and the Murrah Building? The truth is, jihad came to America on 9/11, and every city in America is a potential target.

Headlines of a recent *USA Today* express the worst nightmare of America's intelligence community. Homegrown Islamists are being recruited by foreign governments hostile to the United States, trained in terrorist boot camps, and returned to America with bomb-making knowledge, automatic weapons skills, and a burning desire to kill Americans. That would be *you* and *your* family!

Recently federal officials unsealed terrorist charges against eight new suspects that say they were key actors in a recruitment effort that led young Americans to join al-Shabaab, a violent insurgent group in Somalia with ties to al-Qaeda. The recruitment operation largely focused on Somali-American men from the Minnesota area. The recruits attended training camps in Somalia run by Somali, Arab, and Western instructors who taught them to use machine guns and rocket-propelled grenades and indoctrinated them with anti-American and anti-Israeli beliefs, according to the court documents.

There is evidence the aggressive recruitment of young American Muslims continues. Recently, the Nevada Highway Patrol stopped a rental car carrying five young Somali men who said they were en route to a wedding in San Diego. A lawyer with knowledge of the case said three of the men soon crossed the border and boarded an airplane for destinations unknown.[3]

The day of the bomb will begin like any other day. You will take your children to school, your spouse will go to his or her job, you will arrive at your office and send an email to your child at the university who is trying to cram six years of education into four, as you begin your daily rat race to pay your ever-escalating taxes to fulfill Washington's never-ending pipe dreams.

Suddenly the lights go out, as does everything electrical! Cars and buses are stopping in the middle of the street. People are standing in groups with puzzled faces, asking each other, "What's going on?" "Why is no one's car working?" They reach for their cells phones; they don't work!

Minutes later, there is a thunderous BLAST! The noise is deafening! You see buildings melting like butter before your eyes, now blazing in what appears to be a spontaneous inferno.

Then you see the mushroom cloud. It's surreal!

This can't be happening in America. The unthinkable has become re-ality. The unsinkable ship has just hit the iceberg. Jihad has come to *you*, your children, your family; and in seconds, your life is forever changed.

How will you get in touch with your children?

With your spouse? With your child at the university? You can't; all electronic communication is over!

There will be no warning the Day of the Bomb!

First, catching a city by surprise would increase the destruction and chaos. Second, advance warning would put the mission at risk and have the plot foiled by the FBI before it released its reign of terror. Third, there is no reason to believe that terrorists with "loose nukes" would have only one.

They could set off one bomb and claim that many more were coming, spreading national panic and creating an environment for terrified politi-cians to bow to the demands of radical Islam.

The terrorists have all the advantages. They know when, they know where, and they know how the attack will take place. It will be planned to kill as many as possible. These attacks are meant to break the will of the American people so they won't be able to resist the coming demands that radical Islam will make on the American people to live by the law of Sharia.

Maybe the target will be one of the most prestigious high-rise office buildings in your city, which has proven to be a prime target for radical Muslims in times past. The Twin Towers were selected because they rep-resented American power and wealth.

Maybe the target will be a major shopping center during the holiday season, when it's packed to the walls with unsuspecting Americans who have lived every day of their lives in absolute freedom. It is simply beyond belief that jihad could reach out and destroy their magical lives in an instant.

Just like it was beyond belief that the *Titanic* could ever sink!

Perhaps the seven targets in seven different cities would be seven professional football stadiums across the country, packed with hundreds of thousands of people cheering for their teams to get to the Super Bowl. These cheering fans would never suspect that a very powerful theocratic dictatorship in Iran had the power of nuclear arms and the passion for martyrdom to attempt to crush America in one infamous day.

Think it can't happen?

Think again!

If a bomb in Washington, DC, is successful and the leadership of our country is killed or out of contact, who will lead us? With all electronic systems malfunctioning and without the ability to communicate with the people across the nation, with panic in the streets, with supermarkets filled with screaming, shoving, and shouting Americans who fear extreme hunger or even starvation for their children, who will bring food and water to the cities in devastation? With gun-toting mobs robbing banks, stores, and citizens at will, who will bring law and order? Who will bring medical supplies?

Do you remember Hurricane Katrina? There were people in Louisiana without food, water, shelter, and medical attention for days. Dead people were lying facedown in the street. Dead bodies were floating facedown in the canals.

This chaos and suffering came from one hurricane in one city. What happens when America is hit from coast to coast at one time with nuclear disaster that leaves millions dead and millions more dying from radiation?

Who will make the decisions to chart our course from this national disaster? Whom will we attack? Because these nuclear dirty bombs will be set off by individual terrorist cells, there is no nation we can attack. There is no military solution for terrorism!

The grisly effects of a 10-kiloton ground burst are very clear. One mile in all directions of the downtown area with the high-rise office building, the football stadium, or the shopping mall that was the epicenter of the blast would be totally contaminated.

The massive buildings would be piles of rubble ten to fifteen feet high for one mile north, south, east, and west. There will no human survivors in that one-mile circle of death.

Outside that one-mile circle leveled by the blast, people will be wounded by the flying debris, by instantaneous fires that are an unstoppable inferno, and severe radiation. They stand little chance of survival.

It will be days before emergency workers can get to them because any downtown hospitals would be blasted into rubble, lying in ruins. If emergency workers were instantly available, the victims' burns and acute radiation exposure would require intensive and sustained medical treatment to offer any chance of survival.

Downwind from the detonation point, the cloud of radioactive debris will began to spread. It is the cloud of death! Its shape and size would depend on wind and rain conditions, but within one day, people who live within ten square miles who do not find shelter or flee within hours would receive a lethal dose of radiation. In a city like New York or Los Angeles that could represent more than a million people.

Because there is little that can be done for those in and around the blast zone, medical responders will probably divide the city into zones and concentrate on the population downwind from the epicenter, where the radiation cloud was reduced, thus giving them a greater chance to save some. Those in the one-mile epicenter zone will be written off as hopeless, as will most of the people located on the edge of the one-mile blast zone.

In the months and years following the attack, civic leaders would face this dilemma. If they allowed the residents to return early, those residents would experience a higher cancer rate than the rest of the population. Those unwilling to accept the higher cancer rate would have to abandon their homes. The center of the city would remain too radioactive to build on for a year or more.[4]

As this book goes to print, the United States government has no such plan to protect the citizens of this nation from the impact and effects of a nuclear attack!

I'm confident that if a nuclear attack happens with this administration, and if there are enough people left in Congress to vote on a given bill, someone will quickly craft a bill calling for "the rich" to pay for the damages created by the nuclear attack and someone else will craft a bill blaming George W. Bush because the attack happened!

And I am confident that, after the nuclear attack, Congress will have some committee to write a long and politically correct masterpiece titled "What We Wish We Had Done Before the Bomb!"

For the time being the USS *Titanic* sails into the dark night without binoculars, without the proper flares, without enough lifeboats to prevent disaster, getting intelligence reports from a rope too short to get accurate information, while the band plays on and the iceberg gets closer—all while our leadership continues telling all Americans: "All is well!"

If the headline in your newspaper reads "Iran Has the Bomb!" you should do these things to prepare yourself and your family to live in a world where a nuclear attack is a very real possibility.

1. Have the ability with your own transportation to evacuate the city. Be sure to evacuate immediately, traveling perpendicular to the plume of the blast. Said another way, when you see the mushroom cloud forming in the sky, leave your city in the opposite direction.

   Remember: More people will die from the radiation in that cloud than from the nuclear blast. The radiation can kill you through either radiation burns that will not heal and/or by placing you at much higher risk for cancer for the rest of your life. The radiation is *deadly!*

2. If you are trapped in the city and can't evacuate, get below ground level and stay there for at least three days. If your house has a basement, you are blessed.

   If your house has no basement, be prepared to seal your house or apartment around the windows and doors with duct tape. This will greatly reduce the radiation exposure factor for you and your family.

3. You should have enough food and water stored to supply your family for that three-day period at the very least. Storing enough food for longer periods is advisable because if there are multiple attacks or threats of multiple attacks on America, gas and oil may well be rationed by the government, making it impossible for trucks to bring food and supplies to your local supermarket for days.

4. Get a supply of alternative energy, such as batteries for flashlights and generators for electricity; lighting candles is better than sitting endless hours in the dark.

5. Get a battery-powered radio that will pick up civil defense messages when civilization gets back on its feet.

6. I have been asked this question many times and it's an intelligent question: "Why should we be concerned about Iran getting the bomb? What's the difference between Iran having a nuclear bomb and Russia having a nuclear bomb? Russia has had it for years, and there has not been a problem."

The answer: "During the years of the Cold War, America and Russia had a mutual understanding that if there was a nuclear attack by either side, the other side would execute the MAD Policy! MAD is the acronym for Mutually Assured Destruction.

Basically, the Russians and Americans had reached a common ground of understanding that any attack by the other would guarantee that the one who launched the attack would be exterminated.

The simple truth is that when two rational groups of people come to a common understanding, coexistence can happen.

That's exactly the problem with the leadership of Iran; they are not rational. They are religious fanatics who believe that if they start a global war and their nation and millions of their own people are killed in a nuclear war, they die as martyrs and go immediately to heaven.

Remember: By their own confession, they love death more than life.

They are not afraid to die; they're looking forward to the day. Remember the words of Major Hasan to his fellow radical Islamic terrorist friend just before he murdered thirteen American soldiers at Fort Hood: "I can't wait to join you in the afterlife."

The president of Iran has promised to "wipe Israel off the map" and has threatened a nuclear holocaust. He has also stated that he can see the day when there will no longer be a United States of America. He is a clear and present danger to our national security.

He has promised radical Islamic terrorist groups that he will share with them the nuclear power Iran is developing. It is happening as this book goes to press.

The greatest challenge for our government is not health care: It's stopping Iran from getting nuclear weapons. The only way to win a nuclear war is to make sure it never starts!

The day Iran obtains nuclear weapons, it's a game changer for planet Earth! Life will never be the same!

7. When you pray, pray for America! If we do not use our freedom to defend our freedom, we will lose our freedom.

One of the fundamental truths the Founding Fathers established was the principle that debt made all men slaves. Solomon recorded in his writings: ". . . the borrower *is* servant to the lender" (Proverbs 22:7 NKJV).

America today is swimming in an ocean of debt, and yet we continue to spend money we don't have and bury our children and grandchildren under a mountain of debt making economic slaves of them all.

Soon other nations like China will call for the dumping of the U.S. dollar as the currency for international payment of debt. The nations of the world will respond favorably, and within months, you will see the contents of the next chapter become reality: the *death of the dollar.*

FIVE

Death of the Dollar

I . . . place economy among the first and most important of republican virtues, and public debt as the greatest dangers to be feared . . . to preserve [our] independence, we must not let our rulers load us with perpetual debt. We must make our election between economy and liberty, or profusion and servitude.

—Thomas Jefferson[1]

America's national debt has now become the major national security issue. The following are remarks made by America's foremost leaders who recognize the extreme danger America faces because of our national debt.

Our rising debt levels [pose] a national security threat.
—U.S. Secretary of State Hillary Clinton[2]

The biggest threat we have to our national security is our debt . . . the interest on our debt is $571 billion in 2012 and that's notionally about the size of the Defense Department Budget. It's not sustainable.
—Admiral Michael Mullen, chairman of the Joint Chiefs of Staff[3]

We've reached a point now where there's an intimate link between our solvency and our national security.

—Richard Haass, president,
Council on Foreign Relations[4]

Several months ago, a group of logistics officers at the Industrial College of the Armed Forces developed a national security strategy as a class exercise. Their number one recommendation for maintaining U.S. global leadership was to "restore fiscal responsibility."

—*Washington Post*[5]

The Pentagon sponsored a first-of-its-kind war game . . . on how hostile nations might seek to cripple the U.S. economy with the weapons being stocks, bonds and currencies . . . . It was the first time the Pentagon hosted a purely economic war game.

—Politico.com[6]

The Russians made a "top level approach" to the Chinese that together they might sell big chunks of their GSE holdings [Fannie Mae and Freddie Mac] to force the U.S. to use its emergency authorities to prop up these companies . . . the Chinese declined. . . . The report was deeply troubling . . . heavy selling could create a sudden loss of confidence in the GSEs and shake the capital markets. I waited till I was back home and in a secure environment to inform the president.

—Former U.S. Treasury Secretary
Henry Paulson[7]

We don't have a trillion-dollar debt because we haven't taxed enough. We have a trillion-dollar debt because we spend too much.

—Former U.S. President Ronald Reagan[8]

As if the above statements weren't enough, there's more.

Antonia Orprita reported that "The U.S. supremacy as the top world economy will end sooner than many people believe, so gold is a better investment than the dollar despite it hitting a new record, according to Tom Winnifrith, CEO at financial services firm Rivington Street Holdings.

"The U.S. trade deficit and debt continue to grow and the authorities are reluctant to address the problem, preferring to print money. America is practically owned by China."[9]

With the euro looking about as stable as a bowl of Jell-O and the partisan American media supporting President Obama's "Summer of Recovery," which is a total myth, the U.S. dollar has gotten a stay of execution in the courtroom of global economics.

Jim Amrhein reports that when the economic meltdown began in November of 2007, Alan Greenspan said it was "absolutely conceivable that the Euro will replace the dollar as reserve currency, or will be traded by an equally important reserve currency."[10]

Alan Greenspan's voice echoed the sentiments of other important nations, including China, Russia, India, Brazil, Venezuela, Iran, and others. Let's remember that the UN, OPEC, the International Monetary Fund, and G-20 have all called for the dollar to be replaced as the world reserve currency.

The death of the dollar in the near future is a reality, not hysteria.

Amrhein continues, "Even after the Eurozone gets its act together, we'll still be printing dollars by the truckload, artificially fending off inflation with a bunch of book-cooking hocus-pocus and pursuing (or begging) other nations to underwrite our overspending by purchasing dollar-based debt. That's not how a strong, stable global reserve currency is maintained."[11]

America is now in the economic grip of China because "the debtor [America] is servant to the lender [China]" (Proverbs 22:7).

China, with its economic war chest full of American dollars is cherry-picking and purchasing our finest assets. China is making major moves in the global gold market to position the yuan (Chinese currency) to replace the U.S. dollar as the international currency for world trade.

"With the ascendency of Barak Obama to the presidency, the health-care debacle, the uncertain domestic economy, climate-gate, various

European debt crises, oil spills, and government bailouts and takeovers dominating the news . . . a very significant world monetary development is falling by the wayside . . . the fact that China is doing everything it can to aggregate the bulk of planet Earth's gold inside its borders." [12]

Jim Amrhein reports that China has made three major policy changes aimed at finding and keeping more of the world's gold supplies:

1. China is secretly stockpiling gold.

2. China is lifting the moratorium on private precious metals owner-ship by allowing Chinese citizens to own gold and encouraging them to put 5 percent of their savings in gold and silver.

3. China is strictly banning the export of gold bullion. [13]

"Renowned economist Nouriel Roubini went even further in his state-ment. According to a *Telegraph* UK article from last May, the New York University Professor warned that the yuan was better positioned than the dollar to be the 21st Century reserve currency, and that China's already pushing—via the International Monetary Fund—to make it so." [14]

Hence, the death of the dollar appears imminent, while the Chinese position themselves to become the economic powerhouse of planet Earth. America is putting its faith for the future in paper, promises, and voo-doo economics, while China is becoming more solvent with a currency backed by gold.

The Bloomberg News website reported on September 8, 2010, that "China and Russia plan to start trading in each other's currencies as the world's second-biggest energy consumer and the world's largest energy supplier seek to diminish the dollar's role in global trade." [15]

The screaming headline from Jerome Corsi's Alert reads: "420 BANKS DEMAND ONE WORLD CURRENCY!" [16]

Charles Dallara, the Institute of International Finance's managing di-rector, "encouraged a return to the G-20 commitment to utilize Interna-tional Monetary Fund special drawing rights to create an international *one world currency alternative* to the U.S. dollar as a new standard of foreign-exchange reserves." [17]

Likewise, a July UN report called for the replacement of the dollar as the standard for holding foreign-exchange reserves in the international trade with a new one world currency issued by the International Monetary Fund.[18]

The economic power players of planet Earth have the U.S. dollar in their crosshairs. As America's printing presses monetize our debt, the nations of the world are going for the gold and a divorce from the dollar. The die is cast and the outcome is certain. The end result will affect every person on earth . . . and will devastate America.

MILITARY MIGHT AND ECONOMIC STRENGTH

The two most powerful symbols of American power in the world are the nation's military might and its economic strength. America's military might has been demonstrated numerous times in the past century, from its rescue of European democracies in World War I, to its defeat of the Axis powers in World War II, to its victory in the long Cold War against Soviet expansionism. In 1991, an American-led coalition defeated one of the largest armies in the world in a six-week air attack capped by a four-day ground assault, ejecting Iraq from Kuwait. Twelve years later, a smaller U.S.-led coalition defeated the Iraqi army again, this time in only three weeks, toppling the government. When it comes to military might, the United States is a hyper-power with no equal.

But a nation's military might is founded on its economic strength, for it is a nation's economy that pays for its military forces, their equipment, and training. Here again, the American economy has been the global leader since World War II, to the point that people casually compare the American currency to a deity, referring to the "almighty dollar." There have been other economic heavyweights in world history. In the ancient world, the Greek drachma was "almighty." In their own large spheres of influence, the Chinese liang and Islamic dinar reigned supreme. Then in the modern world, the British pound sterling was an international power for over two centuries.[19] But the fate of the British pound sterling presents a warning sign to the United States. The dominant global currency until World War II, the pound lost that status by 1945; with that development, the United Kingdom lost its position as a global leader, economically and militarily.[20]

The United States is not immune to a similar fate. The clearest threat to America's ability to remain strong, economically and militarily, is the danger posed by the nation's fiscal policies—or lack thereof. The dollar's decline as the world's reserve currency has been driven by decisions and choices made by political leaders, both in terms of changing the foundation of the nation's currency and in pursuing budgetary policies that have led to skyrocketing budget deficits and out-of-this-world debt. In this chapter, we will explore the *twin problems* of *currency health* and *budget health*. But before we can truly understand these twin problems, we first need a brief history on: How did we get where we are now? Where are we going? And why does it matter? The story told here should be of grave concern to every individual who cares about the future health of the nation.

A BRIEF HISTORY OF THE DOLLAR

To understand the current danger to the dollar, we must first understand its history. The dollar has been the world's reserve currency since the end of World War II. It is part of nearly 90 percent of all foreign exchange transactions. Wherever currencies are traded, they are typically converted to dollars first, testifying to the central place of the dollar in the world. This global currency performs several valuable services for the world economy, including serving as a medium of exchange, a store of value, and a unit of account. In other words, a global currency allows people to agree on prices, preserve savings, and measure the worth of objects or services.[21]

Americans have always been suspicious of central banks. The first Bank of the United States was established by Alexander Hamilton, President George Washington's Secretary of the Treasury, but it died in 1811 when Congress voted not to renew its charter. Congress reversed itself a few years later, chartering a Second Bank of the United States in 1816, but President Andrew Jackson saw it as a tool of elite financial interests and made war against the bank, ultimately destroying it. There followed about eighty years of periodic bank panics and financial crises, with a federal government incapable of dealing effectively with the economic disruptions. Things got bad enough in the Panic of 1907 that political leaders turned to banker J. P. Morgan to bail out the system.[22]

At the same time, Americans were arguing over the existence of central banks, they also argued over the foundation of the dollars that would be placed in those banks. Early Americans constantly debated the question of paper money versus gold and silver coins. The idea behind a "gold standard" for currency is that a nation should fix its currency to a specific amount of gold. In theory, any person could go to a bank and redeem his money in gold. This system restrains inflation, since gold can flow in and out of a country depending on how much money is created, and whether that money is seen as credible. But this system also makes it very difficult to fight major wars, and it is no accident that inflation is associated with warfare, as governments print large amounts of paper currency to fund the war effort. President Abraham Lincoln, for example, suspended the gold guarantee for bank notes and printed large quantities of "greenbacks"—paper money not backed by anything but the government's word—to pay for the Union campaign in the Civil War. Prices rose 74 percent from 1861 to 1864, the sharpest spike in inflation since the Revolutionary War. After the war was over, the greenbacks were gradually retired and the nation returned to the gold standard, and over the next two decades, in a period known as the "great deflation," prices fell to their prewar level.[23]

The gold standard remained the global standard, which benefited Great Britain and its British pound sterling. But in the wake of the Panic of 1907, the United States responded by moving toward the creation of another central bank—the Federal Reserve. The Federal Reserve Act, signed by President Woodrow Wilson in December 1913, created a new central bank, composed of a series of regional banks coordinated by a national board of commercial bankers. As European nations abandoned gold again to finance World War I, the American dollar increasingly became a currency of choice in international trade, and the Federal Reserve became the "lender of last resort." Foreigners knew that when they did business in dollars there was an institution backing up those transactions on behalf of American commercial banks.[24]

The Great Depression and World War II wreaked havoc on the world financial system. In the United States, the run on the banks in the early 1930s led to large-scale business failures and high unemployment. Customers demanded gold for their dollars, prompting President Franklin Roosevelt to take the dollar off the gold standard, declare a bank holiday, and attempt the confiscation of privately held gold. Roosevelt issued an executive order that stated, "All persons are hereby required to deliver on or before May 1, 1933, to a Federal Reserve Bank or a branch or agency thereof or to any member bank of the Federal Reserve System all gold coin, gold bullion and gold certificates now owned by them"—to hand over, in fact, their property. The government paid citizens dollars at the official exchange rate of $20.67 an ounce, then devalued the dollar 69 percent by raising the exchange rate to $35 an ounce in 1934.[25] World War II completed the process of devastating the world economy, but by this time the relative health of the American economy—compared to those in war-torn Europe and Asia—left the dollar the king of the world.

The United States became the dominant economic power in 1944. It was then, at a meeting of delegates from forty-four nations in Bretton Woods, New Hampshire, that the dollar became the world's key reserve currency. Famed British economist John Maynard Keynes proposed a new global financial system in which a global currency called a "bancor" would replace gold. But the United States was the real world power as the war began to draw to a close, and it would control events at Bretton Woods. Rejecting Keynes's proposal, the delegates instead agreed to new plan for the dollar to be fixed to gold at a rate of $35 an ounce, with all other currencies in turn fixed to the dollar, the exchange rate depending on how strong the various countries' economies were. Washington agreed to convert foreign central bank dollar holdings into gold upon request. Thus, the dollar would enforce stability in the world by keeping foreign currencies at fixed values, while the dollar itself would remain stable and legitimate by being anchored to gold. In theory, other countries could not expand their money supply irresponsibly by printing currency, since that would undermine their currency's exchange rate with the dollar. Neither could the United States print more money that it could redeem with gold. The Bretton Woods agreement also created the International Monetary Fund (IMF), which had the power to decide whether a country could change its fixed rate against the dollar. Thus, as World War II ended, the American dollar achieved unprecedented status as the one currency against which all others would be measured.[26]

But the seeds of the dollar's decline were planted even before the dollar achieved its dominant status. While John Maynard Keynes did not win the battle at Bretton Woods, he won the larger war when it came to economic policy. The Great Depression ended the earlier economic paradigm that saw balanced budgets as the appropriate goal for the federal government. This older paradigm was seen by Progressive economists as part of a larger Calvinist vision in which individuals were expected to practice self-denial, sacrifice, and delayed gratification, thinking that one's true reward was in the future—in the long run. Keynes is famous for remarking, "In the long run we are all dead." The important thing, he purported, was to enjoy life *now*. Pleasure should be pursued, and suffering is unnecessary. Instead of delayed gratification, we should embrace self-gratification. Part and parcel with this new philosophy was a government program of more liberal credit. Americans could now pursue the "American Dream" of home ownership, as home mortgages moved from seven- and ten-year limits to an astonishing (for the time) twenty years. Consumption became the popular economic philosophy. The suffering and sacrifice of World War II—not just in battle, but also on the home front—solidified this perspective. High personal savings rates during the war led to pent-up consumer demand and massive consumption once the war was over, resulting in inflation. The combination of Roosevelt's large New Deal entitlement programs and the large defense budgets—required by the new Cold War for postwar demobilization that quickly transitioned to a large-standing military—placed the nation's fiscal health in jeopardy.[27]

In the years following Bretton Woods, the key question was whether the United States could continue to convert dollars to gold on demand, and for nearly two decades, the system worked. Inflation and interest rates were relatively low, and the American economy grew at an average annual rate of 6.6 percent. But the world economy grew faster than the supply of gold. Budget deficits began to rise as the United States helped reconstruct Western Europe under the Marshall Plan, then served as the West's primary military defender by trying to contain the Soviet Union, fighting wars in Korea and Vietnam, all the while supporting large New Deal–inspired social programs. The dominant programmatic liberal governing philosophy culminated in President Lyndon Johnson's Great Society, in which the nation embraced massive new spending in such areas as Medicare and Medicaid, student loans, and low-income housing. As the United States printed or borrowed more money to pay the cost of these programs, leading to greater inflation, it also sent billions of dollars overseas for which it had no gold. Other countries became concerned that America would not be able to exchange all of those dollars for gold. A bank run could devastate the world economy.[28]

If the 1944 Bretton Woods agreement signaled the dollar's rise to dominance, its decline could easily be identified as beginning in August 1971. By then, foreigners held more than $45 billion, even though the United States had only $10 billion in gold reserves. In response to this overvaluing of the dollar, President Richard Nixon took the dollar off the gold standard, suspending the right of foreign central banks to convert their dollars to gold. This move, intended at first to be temporary, ended the Bretton Woods agreement and freed other currencies to trade against the dollar and each other. The Smithsonian Agreement replaced Bretton Woods several months later, devaluing the dollar 7.9 percent to $38 an ounce of gold. Just over a year after that, the government devalued the dollar again—11 percent, to $42 an ounce of gold. In March 1973, officials determined that the system was dead, and they abandoned the gold guarantee completely. From now on all currencies, including the dollar, would "float" against each other, finding their own value in the currency market. The only thing backing the dollar now was the faith of the world that the American government was able and willing to honor all dollars. Unrestrained by limited gold supplies or any other tangible object, the government could now print and borrow more dollars than ever.[29]

With Nixon's move, the value of the dollar would be determined by the foreign exchange market. Currency traders would examine the nation's economic policies, looking at such things as budget and trade deficits, interest rates, and inflation, none of which was healthy in the United States in the 1970s. One aftereffect of Nixon's decision was OPEC's 1973 oil boycott, which quadrupled the price of oil. Inflation erodes the value of the dollar, and people do not want to buy dollars when inflation is higher than the interest paid on bonds. Oil, however, is traded in dollars, so a decline in the dollar's value also leads to less money for oil. Using American support for Israel in the Yom Kippur War as their pretext, Arab oil countries compensated for inflation by raising oil prices. The result was even higher inflation (12 percent) and a recession, with unemployment hitting 9 percent—a combination of factors that led to the "stagflation" of the late 1970s. President Jimmy Carter bemoaned the declining dollar in his infamous "crisis of confidence" speech in 1979. During the era of the gold standard, the annual inflation rate was a mere 0.3 percent. In other words, during this era the dollar declined in value at an annual rate of just 0.3 percent. Since moving off the gold standard, a process that began with Roosevelt, inflation has averaged an annual rate more than ten times its gold standard average.[30]

The Federal Reserve, led by Chairman Paul Volcker, responded to Carter's crisis of confidence by dramatically raising interest rates to crush inflation, which peaked at 13 percent. Interest rates approached an unheard-of 20 percent at this time, and unemployment in the ensuing recession exceeded 10 percent. The combination of President Ronald Reagan's tax cuts and Paul Volcker's interest rate hikes worked. Inflation eventually fell to 4 percent, and the stock market began a quarter-century surge that saw the Dow Industrials rise from below 800 to over 14,000. The end of the Cold War and the collapse of the Soviet bloc opened up new markets, solidifying again the dollar's place in the global economy.[31]

However, the prosperity of the late twentieth century hid lingering and persistent weaknesses in the American economy. The tech-stock bubble that burst in 2000 segued directly into a real estate bubble that collapsed with even greater ferocity in 2006. Following a public philosophy that preached home ownership for all—the American Dream—the Federal Reserve kept interest rates exceptionally low and encouraged the development and use of subprime loans to people who had a weak or troubled credit history—another example of Keynes's belief that consumption is good. Many people believed that the nation had entered a new period of "riskless risk," in which housing prices would stay high permanently and homes could be used as short-term investments.[32] The resulting housing crash and loss of confidence in the credit markets had worldwide consequences, as the nation entered what has come to be known as the Great Recession.

By taking the United States off the gold standard, Nixon allowed the government to print large sums of money. The foreign market for those dollars has enabled the nation to borrow money overseas to increase government spending while also cutting taxes—the ultimate example of eating our cake and having it too. That ability has always depended on overseas markets thinking the United States has a sound economy and has not gone too deeply into debt.[33] The financial crisis that hit in 2008 called these assumptions into question, and the result has been a dramatic decline in the value of the dollar. That decline is not all bad. A lower dollar allows American exports to be less expensive overseas, which could aid American manufacturing, perhaps narrowing the trade deficit.

Of course, this also means that imported goods will be more expensive, as will trips to foreign vacation spots.[34] More important, though, the current decline is tied to the fiscal consequences of the financial crisis, consequences that have their roots in earlier decisions.

We've just seen a brief history of the American dollar. Budget deficits and the national debt have come up several times in this history. Before we can understand the *current* danger America faces, we need to take one more trip down the road of history to focus on *budget politics*.

A BRIEF HISTORY OF THE NATIONAL DEBT

There is nothing new about a national debt. The nation was founded in debt necessary to fight the War of Independence. Debt is a completely constitutional phenomenon, for the Constitution grants Congress the power "to borrow Money on the credit of the United States."[35] America's first and greatest Secretary of the Treasury, Alexander Hamilton, said, "A national debt, if it is not excessive, will be to us a national blessing."[36] The obvious question, of course, is how we define "excessive," but Hamilton skillfully used debt management and the creation of a national bank to place the new nation on a firm fiscal foundation.

Battles Over Debt

Just as early American history saw numerous battles over gold, silver, greenbacks, and national banks, so did those battles include fights over debt. The general pattern in American history has been that the national debt rose in times of war and then declined when the war was over. President Andrew Jackson actually succeeded in retiring the national debt completely in 1835, the only president who has accomplished that feat. Unfortunately, the budget surplus and increased money supply that ensued led to increased inflation and speculation. Jackson fought this early real estate bubble by ordering the government to accept only gold and silver in payment for land. Land prices fell, people defaulted on loans, and Wall Street experienced its first great crash, leading to a depression in 1837. The resulting seventy-two-month economic contraction was the longest one in American history, and it destroyed the reelection chances of Jackson's handpicked successor, Martin Van Buren.[37]

The greatest crisis the country had ever faced led to the highest debt up to that time. The debt rose to unheard of levels as Lincoln used deficit spending to pursue the Union effort in the Civil War. Sitting at $2.76 billion in 1866, the debt was forty-two times what it had been just six years earlier. For the next twenty-eight years, however, the government ran budget surpluses in a largely successful effort to reduce the debt, and by the time the depression of 1893 hit, the debt had been reduced by two thirds, dropping to under $1 billion. Even with that depression and more expansive (and thus expensive) foreign policies under presidents William McKinley and Theodore Roosevelt, the national debt remained stable, even declining as a percentage of gross national product (GNP).[38]

It is important to note that the principal revenue source for the federal budget during this time was not a personal income tax. The income tax had a brief early life for a few years during and after the Civil War, but the Supreme Court eventually declared it unconstitutional. The functions of the federal government were capably funded through tariffs and excise taxes.

The First Income Tax

The cause of the income tax was picked up again first by Populists and then by Progressive-era reformers. The same political faction that established the Federal Reserve also pushed for a constitutional amendment making an income tax legitimate. One month before Woodrow Wilson took office, the Sixteenth Amendment was adopted. The main argument for an income tax was based less on government revenue than it was on social engineering. The primary goal of income tax cheerleaders was to change the distribution of wealth. This was true both for the personal income tax and for the corporate income tax. One reason for the lack of political opposition to the income tax was the fact that the original model affected only 2 percent of the population. As much as 98 percent of families were exempted, either due to the high income level taxed or such features as the marital deduction. Tax rates ranged from a low of 1 percent on incomes above $3,000 to a high of 7 percent on incomes over $500,000 (and keep in mind that these are 1913 dollars—again, 98 percent of Americans were not affected).[39]

Once in place, however, funding streams like an income tax are hard to remove. The core impulse of Progressive reformers at the turn of the century was a suspicion of representative democracy and the constitutional system that governed it. Progressive leaders distrusted the popular will, especially as it was manifested in vigorous political parties and big-city political machines. At the same time, Progressives such as Woodrow Wilson believed that the constitutional doctrine of separation of powers was the central defect of the American political system, since it made rapid change difficult. Thus, Progressive reformers sought to distance the popular will from political power by creating new bureaucratic institutions that would allow public issues to be decided and managed by professional experts—technocrats who knew what was right for the nation and could manage it for the common good. Democratic responsiveness was devalued in favor of management by experts who could institute necessary change without the burden of politics—including people who know what the "appropriate" level of wealth is for everyone and who used the income tax code to pursue that goal. Liberal theory sought to raise revenues by raising marginal rates on the incomes of the rich, even as the rich tended to find ways to shelter that income. With the income tax in place, the revenue structure of the federal budget changed from a bias toward tariffs to one dominated by the income tax. Tariffs and excise taxes have moved from providing more than 90 percent of the federal revenues to less than 10 percent today, while income taxes quickly moved to a dominant role in the tax code as early as 1920, and it has been that way ever since. World War I prompted more borrowing and taxing, as spending and the national debt both skyrocketed, but the new income tax was able to produce revenue very quickly.[40]

It is here that John Maynard Keynes reenters our story. For most of American history up to the Great Depression, the standard practice was to increase the national debt to deal with wars or depressions, but then work to draw down that debt (through balanced budgets or budget surpluses) when those times were over. The Great Depression, however, changed that understanding, and the dominant objective of the federal government since then has been to avoid a repeat of that economic disaster. The pay-as-you-go philosophy was abandoned in favor of managed deficit spending. It is common for contemporary fans of balanced budgets to compare the government and the family. Families are told to spend only what they have, or they will have to borrow from someone else, putting themselves in debt. In the same way, we should expect the federal government to spend only what it takes in. Keynes, however, argued that families and the government are not the same things, for families must borrow from others, but a nation can borrow from itself. Thus, deficits are not necessarily bad, and the national debt does not really matter. The result of this economic philosophy was a change in political practice to use higher taxes and higher spending—not to balance the budget or pay down the debt, but to fund popular social programs and appeal to different segments of the population through fiscal policy. Political leaders use the tax code and government programs to give favors to interest groups, none of whom is terribly interested in cutting anything. Even though the Great Depression ended not through social programs, but through World War II, when the war was over, the government's priority was not debt reduction, but management of its new programs.[41]

John Steele Gordon ably summarizes the weaknesses of this system, all of which revolve around human nature. First, the federal government is incapable of controlling a very complex, dynamic, and unpredictable economic system. The law of unintended consequences often rears its ugly head. For example, in 1947 Congress exempted company-provided health insurance from income taxes, causing a large number of people to stop caring as much about health care costs, since their insurance was provided and often paid by their employer. This seemingly innocent element of public policy, coupled with the addition of Medicare and Medicaid in the 1960s, led to the exploding costs of health care we experience today—prompting a major effort by the federal government to control costs through massive health care reform that are largely an unintended and unforeseen development of public policy. Another example of this inability is the luxury tax on boats and airplanes imposed by Congress in 1990. Designed to bring in $16 million, it actually brought in far less, because wealthy individuals simply stopped buying boats and planes, resulting in layoffs in those industries.[42]

Second, the government lacks timely and reliable data to make decisions. It does not know the nation is in a recession for several months, and economic data is always being updated with new information, making the old data used to make policy decisions outdated. Economic theories often assume perfect information, and such a thing simply does not exist.

Third, it is a fact of political life that no elected politician wants to pursue unpopular policies during bad economic times, even if those policies are wise. Politicians are ambitious individuals who always seek reelection, and it is a rare bird that is willing to take the fall for a tough decision. But spending programs create interest groups that seek to expand and perpetuate those programs at the cost of the nation's fiscal health.[43]

President Ronald Reagan succeeded in lowering income tax rates, making tax cuts one of the signature issues of the last thirty years. But despite a more conservative political philosophy, preaching balanced budgets and cuts in government programs, more and more spending is automatic, geared toward huge untouchable entitlements like Social Security and Medicare that are largely beyond political control. The result is ever-higher deficits as the government spends more money on programs the tax system cannot fund. To put the situation in perspective, the 2009 federal budget *deficit* was larger than the entire federal *budget* in 1993, just sixteen years earlier. And increased deficits lead to spiraling debt. It took the government until 1962 to accumulate $300 billion of debt, most of it to fight wars. In the forty-seven years since then, the debt has grown *thirty-nine times* that amount.[44]

This fiscal train wreck has exacerbated the problems with the dollar that are spelled out in the earlier section of this chapter. With the background for these twin problems now explained—the currency health and the budget health (or lack thereof)—we can turn our attention to the most important questions: Why does it matter, and where are we going? What are the dangers facing contemporary America, and what are the larger consequences of this present crisis?

CURRENT DANGERS: HOW DID WE GET WHERE WE ARE?

First, the mismatch between government revenues and government spending is where many of these problems start, so let's begin there. In addition to the growth in spending described above, the recession that began in 2008 greatly exacerbated the fiscal crisis of the nation. Not only did tax revenues decline, but also government spending spiked in an effort to prevent a worse economic disaster. Examples of this increased government spending include $700 billion for the Troubled Asset Relief Program (TARP) bank bailout, supported by President George W. Bush in the waning days of his presidency, and $787 billion for the first economic stimulus program under President Barack Obama in 2009. That additional spending led to a record fiscal year 2009 budget deficit of well over $1 trillion, an amount that was triple that of the previous year—the previous record holder.[45]

Figure 1 graphically illustrates the problem, tracing budget surpluses and deficits from the immediate postwar period in 1946 to estimated figures up to 2015. Although there are more deficit years than surplus years even toward the beginning of this series, deficits for the first two decades appear fairly manageable. Only in the 1960s do they become persistent, before exploding in the 1970s and 1980s. The prosperity of the 1990s— now known to be based on a shaky foundation—led to a brief period of budget surpluses late in the decade, but the tech stock collapse and the terrorist attacks of 9/11 brought the nation back to large deficit spending. Even these large numbers pale in comparison, however, to the massive spike in the deficit propelled by the financial crisis of 2008. More optimistic estimates for the following years still see deficits that are significantly higher than pre–financial crisis numbers. They also optimistically assume a growing economy, and do not account for yet-to-be legislated spending projects, such as large-scale health care reform and possible climate change regulations. In fact, the Obama administration projects deficits may total more than $9 trillion over the next decade.

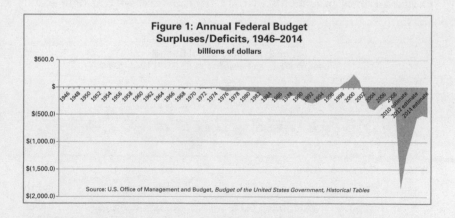

Figure 1: Annual Federal Budget Surpluses/Deficits, 1946–2014
billions of dollars

Source: U.S. Office of Management and Budget, *Budget of the United States Government, Historical Tables*

Another way to understand the deficit problem is to examine budget surpluses and deficits as a percentage of the nation's gross domestic product (GDP). Gross domestic product is the sum of all goods and services produced within the borders of the United States. GDP can be seen as a summary measurement of the overall economic performance of a nation. Growth in the GDP is associated with prosperity; declines are associated with recessions and depressions. The higher a deficit is as a percentage of the GDP, the greater the burden that deficit is on the society. Figure 2 recapitulates the data from Figure 1, this time expressing the surpluses and deficits since World War II as percentages of the nation's GDP. Because of the effects of inflation on the value of the dollar over time, this version of the data is seen as a more accurate and realistic portrayal of the problem. As the figure demonstrates, for most of the postwar era, deficits as a percentage of GDP were lower than they were in World War II. In fact, the deficit in 1943 exceeded 30 percent of GDP—understandable, given that the United States was deeply involved in the greatest war in human history. Until recently, the biggest postwar bulge in the deficit was between the mid-1970s and mid-1990s, when the deficit oscillated between 3 percent and 6 percent of GDP. Again, however, the financial crisis has changed the rules. Deficits as a percentage of GDP tripled from 2008 to 2009, to just under 10 percent. This figure is significantly higher than any other budget since World War II. One analysis suggests that by 2050 federal deficits will comprise 20 percent of GDP.[46] To think of it in another way, the federal government is now beginning to spend money in amounts that are typically necessary to fight world wars.

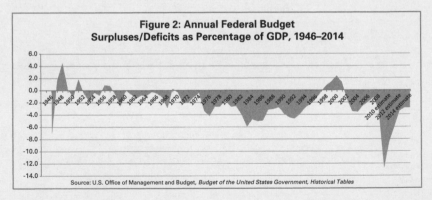

Figure 2: Annual Federal Budget
Surpluses/Deficits as Percentage of GDP, 1946–2014

Source: U.S. Office of Management and Budget, *Budget of the United States Government, Historical Tables*

Finally, we can make inflation-adjusted comparisons between surpluses and deficits by comparing the numbers in constant dollars.

When we use a measurement like constant dollars, we are able to compare values based on one specific date. For example, 2010 dollars are worth significantly less than 1946 dollars, a fact that may serve to exaggerate budget performance. Figure 3 recapitulates the data from the first two figures in constant 2005 dollars—the value of the dollar in 2005. This gives us a very clear picture of changes across time based on one constant standard. Thus, we see sharper turns in both surpluses and deficits since 1946, even in earlier years. What does *not* change is the extreme spike of 2009 and later. Clearly, the financial crisis has rewritten the rules for what we should consider to be "beyond comprehension."

Of course, all of these deficits create ever-higher debt, in numbers that are truly astonishing. Figure 4 traces the growth of the national debt from 1946 to estimated figures for 2015. It is interesting to note the transformation over time. A national debt of $271 billion in 1946 was only marginally higher a decade later. It took ten years for the debt to grow by a third from roughly $300 billion in 1962 to $408 billion in 1971. Then the debt more than doubled in the 1970s (from $381 billion to $909 billion), and tripled in the 1980s (from $909 billion to $3.2 trillion). Growth of the debt slowed down a little in the 1990s, due to the surge in the stock market. It took a full thirteen years for the 1990 level to double. Unfortunately, it has taken only half that time to nearly double once again, from $6.2 trillion in 2002 to almost $12 trillion in 2009. The federal Office of Management and Budget (OMB) estimates that the nation will add over half again to that amount by 2015, a debt level exceeding $19 trillion. On our scorecard, that represents a tripling from the debt's 2002 level.

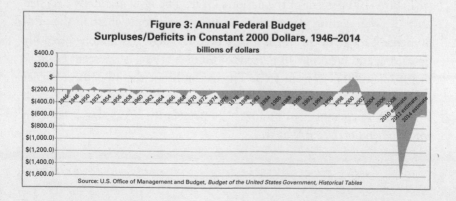

Figure 3: Annual Federal Budget Surpluses/Deficits in Constant 2000 Dollars, 1946–2014
billions of dollars

Source: U.S. Office of Management and Budget, *Budget of the United States Government, Historical Tables*

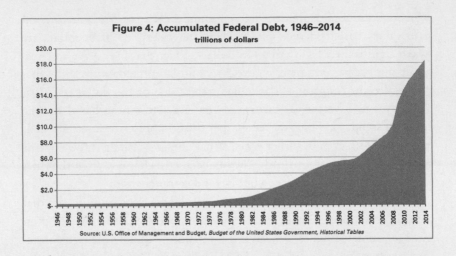

Figure 4: Accumulated Federal Debt, 1946–2014
trillions of dollars

Source: U.S. Office of Management and Budget, *Budget of the United States Government, Historical Tables*

A better method of understanding these numbers is to examine the national debt as a percentage of GDP. Comparing the level of the debt to the GDP is somewhat akin to examining a family's debt load and comparing it to their net worth. We tend to be much more concerned at the prospect of a new college graduate entering the workforce $100,000 in debt from student loans, with no prospects for repayment, than we are over someone carrying over a minor amount on his credit card balance. So it is with the national debt. Figure 5 recapitulates the data from Figure 4, this time expressing the accumulation of the national debt since World War II as percentages of the nation's GDP. Again, we find ourselves approaching debt levels that are typically associated with fully mobilized world war. In fact, the national debt during World War II was well above 100 percent of the nation's GDP. The level gradually declined after the war, coming down to its postwar norm somewhere in the mid-30 percent range in the 1970s. Since then the debt has marched steadily upward again, breaking 40 percent of GDP in 1984, 50 percent of GDP in 1987, and 60 percent in 1991. The nation broke the 80 percent barrier in 2009, and OMB projections indicate that the national debt will push through 90 percent in 2010 to over 100 percent by 2012—levels not seen since the end of World War II.

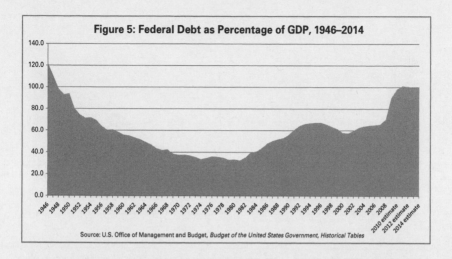

Figure 5: Federal Debt as Percentage of GDP, 1946–2014

Source: U.S. Office of Management and Budget, *Budget of the United States Government, Historical Tables*

Perhaps the most sobering method of understanding the national debt is to examine what it means for each inhabitant of the country. We can think of the debt in per capita terms, which means dividing the entire national debt by the number of people who live in the country—the people ultimately responsible for paying off that debt over time, through taxes or slashed benefit programs. Figure 6 does that, recapitulating the national debt data from 1950 to 2007 (this exercise requires accurate population figures, which come from the U.S. census). For comparison's sake, in 1920 the per capita debt was only $137. By 1940, New Deal spending had raised it to $281 per person. That figure rose sharply in World War II. Nevertheless, we see that the debt per capita was fairly steady until the late 1960s, not rising above $1,700 per person until 1967. Alas, the numbers doubled in the 1970s, moving from $1,858 in 1970 to $3,992 in 1980. In the 1980s, they tripled, to $12,818 in 1990. After leveling out for a few years in the late 1990s, the national debt shot up again to over $29,000 per person in 2007, rising to over $38,000 per person in 2009. That number equates to over $154,000 for a family of four. Budget and population projections from the government estimate a per capita national debt of nearly $59,000 by 2020—a staggering $236,000 for a family of four.[47]

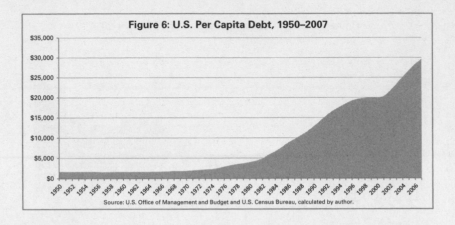

Figure 6: U.S. Per Capita Debt, 1950–2007

Source: U.S. Office of Management and Budget and U.S. Census Bureau, calculated by author.

One of the reasons the level of the debt is so damaging is that a significant portion of the federal budget is now dedicated to paying the interest on that debt. This money does not go to any tangible government program. As with credit cards, borrowing is not free, and the higher the debt, the higher the interest payments. Figure 7 traces the growth of the interest paid on the national debt from 1962 to estimated figures for 2015. As long as the interest stays manageable, it is not a large concern, much as small interest payments on credit cards do not adversely affect a family's budget. When the interest starts chewing up more and more of the total budget, however, things are more worrisome, and that is exactly what has happened in the United States. Net interest on the national debt for the 2008 federal budget was over $252 billion, and government projections see that figure doubling in the next few years. We are fast approaching the point where the interest on the debt will consume more than 10 percent of the total federal budget—hundreds of billions of dollars that could be used either for other purposes or for tax cuts. In fact, interest payments on the debt now comprise the fourth largest category in the budget, after Social Security, Medicare/Medicaid, and national defense. Worse still, these numbers do not tell the whole story, for they do not include the interest expense of intragovernmental debt. This is the debt the government owes to the Social Security Trust Fund, because the government borrows money each year from that fund to pay for normal operating expenses. The true interest on the debt for 2008 was in fact closer to $451 billion. By 2015, it may be as high as $888 billion.[48]

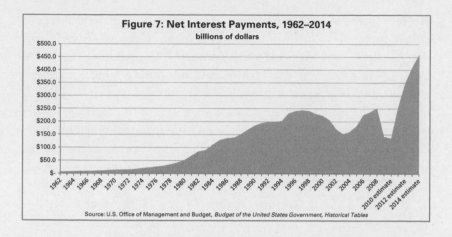

Figure 7: Net Interest Payments, 1962–2014
billions of dollars

Source: U.S. Office of Management and Budget, *Budget of the United States Government, Historical Tables*

It gets worse. The long-term fiscal health of the nation is greatly endangered by the looming financial catastrophes in entitlement programs like Social Security and Medicare. These programs automatically allocate dollars to anyone who qualifies, making them nondiscretionary parts of the federal budget. The number of workers supporting each retiree in America—in other words, the number of people currently paying into these entitlement programs that are supporting current retirees—has dropped from over 5 workers in 1960 to just over 3 in 2008. Projections are that this number will drop even further in the next couple of decades, to 2.2. This means fewer workers supporting more retirees, creating greater stress on the financial health of Social Security and Medicare. Between 2000 and 2030, the sixty-five-and-over set will more than double as the Baby Boomers retire and start to collect their benefits. This cohort will total 20 percent of the population, and entitlement programs that currently comprise 40 percent of the federal budget will jump to 75 percent.[49]

Medicare is in the most dire straits at present. Its insurance benefits have *already* exceeded its tax revenues. Figure 8 displays the growing annual deficits of the Medicare program, with projected deficits of over $50 billion by as early as 2014. The government projects that it will not be able to pay currently scheduled full Medicare benefits as early as 2019—nine years from now. Social Security benefits will begin exceeding its tax revenues as early as 2017, and by the early 2040s will be unable to keep pace with scheduled benefits. The only options to solve this

problem—raise taxes, decrease benefits, or change the retirement age—
are all unpopular. The three major entitlement programs—Social Security, Medicare, and Medicaid—will consume 100 percent of the federal
budget within the next sixty years, crowding out all other budget categories, including interest payments and national security. Figure 9
illustrates the extent to which Social Security and Medicare have out-
stripped spending on national defense and international programs in recent years. One may expect defense spending to level off, as the Obama
administration draws down the war on terror, but no demographic magic
will prevent entitlements from continuing their upward climb. Indeed,
by 2080 the national debt may increase to over 600 percent of GDP—

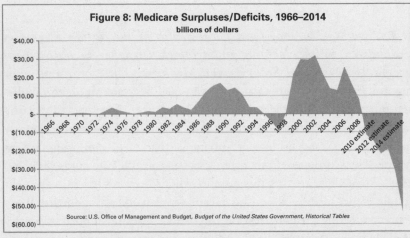

Figure 8: Medicare Surpluses/Deficits, 1966–2014
billions of dollars

Source: U.S. Office of Management and Budget, *Budget of the United States Government, Historical Tables*

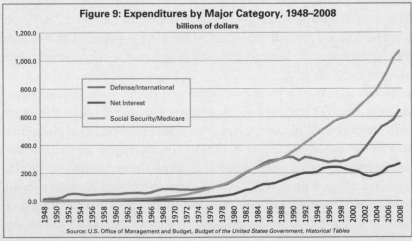

Figure 9: Expenditures by Major Category, 1948–2008
billions of dollars

- Defense/International
- Net Interest
- Social Security/Medicare

Source: U.S. Office of Management and Budget, *Budget of the United States Government, Historical Tables*

almost six times the historical high of 109 percent at the end of World War II.[50] One analysis suggests that, when one adds unlisted liabilities and long-term unfunded retirement and health care commitments to the national debt, the true level of obligations for the nation is a staggering $56 trillion—a figure that works out to roughly $184,000 per American, or an unimaginable $736,000 for a family of four.[51]

Finally, current and future government policies seem designed to do nothing to alleviate the nation's fiscal train wreck—and in fact, they will likely make things worse. The aforementioned TARP legislation and first stimulus plan added almost $1.5 trillion to the federal budget. There is talk of a second stimulus bill, even though by some measurements, the size of the first doubled that of Franklin Roosevelt's New Deal spending as a percentage of GDP. This is also despite the fact that some scholars argue that government stimulus programs do not really work, and in fact are recipes for inflation. Various plans to fulfill the Obama administration's promise of health care reform all attempt to come in, on, or under $1 trillion, but with full implementation delayed for several years (and thus full spending delayed as well), projections are that actual costs will explode to $2.5 trillion between 2014 and 2023. Any deficit cuts will be marginal at best and will not prevent the already ballooning deficits from continuing their upward path. There will unquestionably be tax increases of various types, totaling, perhaps, half a trillion dollars, many of them targeting employers and small businesses, as well as cuts in Medicare reimbursement rates—assuming Congress actually does that. If not, the costs will be even higher.[52]

All of this, in turn, assumes that government estimates of costs and benefits are accurate. But the federal government has done a miserable job of accurately projecting actual costs of health care reform over time. In 1965, Congress estimated that Medicare Part A would cost about $9 billion annually by 1990; instead, the actual cost was $67 billion. In 1967, the House Ways and Means Committee predicted that the entire Medicare program would cost about $12 billion in 1990; instead, the actual cost was $110 billion. In 1988, Congress estimated the cost of Medicare's home care benefit to be $4 billion in 1993—just five years away; instead, the actual cost was $10 billion, more than twice the projected amount. In 1997, Congress established the State Children's Health Insurance Program (SCHIP), planning on appropriating $40 billion over ten years. Congress had to appropriate an additional $283 million in fiscal year 2006 and $650 million in fiscal year 2007 to prevent mass disenrollments. For a variety of reasons, estimates of health care spending are consistently overly optimistic, at ratios that can exceed 10:1. If that pattern holds, a health care overhaul that is projected to cost in the neighborhood of $3.5 trillion over the next fifteen years could, in fact, run much higher—at significant cost to the nation's fiscal sanity.

In addition to all of this is the possible cap-and-trade legislation to address climate change, which some estimate could bring global expenditures of more than $10 trillion over twenty years in energy infrastructure spending alone—forcing us to paraphrase and revise upward. Former Illinois senator Everett Dirksen said it well in his famous quip: "A trillion here, a trillion there, and pretty soon you're talking about real money."[53]

None of This Bodes Well for the Near Future

The hope of some political leaders is that all of this spending will stimulate the economy and that the resulting prosperity, coupled with various political reforms, will solve our debt problem. It seems more likely, however, that any recovery from the recession will not bring jobs back to their former level. The combination of high unemployment and declining home values has led to a decline in consumer activity. Some analysts believe it may take five years or more to recover all the jobs lost in the recession. A record number of Americans are now working part-time because they have no choice, the average workweek is getting shorter (meaning less money in hourly wages), and youth unemployment is approaching 20 percent. The fact that unemployment in recent recessions peaked long after the recessions ended indicates that there are many more jobs to lose. The uncertainty surrounding current policy proposals further exacerbates the problem, for many companies will not engage in new hiring until they have a better idea what is going to happen with health care reform and climate change legislation. Since those programs will significantly change the economic dynamics in America, companies have every incentive not to hire until they know what those programs will look like in their final form and how they will affect them. Reduced business and consumer activity could mean reduced spending on cheaper imported goods from places like China, in turn slowing down its economy and cutting back on the amount of dollars that flow to the Far East—dollars that finance our debt. If the United States must then resort to printing money to finance its debt, the result will certainly be inflation.[54]

But that brings us back to where we started—the death of the dollar. It is time to conclude our journey through fiscal insanity by briefly examining the consequences of these various choices.

LARGER CONSEQUENCES: WHY DOES IT MATTER?

Recall that it is the foreign market for American dollars that has allowed the nation to borrow money overseas to finance our debt. The United States has been able to increase government spending on all sorts of programs while avoiding European-style taxes. Ever since Nixon closed the gold window, the economic stability of the country has been due not to the dollar being tied to a fixed value of gold, but to faith—faith by overseas markets that the United States has a sound economy and has not gone too deeply into debt. The recent decline in the value of the dollar is tied to the financial crisis that began in 2006 and increased in intensity in 2008. That crisis—and the government's response to the crisis—have greatly exacerbated long-existing fiscal problems. The trend lines in the charts in the previous section provide stark evidence of the train wreck facing the nation if it does not find some way to reverse course.

The decline in the dollar is simply the first manifestation of the consequences that await us. Figure 10 provides one piece of evidence for that decline, based on the value of the metal most often associated with the dollar in history: gold. As discussed earlier, the market price of gold was a constant $35 per ounce after Bretton Woods until the late 1960s. Not coincidentally, it was then that our slow-moving fiscal train wreck began to pick up speed. The market price of gold began to outstrip the official price, prompting Nixon to end the gold standard. Gold immediately surged in value, rising to $159 per ounce in 1974. By 1979, gold broke through the $300-per-ounce barrier and, with the exception of a sharp spike in 1980, it tended to oscillate between a low of $270 per ounce and a high around $450 per ounce for the next twenty-six years. When the housing bubble burst in 2006, gold began its current historic rise in value, matching its previous high of just over $600 per ounce in 2006, rising to $768 per ounce two years later, and ending 2009 more than an astonishing $1,100 per ounce.

Of course, one perspective on the *rise* in the value of gold is that it also represents a *decline* in the value of the dollar. By 2003, the dollar had lost 90 percent of its value versus gold since 1971. By 2009, the decline reached 97 percent. Put another way, in 2009 it took thirty-two times as many dollars to buy an ounce of gold as it did in 1971. Gold is often used by investors as a hedge against inflation, which can be triggered by a falling dollar. How far the dollar will fall, one can only guess, but there is clearly room for further movement for gold. Its true peak came in the middle of the stagflation of 1980, when it hit an inflation-adjusted $2,200 per ounce—twice its value in 2009.[55]

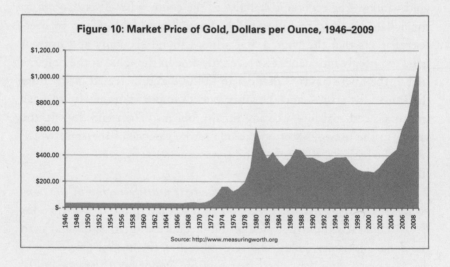

Figure 10: Market Price of Gold, Dollars per Ounce, 1946–2009

Source: http://www.measuringworth.org

In the past thirty years, the United States has moved from being the world's biggest creditor nation to the world's biggest debtor nation. One of the things that made the dollar stable in the 1990s was the willingness of foreign investors to recycle their dollars back into the U.S economy. The nation exports many items overseas, but it imports far more. Cheaper production of goods in places like China allows American companies to close factories in the United States and open new ones overseas, and allows stores like Walmart to sell inexpensive goods brought here from low-wage nations. The result is an annual trade deficit—the difference between the values of what we sell to and buy from other nations.[56] Figure 11 traces trade surpluses and deficits in the United States from 1960 to 2008. Throughout the 1960s, the United States ran slight trade surpluses, averaging over $3 billion per year. The first trade deficit—coincidentally or not—was in 1971. After that, there were only two more surplus years, in 1973 and 1975. Trade deficits in the 1980s averaged $85 billion per year. In the 1990s, they averaged $106 billion per year, with 1999 hitting $265 billion. Since 2000, the trade deficits have continued to soar, averaging over $571 billion per year. The high point was $760 billion in 2006. With the decline of the dollar, the deficits began to draw back, with 2009 seeing a more dramatic fall. As of November 2009, the trade deficit was a "mere" $340 billion.

The trade deficit most famously affects U.S.-China relations, but it exists with Japan and the European Union as well. The advantage of the trade deficit is that Americans enjoy a wide assortment of cheap goods and services from other countries. The disadvantage is that it testifies to the decline in American manufacturing over the past few decades. Also, the trade deficit means that foreign nations like China are stockpiling large amounts of American dollars as reserves to support their own currencies. By 2003, foreign investors owned $9.4 trillion of American assets, while American investors owned just $7.2 trillion of foreign assets.[57] As long as foreign investors recycle their dollars into the U.S. economy, things will remain stable.

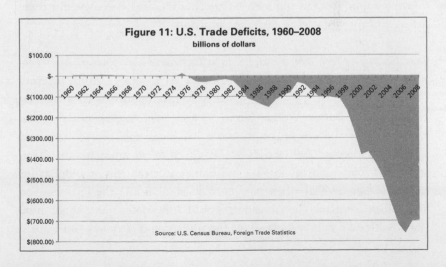

Figure 11: U.S. Trade Deficits, 1960–2008
billions of dollars

Source: U.S. Census Bureau, Foreign Trade Statistics

The fear is that foreign investors may someday take stock of America's shaky fiscal situation and decide that the country is no longer worthy of the faith they have placed in it for so many years. If that occurs, we may find foreign countries dumping their dollars. Dumping would occur if foreign nations lost confidence in the dollar, perhaps due to the frightening trends illustrated in this chapter. A dollar collapse could result from deflation, hyperinflation, or the American government defaulting on its debt payments. These countries might decide to diversify their foreign-exchange reserves, meaning they would dump dollars in favor of the euro or the yen. In fact, in 2005 reports came out that the central bank in South Korea was planning to do precisely that; as a result, the dollar tumbled against all foreign currencies, and the stock market suffered its biggest decline in nearly two years.[58] In addition to cheaper imports, a strong dollar keeps mortgage rates lower and helps fund the budget deficit. All of that changes with a weaker dollar. In many ways, the U.S. economy is as much dependent on foreign cash as it is on foreign oil. One analyst said it best: "Having the reserve currency status is like being able to write check after check and not have anyone cash them. But when you lose the reserve currency status, it's as if all those checks are taken out from under the mattress, and suddenly cashed."[59]

It is not clear what currency could replace the dollar as the world's reserve currency. Many scholars and analysts advocate using the IMF's Special Drawing Rights (SDRs) as the basis for a new world currency. Certainly, the euro is an option, and there has been talk about an "Asian Currency unit" that would serve as another regional currency, but there are significant obstacles to such developments.[60]

Just because there are obstacles to alternative currencies, however, does not mean the threat does not exist. At the G8 summit meeting in July 2009, Russian President Dmitry Medvedev displayed a coin labeled "United Future World Currency" and advocated diversifying the global currency system away from the dollar, a call echoed by France and China. An October 2009 report by *The Independent* suggested that Arab states had joined China, Russia, and France to stop using the dollar for oil trading in favor of a basket of currencies including the Japanese yen and Chinese yuan. The transition would supposedly take about nine years, with gold perhaps serving as the transitional currency until 2018.

Brazil and India are reportedly interested, and the United Nations Conference on Trade and Development also reported on the desirability of shifting away from the dollar to some other system. Such a shift would make it harder for the United States to borrow overseas to finance its budget and trade deficits, leading to much higher interest rates as well as inflation. Gold, in turn, would continue to rise in value. Some analysts even speculate that a dollar collapse could prompt another attempt by the government at 1930s-style confiscation—not gold coins or bullion this time, but assets in 401(k)s and IRAs.[61]

Just as disturbing, it is becoming very clear that these developments are leading to reducing the United States' leverage with other countries. China is the largest foreign lender to the United States. In July 2009, Chinese officials questioned their American counterparts about health care reform and how it would affect the budget deficit. The Chinese wanted to know that the United States would be able to pay them back for financing our debt. The result was a very conciliatory visit by President Obama to China in November 2009—avoiding any earlier meetings with the Dalai Lama and attempting not to antagonize Beijing. China wants to replace the United States as the dominant power in the Pacific region, a move that would have potentially high consequences for the security of Taiwan, freedom for Tibet, and hope for the many sufferers of human rights abuses in the People's Republic of China. Close American ties to China would also have profoundly negative consequences when the China economic bubble bursts. China is attempting to work around some severe internal problems, not the least of which is its attempt to, in the words of David Smick, "Marry a market economy with a Marxist political regime." Such a combination seems unsustainable in the long run, especially considering the demographic implications of China's one-child policy, which has led to a surplus of males over females. Highly accelerated military spending may be one way to absorb the excess males. The result of a Chinese bubble burst would be massive deflation, rising unemployment, stock market collapses, and long-term economic stagnation. One possible response to this prospect sees China withdrawing its reserves from the global system to use them at home. Either way, American dependence on China has profound dangers.[62]

CONCLUSION

We return now to the larger question of the economic strength of the United States. The only reason the dollar has weathered the storm of the financial crisis so far is that the recession hit Europe and Japan worse than the United States. Interest rates will rise eventually, and when they do, the cost of government debt will rise as well. A mere 2 percent rise in interest rates would cause servicing of a $10 trillion debt to cost an extra $100 billion. If current trend lines continue, there is a very real possibility of the nation defaulting on the national debt—or attempting to avoid that prospect by printing new dollars into a hyperinflationary era. So, while there is no single currency that can replace the dollar any time soon, it is clear that the dollar is losing dominance to other currencies. It took decades for the British pound sterling to lose its place to the dollar, and it may take as long for the dollar to do the same. But whether several countries catch up to the United States and compete for dominance—leading perhaps to separate regional currency blocs—or one alternative currency rises to displace the dollar completely, losing its status as the world's reserve currency means the United States loses its status as an economic superpower. If that happens, there will be fewer resources available for the armed forces, compromising the nation's status as a military superpower as well. Historian Niall Ferguson notes that this pattern of imperial decline has been repeated numerous times in world history.[63]

These developments all come back to human choices. By moving off the gold standard, the United States can print large quantities of dollars, which will come at a cost when the market thinks the nation has gone too deeply into debt—which it surely must conclude at some point. By pursuing temporary increases in government spending to deal with the financial crisis, political leaders lay the foundation for new permanent programs and even higher government spending and debt. And when one segment of the population derives benefits from government policies, whether through programs or tax breaks, it is probably a law of human nature that said group will seek to maintain those benefits. Many Americans now think the government is responsible for economic growth and welfare. They have bought into Franklin Roosevelt's argument that government should guarantee not just the traditional natural rights to life, liberty, and the pursuit of happiness, but also "freedom from want" and "freedom from fear"—objectives beyond the ability of any human institution to satisfy. These unreasonable expectations represent a shift in perspective from thinking that we as individuals are responsible for our well-being to a public philosophy of entitlement. We expect the government to do more for us.[64] And because we get the government we deserve, government increases in size to accommodate those expectations. The attempt to ignore human nature has led us to where we are today.

The United States could hardly be in a worse position had its greatest enemy engineered it. But perhaps we have done his work for him. John Maynard Keynes once wrote, "Lenin is said to have declared that the best way to destroy the Capitalist System was to debauch the currency. Lenin was certainly right. There is no subtler, no surer means of overturning the existing basis of society than to debauch the currency."[65] What Keynes—and Lenin—said concerning inflation could easily be applied to the general state of the dollar and the American economy. Decisions, great and small, from philosophers and political leaders rejecting time-honored wisdom to a population too willing to buy what they were selling, embrace conspicuous consumption, and refuse to say no to government overreach, have led us to this point. It will take a new pattern of choices to reverse direction. The question is whether there are any leaders willing to articulate such a vision—and whether the population is willing to follow. If that change in direction is not effected soon, we may very well witness the death of the dollar—killed by our own hands.

SIX

The Rejection of Israel

AMERICA'S REJECTION OF ISRAEL

In 1776 when the founding fathers pledged "their lives, their fortunes and their sacred honor"[1] to birth America, the beacon of hope circumscribed the earth, inviting "your tired, your poor, your huddled masses longing to be free."[2]

The birth of America would not have become reality without the contribution of the Jewish community in America and Europe. One of the many acts of heroism and humanitarian aide is the amazing story of Philadelphia banker, Haym Salomon.

In August of 1781, the Continental Army had trapped Lt. General Charles Cornwallis in the little Virginia coastal town of Yorktown. George Washington and the main army and the Count de Rochambeau with his French Army decided to march from the Hudson Highlands to Yorktown and deliver the final blow. But Washington's war chest was completely empty, as was that of Congress.

Washington determined that he needed a large sum of money to finance the campaign. When Morris told him there were no funds and no credit available, Washington gave him a simple but eloquent order: "Send for Haym Salomon." Haym again came through, and the money was raised. Washington conducted the Yorktown campaign that proved to be the final battle of the Revolution, thanks to Haym Salomon.[3]

According to Peter Wiernik in *History of the Jews in America*:

> Salomon negotiated the sale of a majority of the war aide from France and Holland, selling bills of exchange to American merchants. Salomon also personally supported various members of the Continental Congress during their stay in Philadelphia, including James Madison and James Wilson. Acting as the patriot he was, he requested below market interest rates, and he never asked for repayment.[4]

The Revolutionary War ended with the Treaty of Paris, signed on September 3, 1783; but the financial problems of America continued. It was Haym Salomon who managed, time after time, to raise the money to fund the dreams of freedom of America.

The many contributions of the Jewish people in the birth, growth, and development of America in the fields of medicine, science, arts, the federal judiciary, politics, the military, education, and humanitarian causes is endless and monumental. America has been the nation of refuge for the Jewish people who were scattered across the face of the earth for centuries in search of a home. In the irony of history, the Jewish people had a God-given home, but were homeless for centuries.

The bond between America and the Jewish people was strengthened on May 15, 1948, when President Harry Truman recognized the rebirth of the State of Israel eleven minutes after Prime Minister Ben Gurion read the Israeli declaration of statehood.

Every president from George Washington to George Bush has been a bold defender of the State of Israel. Then came President Barak Obama and the change no one could have possibly predicted became a shocking reality. The President of the United States was rejecting Israel boldly and without apology, demanding a "no growth" policy in the settlements and no homes to be built in Jerusalem. Why would he do this?

In his book, *The Grand Jihad: How Islam and the Left Sabotage America*, Andrew McCarthy explains President Obama's full-waist bow to the monarch of Saudi Arabia, saying:

> So, of all the planet's potentates, why would an American president demean his station in homage to this one? Because Saudi Arabia is

the cradle of Islam. More specifically, it is the bottomless purse and symbolic crown of a movement which aims at nothing less than supplanting Western political, economic and cultural values. The subversion of those values is Obama's fondest wish: the work of his presidency, the hope behind the change. The President was bowing to a shared dream."[5]

The sharing of the Islamic dream makes it possible to understand President Obama's rejection of Israel, America's most reliable ally for more than sixty years, as well as the only democracy in the Middle East.

In a recent Gallup poll, 67 percent of Americans said they had a favorable opinion of Israel while 17 percent had a favorable opinion of Congress. Recognizing the broad base of public support for Israel, two thirds of the U.S. House of Representatives signed a letter to Secretary of State Clinton declaring: "We are writing to reaffirm our commitment to the unbreakable bond that exists between our country and the State of Israel and to express to you our deep concern over recent tension."[6]

The "recent tension" was a reference to Prime Minister Netanyahu's visit to the White House. The president refused to take a picture with Prime Minister Netanyahu, there was no press conference, there was no state dinner, and there were no warm handshakes.

The president of the United States left the prime minister of Israel sitting alone in the Oval Office while he went into the White House to have supper with his family. Never in the history of America had a visiting head of state been so shabbily treated.

The president lectured the prime minister on the nerve of Israel to build housing units in the City of Jerusalem. Question: By what authority does the president of the United States have to tell the people of Israel what they can build and where? The State of Israel is not a vassal state of the United States. Israel is a democracy with the right of self-determination without pressure from the White House.

In March of 2010, Secretary of State Hilary Clinton spent forty-five minutes on the telephone lecturing Prime Minister Netanyahu for building housing units in Jerusalem for the Jewish people, on land that President Obama intends to give to the Palestinians in some future obscene peace offering.

Writing in the *Australian* about the announcement of planned housing construction in Jerusalem, Greg Sheridon, the paper's foreign editor, observed, "Barak Obama's anti-Israel jihad is one of the most irresponsible policy lurches by any modern American President."

In September 2009, President Obama announced that the United States "does not accept the legitimacy of continued Israeli settlements," otherwise known as Jewish communities on Jewish land in the State of Israel. Israel must "end the occupation that began in 1967."[7]

Let's take a snapshot of history. Israel was attacked in 1967 in the Six Day War by Arab armies. The Israelis won a stunning and decisive victory including the Western Wall in Jerusalem. Now the president of the United States wants Israel to give back the land the Israelis won in a war the Arabs started. He probably would like for Arizona, Texas, and California to end their occupation of Mexican territory brutally seized in the first half of the nineteenth century. The same logic could apply.

Iran joined the nuclear club as America waved limp-wristed sanctions at their efforts. The president struggles to find common ground with Ahmadinejad of Iran and his theocratic dictatorship, which murdered Iran citizens on the streets as they were protesting for freedom.

Why is it that the president has infinite patience with radical Islamic terrorists and theocratic dictators but zero tolerance for the nation of Holocaust survivors who want to build homes in their God-given land?

Following the midterm elections in November 2010, I believe the president will begin a major political push following the election to divide the city of Jerusalem. The pitch will be that the Palestinians should be given East Jerusalem as their price for peace. And the Jewish people will be asked if they would rather have part of Jerusalem and live in peace or have all of Jerusalem and constant war.

Who is the wise man?

The sages of Israel say the wise man is the man who sees the future.

Who is the fool? The prophet Isaiah says, "Woe to those who call evil good and good evil" (Isaiah 5:20).

America is lost in a politically correct fog that lacks moral clarity. We can't see the future because we lack the courage to admit the reality that radical Islam is the enemy of every free society. Our willingness to look at evil and call it good is moral insanity and treason against freedom.

And to make matters worse: if America puts pressure on Israel to divide the city of Jerusalem, the judgment of God will come to America. The prophet Joel states this concept clearly in Joel 3:2 saying:

I will also gather all nations . . . and I will enter into judgment with them . . . on account of My people, My heritage Israel, whom they have scattered among the nations; they have also divided up My land.
—*Joel 3:2 NKJV*

ISRAEL: LAND OF COVENANT

Israel is unlike any nation on the face of planet Earth: Israel is the only nation created by a sovereign act of God who entered into an eternal blood covenant with Abraham 3,500 years ago.

God told Abraham to leave his land, his birthplace, and his father's house and travel to "a land that I will show you" (Genesis 12:1 NKJV). Seven times God promised the land to Abraham, once to Isaac, and three times to Jacob.

The covenant for this land that God Almighty loves and that radical Islam passionately hates is recorded in Genesis 17:7–8. God speaks to Abraham, saying: "And I will establish My covenant between Me and you and your descendants after you in their generations, for an *everlasting covenant,* to be God to you and your descendants after you. Also I give to you and your descendants after you the land in which you are a stranger, all the land of Canaan, as an *everlasting possession;* and I will be their God."

When Abraham was informed by the Almighty that he would have a son at the age of approximately one hundred years and his wife Sarah, whose womb was dead would come to life and give birth to Isaac at the age of ninety, Abraham pled with God to allow Ishmael (father of the Arabs), to be included in the covenant. God's answer was clear and concise:

"No, Sarah your wife shall bear you a son, and you shall call his name Isaac; I will establish My covenant with him for an everlasting *covenant, and with his descendants after him.*
—*Genesis 17:19 NKJV*

The book of Genesis ends with Joseph telling his brothers, "God will surely come to your aid and take you up out of this land [Egypt] to the *land He promised* [Israel] on oath to Abraham, Isaac and Jacob" (Genesis 50:24 NIV).

The book of Exodus opens with God commanding Moses to lead the Jewish people to the "land flowing with milk and honey" (Exodus 3:8 NKJV). The night of the first Passover began a forty-year journey for the Jewish people through a barren wilderness. It was a journey of triumph and tragedy, a journey of endless tears and horrific trials.

They were bound for the Promised Land with the cloud by day and the fire by night as a testimonial of God's presence and guidance. They received the Torah of God at Sinai; they received gushing water from a smitten rock from the rod of Moses; they received manna from heaven as the Shekinah glory of God hovered over the Tabernacle, reminding them that their God was Jehovah Shammah: The Lord Is There.

The Jewish connection to the land of Israel did not begin in May 1948 with an emotional declaration at the UN as a result of the Holocaust. It began 3,500 years ago by the will of God to a chosen people who were destined not to live just anywhere on planet Earth but a unique and special place called Israel.

Moses told the children of Israel when they were in sight of the land of Israel that it was a "land flowing with milk and honey."

> *The land you are entering to take over is not like the land of Egypt, from which you have come, where you planted your seed and irrigated it by foot as in a vegetable garden. But the land you are crossing the Jordan to take possession of is a land of mountains and valleys that drinks rain from heaven.* It is a land the LORD your God cares for; *the eyes of the LORD your God are continually on it from the beginning of the year to its end.*
> —*Deuteronomy 11:10–12 NIV*

Israel is a nation God loves, God created, God defends, and whose eyes are upon it continuously.

In the first battle, the Jewish people had to fight defending themselves against the Amalekites after crossing the Red Sea:

So Joshua fought the Amalekites as Moses had ordered, and Moses,
Aaron and Hur went to the top of the hill. As long as Moses held up
his hands, the Israelites were winning, but whenever he lowered his
hands, the Amalekites were winning.

—*Exodus 17:10–11 NIV*

The point is this: When Israel looked up to God, their source, they won!
When they looked down, they lost. The secret of Israel's power is not in
horses and chariots; the secret of Israel's power is the God of Abraham,
Isaac, and Jacob.

The spirit of Israel is captured by the words of the prophet Zechariah:

"Not by might nor by power, but by my Spirit," says the LORD
Almighty.

—*Zechariah 4:6 NIV*

God's pledge to curse any nation that attacked Israel is demonstrated in
the attack of the Amalekites upon Israel.

Then the LORD *said to Moses, "Write this* for *a memorial in the*
book and recount it in the hearing of Joshua, that I will utterly blot
out the remembrance of Amalek from under heaven. . . . Because the
LORD *has sworn: the* LORD *will have war* with Amalek from
generation to generation."

—*Exodus 17:14, 16 NKJV*

The rebirth of Israel on May 14, 1948, was the literal fulfillment of the
promises made by the ancient prophets of Israel. It was the literal fulfillment of the prophet Isaiah who wrote:

Who has heard such a thing? Who has seen such things? Shall the earth
be made to give birth in one day? Or shall a nation be born at once?

—*Isaiah 66:8 NKJV*

My father, an ordained minister of the gospel for fifty-plus years, and I
were sitting at the kitchen table in our home listening to the radio on that
historic day when Israel was reborn. When the radio announcer declared

that the United Nations had recognized the State of Israel, my father, with tears in his eyes, said, "This is the greatest miracle of the twentieth century."

The UN declaration granting statehood to Israel and a homeland for the Jews of the world was recognized by President Harry Truman eleven minutes later. England abstained from the vote, refusing to support the Jews having a homeland to be called Israel. England's long anti-Semitic roots bore bitter fruit on that historic day.

Why is this divine covenant for a specific land to the Jewish people so crucial in the twenty-first century? It's urgent because World War III is about to begin over the failure of humanity to recognize Israel's historic right to the land.

British Prime Minister Benjamin Disraeli, who despite the fact that he had been baptized as a Christian, retained enormous pride in his Jewish ancestry, said in a reply to an insult by the Irish Catholic Daniel O'Connell, "Yes, I am a Jew, and when the ancestors of the right honorable gentleman were brutal savages in an unknown land, mine were priests in the Temple of Solomon."

The point is this: Jerusalem was the capital of Israel long before Berlin, Paris, or New York existed. The city of Jerusalem has been the capital of Israel and the Jewish people since King David defeated the Jebusites there 3,000 years ago.

How strange that ignorant and uninformed leaders in the twenty-first century believe that the ancient biblical city should not be Jewish. The Jewish people have more claim to Jerusalem than the French to Paris or the Germans to Berlin or the British to London.

THE BOUNDARIES OF ISRAEL

The boundaries of this sacred real estate transaction encompass an area far greater than the State of Israel presently controls. Genesis 15:18 states that the land God gave to Abraham, Isaac, and Jacob three thousand five hundred years ago stretches from the Mediterranean Sea on the west to the Euphrates River on the east.

Ezekiel declares the north boundary to be at Hamath, one hundred miles north of Damascus (see Ezekiel 48:1) and the southern boundary at Kadesh, about one hundred miles south of Jerusalem (see Ezekiel

48:28). When Messiah comes, Israel will gain control of every square inch of the promised land given by God to Abraham and the Jewish people for an everlasting possession.

If you look at a map of the Middle East and fix the boundaries recorded in Scripture, the day will come when Israel will own and control all of present-day Israel, including Jerusalem, Lebanon, the West Bank of Jordan, and most of Syria, Iraq, and Saudi Arabia. I believe Messiah will come, and though he delays his coming, he will restore to Israel the promised land given by a sovereign act of God 3,500 years ago as the nations of the world gnash their teeth in anguish.

THE HISTORY OF REJECTION

There is a supernatural curse attached to the land of Israel. It is a divine curse from God himself to men and nations who, with malice aforethought, do harm to the Jewish people or attack the State of Israel.

The prophet Obadiah writes:

"As you have done [to Israel], it shall be done to you; Your reprisal shall return upon your own head."

—Obadiah 1:15 NKJV

The prophet Joel speaks of God's judgment upon nations who divide the land of Israel, which includes the city of Jerusalem, saying:

I will also gather all nations . . . and I will enter into judgment there on account of My people, My heritage Israel, whom they have scattered among the nations; they have also divided up My land.

—Joel 3:2–3 NKJV

The prophet Jeremiah writes that any nation that attempts to seize Jewish land will lose their land:

The inheritance which I have caused My people Israel to inherit [the promised land]—behold, I will pluck them out of their land.

—Jeremiah 12:14 NKJV

The prophet Zechariah writes:

> For thus says the LORD of hosts: "He sent Me after glory, to the
> nations which plunder you; for he who touches you [the Jewish people]
> touches the apple of His eye. For surely I will shake My hand against
> them, and they shall become spoil for their servants."
> —Zechariah 2:8–9 NKJV

God made this promise to Abraham and his descendants in the Book of
Genesis, and the boneyard of human history is filled with nations who
failed to get the promise that the curse of God Almighty would come to
any people or nation that oppress Israel or the Jewish people.

The Genesis account reads: "I will curse him who curses you" (Genesis 12:3 NKJV).

Let's walk through the pages of world history and discover men and
nations who oppressed the Jewish people and died under the curse of
God. We will discover that what was done to Israel by men and nations,
God did exactly to the oppressors of Israel and the Jewish people.

We will also look into the future at nations seen nightly cursing
Israel and the Jewish people over television and see the judgment of God
crushing those nations and their armies in the future. The prophet Isaiah
writes:

> "I am God, and there is none like Me, declaring the end from the
> beginning, and from ancient times things that are not yet done,
> saying, 'My counsel shall stand, and I will do all My pleasure.'"
> —Isaiah 46:9–10 NKJV

PHARAOH'S REJECTION: PHARAOH DROWNS
IN HIS SELF-FULFILLING PROPHECY

The Egyptian Pharaoh who held the children of Israel captive had a plan
to kill the Jews by forcing the midwives of Egypt to drown newborn Jewish male babies in the river (see Exodus 1:22).

Why did Pharaoh hate the Jews with such malice that he wanted to
kill their male children? Why were the Jews living in Egypt? To understand how the Hebrew children ended up in a foreign land, from which

they would make an exodus after 430 years of captivity, we must start from the beginning in the book of Genesis.

Jacob, who would later be known as Israel, was the grandson of Abraham; he lived in Canaan and had twelve sons.

Jacob's favorite son was Joseph, who was given a coat of many colors by his father that was suited for royalty. Jacob's favoritism towards Joseph caused his eleven brothers to hate him enough to kill him. In the course of time, they sold Joseph to the Midianites, who took him into Egypt and sold him a second time to Potiphar, a wealthy Egyptian who served in Pharaoh's court.

There was a problem!

Potiphar's desperate housewife lusted after beautiful Joseph and tried repeatedly to seduce him. When Joseph repeatedly refused, Potiphar's wife falsely accused Joseph of rape. He was sent to prison, unknowingly awaiting the day of God's promotion to the palace of Pharaoh— promotion to privilege and power that the mind of a prisoner could never have comprehended.

When Joseph became prime minister in Egypt, an empty stomach drove his brothers into Egypt searching for food. Upon arriving in Egypt, the sons of Israel were forced to appear before the prime minister, their brother Joseph, to receive permission to buy grain. On their third visit into Egypt, Joseph revealed himself to his brothers, who had presumed he was dead.

The reconciled family brought unity, and unity brought the blessing of God. King David writes, "Behold, how good and pleasant *it is* For brethren to dwell together in unity! . . . For there the LORD commanded the blessing" (Psalm 133:1, 3 NKJV).

A family of seventy entered the land of Egypt where they would become a nation of millions in 430 years of slavery.

The Bible says, "But the children of Israel were fruitful and increased abundantly, multiplied and grew exceedingly mighty; and the land was filled with them" (Exodus 1:7 NKJV).

When Joseph died, there arose in Egypt a pharaoh who knew not Joseph. That pharaoh began to dread the children of Israel and feared that Egypt could be taken over by the Israelites should they ever meet in battle. Pharaoh said to his people, "Let us deal shrewdly with them, lest they multiply, and it happen, in the event of war, that they also join our enemies and fight against us, and so go up out of the land" (Exodus 1:10 NKJV). So Pharaoh oppressed the children of Israel and forced them to become Egyptian slaves.

Unsatisfied by their bondage alone, Pharaoh planned to decimate the children of Israel, lest they become more powerful than Egypt. In doing so, he commanded the Hebrew midwives to kill any male babies that were born in Egypt.

"But the midwives feared God, and did not do as the king of Egypt commanded them, but saved the male children alive" (Exodus 1:17 NKJV).

As a result, God blessed the midwives and gave them households of their own, and the children of Israel continued to multiply and prosper. Still determined to annihilate the Jewish people, Pharaoh commanded that every Hebrew baby boy be drowned in the river.

About this time, Jacob's great-grandson Moses was born. In an effort to save him from being drowned, Moses was placed in a basket and put at the river's edge where Pharaoh's daughter was known to bathe. All went according to plan. Pharaoh's daughter discovered Moses in the basket, took compassion on him, and raised him as her own son. Moreover, because Pharaoh's daughter hired Moses' biological mother to be his wet nurse, Moses grew up knowing he was a Hebrew and understood his Jewish legacy.

As an adult and living as the prince of Egypt, Moses witnessed the beating of a Hebrew slave. He entered the fight, killed the Egyptian, and buried him in the sand. Having broken the law of Egypt and incurred the wrath of Pharaoh, Moses fled for his life to the depths of the wilderness.

Here he married Zipporah and became a father to Gershom, meaning, "I have been a stranger in a foreign land" (Exodus 2:22 NKJV). As Moses was tending the flock of Jethro, his father-in-law, he saw the burning bush that was not consumed by the fire and heard the voice of God commanding him to return to Egypt to liberate the Jewish people from bondage.

As an eighty-year-old man, Moses returned to Egypt to lead the Jewish people out of Egyptian captivity. Moses begrudgingly accepted this role, and the children of Israel accepted him as their deliverer. Pharaoh, however, did not accept Moses' request to free the Hebrew children.

With every one of Pharaoh's refusals to liberate the children of Israel,

God sent plagues upon the land. Miraculously, the plagues affected only the Egyptians and left the Hebrew children unscathed. Ten plagues befell the Egyptian people. Why ten plagues?

There were ten plagues, because Egypt served ten major gods. With each plague, God Almighty specifically destroyed one of the major gods of Egypt. The Jewish people had lived for 430 years in a land of idolatry with gods you could see and touch. They were about to be introduced to the God no one could see or touch but who had all power in heaven and on earth.

Whether it was frogs, lice, locusts, disease, hail, or darkness, nothing was compelling enough to motivate Pharaoh to release the children of Israel until the tenth plague arrived. The final plague was the death of all of the Egyptians' firstborn. By God's instruction, the Israelites put the blood of a lamb on their doorposts and were spared the Angel of Death. With Pharaoh's own son dead in his bed, he told Moses and the children of Israel to leave the land of Egypt.

Despite Pharaoh allowing the Hebrew children to flee, Pharaoh quickly changed his mind and came after them. Ever faithful as the defender of Israel, the Lord prepared Moses for what was to come. The Lord said to Moses: "I will harden Pharaoh's heart, so that he will pursue them; and I will gain honor over Pharaoh and over all his army, that the Egyptians may know that I *am* the LORD" (Exodus 14:4 NKJV).

As the children of Israel marched out of Egypt with all their animals and carts loaded with the wealth of Egypt, Pharaoh and his army pursued them with a rage fueled by the death of his son and the firstborn of all Egypt.

As Moses and the children of Israel came upon the Red Sea, God prepared to remove Egypt's chief god, Pharaoh himself. The Lord divided the waters so that the children of Israel were able to walk through on dry ground. As the Hebrew children crossed the sea, Pharaoh's enraged army pursued the Jewish people.

Once the children of Israel successfully crossed the Red Sea, the Lord caused the walls of water, which had previously framed a dry pathway, to fall upon the Egyptians. The Word says, "Then the waters returned and covered the chariots, the horsemen, *and* all the army of Pharaoh that came into the sea after them. Not so much as one of them remained" (Exodus 14:28 NKJV).

Little did Pharaoh know that when he plotted to exterminate the children of Israel by drowning their sons in water, that he was merely forecasting the means of his own fate. Exactly what he had done to the Jewish people was done to him by the hand of God.[8] "I will curse those who curse you" could have been chiseled upon his royal headstone.

HAMAN'S AND HITLER'S REJECTION: THE SONS OF HAMAN AND THE TRIAL AT NUREMBERG

The Sages tell us to study Jewish history carefully— for everything that happened to our forebears, is bound to recur with us—their descendants.[9]

To make the connection between the ancient account of Queen Esther and the part she played in saving the Jewish people from extermination and the Nuremberg Trials requires careful historic examination. An assessment of Hebrew Scripture in the book of Esther reveals signs that foreshadow the hanging of Hitler's Nazis at Nuremberg.

Before comparing the hangings of Haman's sons and the Nuremberg war criminals collectively, it is first necessary to consider the accounts separately.

Esther, Haman, and the Feast of Purim

Purim is a Jewish celebration commemorating Queen Esther's salvation of the Jewish people. The book of Queen Esther holds the narrative of Esther's rise to become queen in the kingdom of Ahasuerus and her supernatural intervention on behalf of her people, the Jews, that ultimately saved them from extermination and the first proposed holocaust.

The Story of Esther

An orphan who was raised by her older cousin Mordecai, Esther was a beautiful young Jewish woman. At the time, King Ahasuerus was in search for a new queen, and it was decreed that all young virgins be taken into the king's palace and cared for by the custodian of the women.

Accordingly, Esther was taken with the rest of the young virgins who resided in the kingdom. Before leaving for the king's palace Mordecai urged Esther not to reveal her Jewish roots to the king. Submitting to his paternal authority, she obeyed the command and kept her Jewish heritage a secret. Ultimately, Esther found favor with King Ahasuerus, as he loved her more than he loved all the other young women. Esther, a Jewish woman, was made queen of Persia—today's modern Iran.

Daily, Mordecai sat within the king's gate in an effort to learn of Queen Esther's welfare. While there, Mordecai became aware that two of the King's doorkeepers plotted to harm King Ahasuerus. Mordecai revealed the plot to Queen Esther who, in turn, relayed the message to the king on behalf of Mordecai. As a result, the doorkeepers were hanged and the entire incident was recorded in the king's book of chronicles.

After this, the king promoted one of his men, Haman, to the second highest seat in the kingdom. With this promotion the king commanded his servants to bow and pay homage to Haman. Mordecai, being a Jew, refused to bow to Haman. Haman was "filled with wrath" (Esther 3:5 NKJV).

Once Haman learned Mordecai was a Jew, Haman conspired not only to kill Mordecai, but the entire Jewish population throughout the kingdom of Persia. At this time in world history, the vast majority of Jews lived in Persia. Haman sought an audience with the king and requested a decree be written commanding the destruction of all Jewish men, women, and children, and the plunder of their possessions.

The king, still not knowing that his queen was a Jew, consented to Haman's request and allowed to be written the decree that commanded the total destruction of the Jewish people to fall on the thirteenth day of the twelfth month. The decree was sealed with the king's signet ring and dispersed throughout the kingdom. This decree was made according to the law of the Medes and the Persians, which meant the king himself could not rescind his own decree. It appeared the Jews were doomed to death.

Mordecai told Esther of the king's decree and commanded her to go before the king to plead for the lives of the Jewish people to be spared. Mordecai sent the following message to Esther: "Do not think in your heart that you will escape in the king's palace any more than all the other Jews. For if you remain completely silent at this time, relief and deliverance will arise for the Jews from another place, but you and your father's house will perish. Yet who knows whether you have come to the kingdom for *such* a time as this?" (Esther 4:13–14 NKJV).

Although Esther was queen, she was not permitted to appear before the king unless summoned. Anyone who appeared before the king without being summoned by him would be put to death unless the king held out his scepter as a sign he consented to his or her presence.

Considering the possibility of her death for appearing before the king without his royal invitation, Esther requested that Mordecai and the rest of the Jewish people in the kingdom fast and pray on her behalf that she find favor with King Ahasuerus. Determined to protect her people from certain death, Esther resolved to break the king's law, seeking him without invitation, saying, "I will go to the king, which *is* against the law; and if I perish, I perish!" (Esther 4:16 NKJV).

In answer to her prayers, Esther found favor with the king when she entered his court. He asked, "What do you wish, Queen Esther? What *is* your request? It shall be given to you—up to half the kingdom!" (Esther 5:3 NKJV).

Esther asked that Haman and the king attend a banquet that she would prepare; there she would tell the king her request. When Haman learned that he was invited to a private banquet with the king and queen, he was elated that his political star was rising.

Haman saw Mordecai at the king's gate. When Mordecai failed to bow to him, Haman's hatred for him grew. In an effort to conceal his indignation, Haman's family suggested that he make a gallows and ask the king to hang Mordecai for his failure to bow before him. Haman was pleased by this idea and instructed that Mordecai be hanged on that gallows.

The Demise of Haman

That evening, King Ahasuerus could not fall asleep. Consequently, the king requested that the record of chronicles be read to him. As the chronicles were being read, the king heard the account of Mordecai and the role he played in protecting him from the doorkeepers' plot. In light of this, the king sought to reward Mordecai for saving his life. As Haman walked into the king's court to seek Mordecai's execution, King Ahasuerus asked Haman, "What shall be done for the man whom the king delights to honor?" (Esther 6:6 NKJV).

Thinking the king wanted to honor him, Haman suggested that a royal robe the king had worn be put on the man and that he ride a royal horse the king had ridden in a parade that honored him. The king agreed and mandated Haman to honor Mordecai in exactly that manner. In shock, Haman was mortified.

Defeated and deflated, Haman returned to his home to relay all that had happened to his wife. Prophetically, Haman's wife said to him, "If Mordecai, before whom you have begun to fall, is of Jewish descent, you will not prevail against him but will surely fall before him" (Esther 6:13 NKJV).

Not long after that, Haman was ushered to the private banquet hosted by Queen Esther and attended by the king. When King Ahasuerus asked the queen to make her request known, Esther begged that her life and the lives of her people be spared.

Confused by her request, as he had been unaware that she was a Jew, the king asked Esther who had ordered such a vicious decree. Queen Esther lifted her right hand, pointed her slender forefinger in the face of Haman, and said, "The adversary and enemy *is* this wicked Haman!" (Esther 7:6 NKJV).

The king was enraged by Haman's actions. One of the king's servants pointed out the gallows that Haman had constructed for Mordecai, and the king commanded Haman—and eventually his sons as well—be hanged on it. So, Haman died hanging from his neck on the very gallows he built for Mordecai. Mordecai, on the other hand, was given Haman's signet ring by the king and appointed over the house of Haman.

Esther was still determined to save her people. However, because the decree aimed at exterminating the Jews was sealed with the king's signet ring, the king was powerless to revoke it. But, the king allowed Esther to write an alternative decree in an effort to save the lives of the Jewish people.

She did so, and the new decree permitted the Jews to defend themselves from anyone who tried to take their lives. The Jews fought fiercely and, in the end, destroyed all their enemies. Once Queen Esther and her people were saved, King Ahasuerus asked if she had any further requests. Her response was, "let Haman's ten sons be hanged on the gallows" (Esther 9:13 NKJV). The king obliged and like their father before them, Haman's sons were hanged.

On the very day that Haman sought to have the Jews exterminated, the Jewish people assembled and celebrated with a day of feasting and gladness instead. They called the celebration Purim, after the name Pur—which means "the lot," since Haman had cast the lot to destroy the Jewish people (see Esther 9:24–26).

After overcoming their enemies, all of the Jews in the land were determined to commemorate their salvation annually: "The Jews established and imposed it upon themselves and their descendants and all who would join them, that without fail they should celebrate these two days every year . . . that these days should be remembered and kept throughout every generation . . . that these days of Purim should not fail *to be observed* among the Jews, and that the memory of them should not perish among their descendants" (Esther 9:27–28 NKJV).

The Nuremberg Trials

The wrongs which we seek to condemn and punish have been
so calculated, so malignant, and so devastating that civilization
cannot tolerate their being ignored because it cannot survive
their being repeated . . . that four great nations, flushed with
victory and stung with injury, stay the hand of vengeance and
voluntarily submit their captive enemies to judgment of the
law is one of the most significant tributes that power has ever
paid to reason.[10]

　—United States Supreme Court Justice Robert Jackson's excerpt
from his opening statement at the first Nuremberg Trial

In 1944, as victory over the Third Reich approached, President Franklin D. Roosevelt sought a strategy from the U.S. War Department to determine how Hitler's Nazi war criminals would be brought to justice.[11] The United Kingdom exercised a comparable approach as the British War Cabinet was brainstorming similar plans as early as December 1942.[12] Ultimately, the result was the International Military Tribunal (IMT), a court created under the Allied powers, as a multinational and multijurisdictional mechanism to bring some of the greatest Nazi offenders to justice.

The IMT would take place in Nuremberg, Germany. The geographic symbolism in choosing Nuremberg is not to be overlooked. Nuremberg was home to major Nazi rallies and conferences.[13] In fact, one of these conferences birthed two laws known as "the Nuremberg Laws." Collectively, these laws were aimed at denying Jews their citizenship rights in addition to criminalizing marriage and "extramarital intercourse between Jews and Germans."[14]

However, with the Nuremberg Trials taking place there, the city whose very name belonged to laws that deprived Jews of their liberties as German citizens, a city once known for its Nazi party rallies, would now be made infamous as the city where some of the Nazi party's most atrocious players met their fate at the gallows of justice.

Some decry that the Nuremberg Trials were ex post facto (literally, "after the fact") justice. Naysayers complained that because the Nuremberg defendants were charged with violating laws that did not exist at the time their crimes were committed, but rather laws that were created by the IMT after their capture, the judicial procedure that ultimately condemned them to death was unfair.

Supreme Court Justice Robert Jackson, who would oversee the trial, offered a rebuttal to such a suggestion, undermining any allegation of ex post facto justice in saying, "What we propose is to punish acts which have been regarded as criminal since the time of Cain and have been so written in every civilized code."[15]

Although Nuremberg would eventually host thirteen trials against various war criminals, the first trial would be the most notoriously remembered, as it was against the highest-ranking Nazis, whose deaths all but overshadowed their heinous lives. With twenty-four defendants and the four Allied nations as plaintiffs, the first trial at Nuremberg would last ten months and result in eleven of the defendants being sentenced to death by hanging.[16]

Despite claims that Nuremberg was nothing more than "victors' justice," after copious amounts of incriminating evidence describing the atrocities committed by the defendants was shown at trial, one did not have to possess a great legal mind to concede that the accused deserved a fate worse than death. Some examples of the prosecution's evidence consisted of the following:

USA Exhibit #253: tanned human tattooed skin from concentration camp victims, preserved for Isle Hoch, the wife of the commandant of Buchenwald, who liked to have the flesh fashioned into lampshades and other household objects for her home.

USA Exhibit #254: the fist-shaped shrunken head of an executed Pole, used by Isle Koch as a paperweight.[17]

If the physical evidence left any doubt as to the extent of the grotesque disregard the defendants displayed for human life, such doubts would be eradicated by witness statements. Such witnesses included Marie-Claude Vaillant-Couturier, a young French woman and concentration camp survivor who testified the Nazi orchestra played jovially as those fated for the gas chambers were segregated from those who would be used for labor. Vaillant-Couturier went on to explain that as she slept, she was "awakened by horrible cries. The next day we learned that the Nazis had run out of gas and the children had been hurled into the furnaces alive."[18]

While the eleven death sentences that resulted from the first Nuremberg trial were handed down on October 1, the hangings were not scheduled to take place until October 16, 1946. Additionally, although eleven criminals were scheduled to be hanged, only ten men would swing from the gallows that day. The most prominent defendant, Hermann Wilhelm Goering, an arrogant and unrepentant man who rationalized his actions as simply following orders, escaped the noose only hours before his slated execution. He committed suicide by ingesting a vial of potassium cyanide.[19] An interpreter at the trial described Goering as one who possessed "manipulative behavior" that became "an irritant to the court."[20] The interpreter went on to say: "If one can speak of a dominant personality in the dock, Hermann Goering definitely fits that description as the leading defendant . . . I recall him sitting in the first seat in the front row of the dock, often with supercilious smile, perhaps knowing that he would cheat the hangman."[21]

Goering did indeed cheat the hangman. Late at night on October 15, 1946, Burton C. Andrus, the American commandant of the Nuremburg prison, instead of formally reading Goering his death sentence, discovered him dying in his prison cell. *Newsweek* reported, "Hermann Wilhelm Goering, lying on his small iron cot in Cell No. 5 and wearing black silk pajamas and a blue shirt, crushed between his teeth a glass vial of potassium cyanide, gasped, twitched, and died."[22] With Goering dead, prison guards, "determined that no other victim should escape them," immediately bound the remaining ten defendants and promptly escorted them to the Nuremberg gymnasium, the location where the hangings would take place.[23] At 1:11 a.m. the first of the condemned Nazis walked the thirteen steps to the platform of the gallows; by 2:57 a.m. the last of the Nazi war criminals were pronounced dead.

The mystery surrounding Goering's suicide still lingers today. It is not clear exactly how he came into possession of the poison that ended his life or how his suicide was timed so perfectly, two and a half hours before his execution would have taken place.[24] His person, as well as his prison cell, was routinely inspected, and the prisoners were not made aware of the hour their hangings were scheduled to take place.[25] What is known is that near the start of the trial, Goering bragged to one of the defense lawyers that "they will never hang me."[26] He was right. After Goering's body was discovered, it was photographed as proof of death with "one eye open and the other closed." It is as if he were "winking at the fate he had avoided."[27]

Law school professor Donald E. Wilkes describes the hangings as bearing a "stern, unadorned, Old Testament righteousness." Referring to a witness's impression of the executions, he notes: "It was a grim pitiless scene. But for those who had sat through the horrors of and tortures of the trial, who had learned of men dangled from butcher hooks, of women mutilated and children jammed into gas chambers, of mankind subject to degradation, destruction, and terror, the scene conjured a vision of stark, almost biblical justice."[28]

The Connection Between Haman and Hitler

There are many signs in the book of Esther that foreshadow the hanging of the Nazi war criminals at Nuremberg. For instance:

1. 1946 was the year the Nazi war criminals were hanged.

Throughout the Torah, there are various places where letters are written smaller or larger than the surrounding text. Writing certain letters in larger or smaller text is an archaic Hebrew tradition that has been kept since the time of the scribes; the explanation as to why certain letters are written differently is not always ascertainable.[29]

In Esther 9:7–9, the names of Haman's ten sons are listed. Within those verses, the following Hebrew letters are written in a small script, *"tav," "shin,"* and *"zain."* Additionally, the Hebrew letter *"vav"* is written in a larger script than the rest of the text.[30] Since the Jewish calendar year is represented by Hebrew letters, the smaller letters, *"tav," "shin,"* and *"zain"* refer to Jewish calendar year 707. Meanwhile, the large letter *"vav"* equals 6, which is referring to the sixth millennium.[31]

Therefore, when reading all of these letters together, they collectively refer to the 707th year of the sixth millennium, or the year 5707 on the Jewish calendar.[32] Consequently, the year 5707 is the year 1946 on the civil calendar.[33]

2. The Nazi war criminals' death sentences were carried out on October 16, 1946.

> *"On the seventh day of the Sukkot holiday, i.e. Hoshana Raba, the judgment of the nations of the world is finalized. Sentences are issued from the residence of the King. Judgments are aroused and executed on that day."*[34]

Sukkot, also known as the Feast of Tabernacles, is a weeklong holiday memorializing the forty years the children of Israel spent wandering in the desert after their release from Pharaoh's captivity. Sukkot, which translates as "booths," refers to the temporary shelters that the Jews lived in during their time in the desert. In the Jewish tradition, the seventh and final day of Sukkot is called Hoshana Raba, which is the day that marks the judgment of the nations of the world.[35] According to the Jews, "God judges the world on Rosh Hashanah and concludes the verdict on Yom Kippur," then, on Hoshana Raba, the verdict receives its final seal.[36]

The significance of Hoshana Roba, as it relates to Nuremberg, is that in the year 1946, Hoshana Raba fell on October 16, the very day the condemned were hung from Nuremberg's gallows. Although the trial for those accused of Nazi war crimes ended in June of that same year, "sentencing was repeatedly postponed due to appeals for amnesty."[37] As a result, the sentencing was not handed down until the beginning of October and then carried out on October 16, the day of the judgment of nations.

3. Esther asked the king to hang the sons of Haman "tomorrow."

While the book of Esther never specifically mentions the name of God in its text, the word *king* is found throughout, and according to Talmudic scholars, has a double meaning. Within the text, the terms "king" and "King Ahasuerus" are used. Whenever it reads "King Ahasuerus," the Scriptures are referencing Esther's husband. However, when the word "king" stands alone, without the succession of the proper noun, "Ahasuerus," then the word takes on a double meaning; it can be referring to both King Ahasuerus and to God.[38] In the book of Esther, the queen asked the king to hang Haman's sons tomorrow. She said, "If it pleases the king, let it be granted to the Jews who *are* in Shushan to do again tomorrow according to today's decree, and let Haman's ten sons be hanged on the gallows" (Esther 9:13 NKJV).

In verse thirteen, the word "king" stands alone. Therefore, Queen Esther was not only asking King Ahasuerus to hang Haman's sons, she was also supplicating the same request to God. Furthermore, she asks the king to hang Haman's sons "tomorrow." This is important because in the Talmudic tradition, the word "tomorrow" does not necessarily mean the twenty-four-hour period that follows today. In fact, the word "tomorrow" basically means, "at some point in the future."[39]

Therefore, not only did Queen Esther ask King Ahasuerus to hang Haman's sons tomorrow, she was also praying that God would do the same "at some point in the future." Furthermore, while Haman's biological sons were indeed hanged by King Ahasuerus, it can be said that the Nazi war criminals who were hanged at Nuremberg are surely the spiritual sons of Haman.[40]

Haman is described as "the enemy of all the Jews" who "plotted against the Jews to annihilate them . . . to consume them and destroy them" (Esther 9:24 NKJV). This evil description is one that fits both Haman and his ideological progeny, the Nazis.

4. Ten were hanged.

As previously mentioned, eleven Nazis were sentenced to die on November 16, 1946. However, due to Goering's suicide, only ten were hanged—the exact number of Haman's sons.

5. The number 13.

Every Hebrew number has a meaning correlated with it. For instance, the number 12 is a perfect number that relates perfection of government or perfect rule.[41] A prime example of this number at work is Jesus and his twelve disciples.

However, one added to the perfect number 12 yields 13, which is imperfection. The first time the number 13 appears in Scripture, it reads, "Twelve years they served Cherdorlaomer, and the thirteenth year they rebelled."[42] Bible scholar E. W. Bullinger noted that in the Bible, "every occurrence of the number thirteen, and likewise every multiple of it, stands in connection with rebellion, apostasy, defection, corruption, disintegration, revelation or some kindred idea."[43]

Notice that in the book of Esther, Haman demanded that the Jews be annihilated on the thirteenth day of the month: "And the letters were sent by couriers into all the king's provinces, to destroy, to kill, and to annihilate all the Jews, both young and old, little children and women, in one day, on the thirteenth day of the twelfth month, which is the month of Adar, and to plunder their possessions" (Esther 3:13 NKJV).

It is not a coincidence that these words are written in that particular chapter's *thirteenth* verse. With that in mind, see also that Esther asks the king to hang Haman's sons in the *thirteenth* verse of chapter nine. Ironically, the criminals at Nuremberg had to climb 13 steps to the top of their gallows. Additionally, Nuremberg ultimately held 13 trials against Nazi war criminals. Is this a coincidence? I think not.

6. Both the Nuremberg war criminals and Haman were hanged on their own property.

It is worth mentioning that both Haman and the Nazi war criminals met their fates on their own property. Haman was hanged at his own house on the gallows that he had built for Mordecai. Similarly, the Nazi war criminals were hanged in Nuremburg, which was the home of the

Reichsparteigelande, the Nazi Party rally grounds. So, both Haman and his ideological offspring met their fate in exactly the same surroundings.

7. The Feast of Purim

Hitler's hatred for the book of Esther has been described the following way: "Hitler harbored a venomous hatred for the book of Esther, and the holiday of Purim. 'Unless Germany is victorious,' he proclaimed, 'Jewry could then celebrate the destruction of Europe by a second triumphant Purim Festival.' When Hitler invaded Poland in 1939, he banned the reading of the book of Esther and ordered that all synagogues be closed and barred on the holiday of Purim. On Purim in 1942, in one town in Nazi occupied Poland, ten Jews were hanged by Hitler's SS, in a sadistic parody of events in the book of Esther."[44]

This same sentiment resonated on October 16, 1946, when the ten war criminals met their fates. While not all of the condemned spoke last words, the tenth and final criminal that was executed, Julius Streicher, had plenty to say: "Only Julius Streicher went without dignity. He had to be pushed across the floor, wide-eyed and screaming: 'Heil Hitler!' Mounting the steps he cried out: 'And now I go to God.' He stared at the witnesses facing the gallows and shouted: 'Purimfest, 1946.' "[45]

8. The manner in which they killed is the manner in which they died.

Haman built a gallows intending to hang Mordecai on it. Similarly, the Nazis hanged Jews in effigy on Purim in 1942 (as noted above) and routinely executed the Jewish people with hanging throughout the Holocaust. What they had done to the Jewish people, in turn, was exactly done to them.

Without a doubt, the hanging of the Nazi war criminals as foretold by the book of Esther cannot be explained away by irony and coincidence. There is nothing that is not hinted in the Torah.[46]

"And I will curse him who curses you . . ."

—*Genesis 12:3 NKJV*

ENGLAND'S REJECTION UNDER THE
REIGN OF "EDWARD THE HAMMER"

Winston Churchill called Edward I one of the greatest kings in European history. It was under Edward's rule in the late 1200s that Wales and Cornwall were merged into the British crown and Scotland and Ireland were invaded and occupied.

Edward I was also the first European monarch to set up an effective administrative bureaucracy to survey and perform a census of his kingdom, and establish laws and political divisions.

Edward I also embraced the financial power of the Jewish people. The English Jews were not allowed to own land or hold public office, and they could not join most of the trades or professions. They soon discovered that money could be the secret of their survival, and many acquired great wealth.

Ever resourceful, Edward I found a way to separate the Jewish people from their money. First, he borrowed from them to finance his imperial ambitions, and then, rather than repaying the debt, Edward I simply expelled the Jews from England. Edward I was uniquely inventive: He kicked the Jews out of England twice. After a time, he invited the Jews back to their English homeland, borrowed more money, and then expelled them again.

The anti-Semitic roots of England run deep and long. On November 29, 1947, the United Nations Partition Plan for Palestine was adopted by a decision of the general assembly. The resolution was approved by a vote of 33 to 13 with 10 abstentions. England was one of the abstentions refusing to support the birth of a Jewish state.

Recently, Diana and I went to London and, with the assistance of some very gracious and politically well-connected friends, were given an audience with one of the most powerful and influential members of the British government. My intention was to seek his blessing and guidance in having a "Night to Honor Israel" in the Royal Albert Hall for the greater London area.

Diana and I were ushered into his elegant office. We introduced ourselves with Diana pouring on her considerable charm. It was like water off the proverbial duck's back. I was reminded of that old country song: "Is It Cold in Here or Is That Just You?"

We presented the concepts, purposes, and objectives of a "Night to Honor Israel" clearly and concisely. Diana and I waited for his response from a face that reflected no emotion. His statement I will never forget.

With all the frigidity of a massive iceberg, he folded his hands on the desk, raised his eyebrows, and said, "There are times in history when doing nothing is the best thing to do; this is one of those times in history."

Diana and I thanked the politician for his time and left his office with a blast of frigid air following us through the door.

The anti-Semitic climate in England today is covered well by Melanie Phillips in her chilling book, *Londonistan,* graphically describing how radical Islam is rapidly gaining control of Britain.

Britain has become a largely post-Christian society, where traditional morality has been systematically undermined and replaced by an "anything goes" culture in which autonomous decisions about codes of behavior have become unchallenged rights.

"Judaism and Christianity, the creeds that form the bedrock of Western civilization, have been pushed aside and their place filled by a plethora of paranormal activities and cults. So much so that now prisoners are allowed to practice paganism in their cells . . . and a Royal Navy sailor was given the legal right to carry out satanic rituals and worship the devil aboard the frigate HMS *Cumberland.*" [47]

"The issues of Iraq, America, and Israel are now conflated in the British public mind in a poisonous stew of irrationality, prejudice, ignorance, and fear. Britons believe that the only reason they are currently threatened by Islamic terror is the UK's support for America in Iraq. They think the main reason for Muslim rage is the behavior of Israel towards the Palestinians, and that America made itself a target simply because of its support for Israel. 'Middle Britain' thinks that America is the fount of all evil and that Israel poses the greatest threat to world peace. The daily invective against Jews, Israelis, and evil Americans upon young Muslims who were already inflamed against the West has turned up the temperature to the boiling point. The relentless demonization of America and Israel by the British media has acted as a powerful recruiting sergeant for the jihad and has entrenched *Londonistan* in Britain's national psyche." [48]

The emergence of "Londonistan" should be of the greatest concern to America, for which it poses acute danger. Clearly, the fact that Britain has become Europe's radical Islamic terror factory presents immediate and obvious risks to America's physical security.

As the Pentagon briefing paper observed, "America's political leaders still think Muslim terrorists, even suicide bombers, are mindless criminals motivated by 'hatred of our freedoms' rather than religious zealots motivated by their faith. And as a result we have no real strategic plan for winning a war against jihadist." [49]

Think about it!

Great Britain began down the road of anti-Semitism by kicking the Jews out of England after taking their money. They kicked out the seed of Abraham, who were loving, peaceful, and law-abiding.

In 1947, they voted against the Jewish people having a homeland in Palestine. Currently, England is charging members of the Israeli government as war criminals for their role in defending Israel from the rocket attacks of Hamas.

Today, England is flooded by the soldiers of Allah who love war, live by their own law, and threaten to kill anyone who rejects their faith. There comes this haunting refrain that none should ever forget: "I will curse those who curse you."

THE VOYAGE OF THE DAMNED: CUBA'S REJECTION

Herbert Karliner: A Survivor's Story

Herbert Karliner was just twelve years old when he sailed on the SS *St. Louis* with his parents and three siblings. A young boy who lived through Kristallnacht, the voyage of the *St. Louis,* and ultimately his family's demise in the concentration camps, Herbert is a survivor. The son of religious Jews, Herbert attended services at his synagogue every Friday and Saturday.

During Kristallnacht, as his family's synagogue burned, Herbert's father tried to save the Torah, but the Nazi guard stopped him. In addition to their place of worship being destroyed, their family business was also vandalized. Later that evening, Herbert's father Joseph was arrested and taken to Buchenwald. Once a multigenerational member of his community, Herbert was now no longer allowed to attend school and would be "kicked around just walking on the same sidewalk as the

Aryan people."[50] After Kristallnacht, Herbert's life would never be the same.

Following these tragic events, Herbert's mother was informed that in order to secure her husband's release from Buchenwald, she had to obtain visas for another country as proof that she and her family would leave Germany. Despite having to sell their home and business at Gestapo-mandated prices, Herbert's mother paid inflated fees to secure landing permits in Cuba for her family. The Karliners planned to stay there until their quota number was called for entrance into the United States. Upon securing the permits to leave Germany, Joseph Karliner returned home after three weeks in Buchenwald. Described by his son Herbert as "unrecognizable," Joseph would not open up about his experiences at the concentration camp until the family was well on their way to Cuba.[51] Although his father was hesitant to describe what he had gone through, Herbert's uncle had been sent to Dachau a year earlier, never to return. Even at the young age of twelve, Hebert said he "already knew what it meant to go to a camp."[52]

Well on his way to Cuba and hopeful that the worst was behind him, Herbert enjoyed the sense of adventure he felt cruising aboard such a grand ship. Unfortunately, his high spirits would not last long as he and his family quickly realized they would not be able to disembark in Cuba. His sense of adventure had now turned to panic as the passengers sent telegrams looking for a savior. "We sent a plea to Mrs. Roosevelt to allow only the children to enter the U.S., but it came to deaf ears . . . we had to return to Europe knowing full well what it meant."[53] After hanging in limbo on board the *St. Louis,* the Karliners were told that help had been found.

Still uneasy about what the future held, Herbert and his family were taken to France where his older sister and his parents were sent to a tiny village. Meanwhile he, his brother, and his younger sister were taken to a children's home.

He would later celebrate his Bar Mitzvah in that home, as he recalls it: "We were a bunch of boys together, without our parents there, and it was very sad."[54] The following year, in 1940, Herbert's parents came to visit their three children at the home. Upset by the poor accommodations, the Karliners decided to take their youngest daughter back to the village with them; this would ultimately cost the girl her life.

In the end, Herbert's mother, father, and two sisters were killed at

Auschwitz; only Herbert and his brother survived. Herbert would not discover this until the American troops arrived in Paris. With nowhere to go, Herbert was sent by a Jewish humanitarian organization to be a counselor in order to receive groups of Jewish children from various liberated concentration camps. Karliner describes the experience: "It was awful . . . children from all nationalities . . . not even speaking the same language, not understanding one another and behaving like cave men; all sick and so pitiful."

After the dust settled in Europe, Herbert and his brother were able to move to America to live with their uncle in 1946.

As a twelve-year-old boy admiring the beaches of Florida from the deck of the *St. Louis* in 1939, Herbert made a promise to himself that he would come back to Miami one day. After moving to America, he kept that promise to himself and went to work in Miami in 1949. However, his new sense of freedom was quickly stripped away since he was drafted into the U.S. Army one year later. A young man who had lived through the worst war the world had ever seen went and proudly served his new country. After deployments to Korea and Japan, Herbert kept the promise he made to himself and finally put down his roots in Miami Beach in 1954. Currently retired and still living in Miami Beach, Herbert is eighty-six years old. He has been married to his wife Vera for forty-eight years and has two daughters.

Herbert remembers his voyage on the *St. Louis,* and with his white hair blowing in the sea breeze, he stares at Florida's crystal waters and says, "I promised myself I would come back to Miami one day . . . it took me a long time . . . but I made it." [55]

Cuba and the Voyage of the SS *St. Louis*

At first, many would not be able to see the likeness between the plight of present-day Cuban political refugees and the Jewish people trapped in the jaws of the Third Reich. However, one need look no further than the 936 Jewish refugees aboard the *St. Louis* to see the striking similarities between the shared fate of those aboard the *St. Louis* and those Cubans who have unsuccessfully fled their nation since Castro's Revolution of 1958.

Indeed, while the circumstances surrounding their stories may be different and although they are separated by cultures and generations, taking to the ocean's waters in overcrowded boats hoping it would carry them to a better life is the tie that binds the two.

In order to understand the voyage of the damned—the *St. Louis* voyage to Cuba—one must start in Paris, France, on November 7, 1938. It was on this day that Ernst von Rath, the third secretary of the German embassy in Paris, was shot and killed by Herschel Grynszpan, a Polish Jew.[56] Grynszpan was "outraged at the brutal expulsion from Germany of 10,000 long-resident Polish Jews with nothing but the clothes on their backs and about four dollars each, who were poorly treated by the Poles when they were dumped at the frontier."[57] As a result of the shooting, one of the most violent pogroms was carried out against Germany's entire Jewish population.

Known as "Kristallnacht," or the "Night of Broken Glass," from November 9 to 10, 1938, the Jews of Germany were attacked, their synagogues vandalized, and their businesses and homes looted and destroyed. When the dust settled after the two-day attack, ninety-one Jews had been murdered, thousands injured, and over twenty thousand sent to concentration camps.[58]

To add insult to serious injury, the nation's Jews were held liable for the Kristallnacht pogrom and a fine of $400 million was imposed upon Germany's half million Jewish population.[59] Though the world did not realize it then, Kristallnacht marked the beginning of the Holocaust and the systematic extermination of the Jewish people.

After those fateful nights in November, the world was put on notice of the horrors that plagued Hitler's victims. The Jewish people quickly realized their window of opportunity to flee Hitler's Germany was growing smaller by the day. Leaving, however, was not easy. Refugees were not welcome with open arms, as many countries had immigration quotas, most notably the United States.

As a result, visas were hard to come by. Not only was money required to gain entry into a new nation, but Jews also had to pay just to leave Germany. This made travel cost prohibitive, since they had already been experiencing financial oppression under the Nazi regime.[60]

Despite these hurdles, immigration was the only way for German Jews to escape the oppressive regime that plagued them. And, for the 936 who booked passage aboard the SS *St. Louis,* it seemed like their only hope of survival.

Cuba appeared to be a suitable destination for refugees fleeing Germany. Jewish refugees were welcomed in Cuba, and the nation had received 1,500 of them in 1938 alone.[61] With its close proximity to America, Cuba was a choice location for refugees to find temporary solace while waiting to make America's immigration quota.[62] However, unbeknownst to those aboard the *St. Louis,* their arrival in Cuba was doomed before the ship even set sail from its German port in mid-May 1939.

In 1939, there were more than six thousand Jews living in Cuba, mostly in the port city of Havana.[63] Early that same year, immigration levels spiked, and in one twenty-four-hour period some twelve hundred refugees had arrived from various European nations.[64] With local constituents growing more discontent upon the arrival of more refugees, the government passed Decree 55 in the beginning of 1939.[65]

This decree was aimed at curbing immigration to Cuba by requiring refugees to pay a $500 bond to Cuba, ensuring they would not become permanent wards of the island nation.[66] Decree 55 stated tourists were still welcome in Cuba and as such were not required to pay bonds or obtain visas. Manuel Benitez, the corrupt director-general of immigration, saw the new law as an opportunity to generate personal wealth for himself. Accordingly, Benitez began to issue "landing certificates" to all tourists at the cost of $150 each. Benitez used these certificates as a tool to allow refugees to land in Cuba as tourists. The certificates appeared authentic, and even made to look like visas.[67] As a result, those looking to profit off the desperate Jewish immigrants would buy these certificates in bulk and resell them at inflated prices.[68] Benitez's plan to reap personal wealth as a result of the loophole in Decree 55 was successful, much to the chagrin of President Federico Laredo Brú. Additionally, Benitez had the benefit of being protected by Cuba's military leader Colonel Fulgencio Batista, a man whose influence was growing with Cubans. Because Batista had the power of the military behind him, Cuba's President Brú was unable to force Benitez to share his profits.[69]

In an effort to dry up Benitez's steady profit stream, President Brú's government took swift action to end Benitez's power to issue landing certificates.[70] The desired result would be twofold:

1. Closing the immigration loophole would no longer allow Benitez to cash in at Cuba's expense.

2. President Brú would gain favor from the Cubans in not allowing more refugees to enter the nation.

Prior to the *St. Louis*'s arrival in Cuba, Germany sent Nazi "provocateurs" to incite local anti-Semitic sentiment.[71] This was not a difficult task, since Cuba's economy was weak and the native population did not want to see the influx of more Jewish refugees, as many believed Cuba was already being overrun with Jews.[72] Therefore, to stay in good graces with the locals, Brú's government issued Decree 937 in May 1939. Decree 937 made the landing permit of passengers on board the *St. Louis* null and void. They had to find another way to buy their way off the ship, after having already paid an exorbitant amount under the original law.

As a result, the landing certificates, which the *St. Louis* passengers believed would grant them temporary stay in Cuba, were invalidated and would no longer grant refugee access to Cuba. Despite the fact that the Hamburg-America Line was aware of this change in Cuba's immigration policy prior to the *St. Louis* setting sail, it looked the other way and allowed the ship to depart.[73] Truthfully, the Hamburg-America Line did not care whether or not the passengers on the *St. Louis* were ever allowed to disembark in Cuba or any other port for that matter. In fact, the Hamburg-America Line charged its passengers 230 Reichsmarks, on top of the cost for their passage, in the event that the *St. Louis* had to make an "unplanned" trip back to Germany.[74]

Designed as the ultimate propaganda tool by the Nazis, the voyage of the *St. Louis* was intended to serve as a microcosm of the anti-Semitic attitude that spanned from one coast of the Atlantic to the other. Nazi Germany watched the *St. Louis* set sail, hoping that if Cuba refused to admit the Jewish refugees then the increasingly isolationist United States would do the same.[75] They were right.

The true tenor of those aboard the ship may never be fully realized. The captain of the ship, Gustav Schroeder, described by one of the survivors of the *St. Louis* as a compassionate man who ordered decent treatment for his Jewish passengers, noted in his diary at the outset of the trip that, "There is a somewhat nervous disposition among the passengers. Despite this, everyone seems convinced they will never see Germany again."[76]

As the *St. Louis* sailed closer to Cuba, Captain Schroeder was notified that the landing certificates held by most of those on board had been invalidated and would no longer be honored once the ship arrived.[77] Upon hearing that Cuba would not be allowing the passengers to disembark, Moritz Weiler, a man escaping Germany with his wife, succumbed to a deadly heart attack.[78] With no place to store the corpse, Mr. Weiler's body was buried at sea.[79]

This would not be the only fatality aboard during the journey. Less than an hour later, a despondent member of the crew threw himself overboard at the exact spot where Weiler's maritime funeral had taken place.[80] Unfortunately, the morbid mood on the *St. Louis* would only be exacerbated once it reached its destination.

The *St. Louis* arrived in Cuba on May 27. Only twenty-two of its Jewish passengers had the money required to pay the $500 bond in compliance with Cuba's newly refined immigration laws.[81] Therefore, they, along with six other non-Jewish passengers, were the only ones allowed to disembark.[82] While Colonel Batista had the influence to intercede on behalf of those who remained onboard "he dodged the issue, claiming to be ill with the grippe."[83] As the *St. Louis* sat anchored in Cuba's port, the publicity surrounding the ship and the plight of the refugees became a worldwide controversy.

While the ship idled in Cuba's harbor for days, Max Lowe, a Jewish man traveling with his wife and children, went to the location on deck where Mr. Weiler had been buried at sea days before. In an effort to end his life, Lowe slashed his wrists, threw himself overboard, and attempted to pull his own veins out of his arms.[84] Lowe's suicide was interrupted when a Cuban police boat pulled him from the water and sent him to a hospital.[85] Ironically, Lowe, who wanted to die, ended up being saved by the Cubans. Meanwhile, his family was left behind on the ship and prohibited from disembarking in order to accompany Lowe to the hospital.[86]

With seemingly little hope of being admitted into Cuba and increasingly morose events happening on board, Captain Schroeder, concerned about mass suicide attempts, created "suicide patrols" to prevent any additional passengers from taking their own lives.[87] The captain's apprehension was not unfounded. Jules Wallerstein, a young boy traveling with his family, said his father indicated that the passengers would commit suicide should the ship go back to Germany.

Wallerstein stated, "To me that was a shocker, I was twelve years old and realized it was the end of my life. My parents knew that if we went back the trains would be waiting for us."[88] Finally, the *St. Louis* was ordered out of Cuba's waters and Captain Schroeder turned northbound toward Florida.

In what seemed to be an answer to prayer, while the ship was four miles off the Floridian coast, the *St. Louis* was called back to Cuban waters. President Brú did not want to allow the passengers aboard the *St. Louis* into Cuba—doing so would make him appear politically vulnerable. He was struggling to hold on to his power, with Batista's influence and command as it was.[89] Additionally, President Brú felt he had to "maintain the prestige of the Cuban government vis-à-vis the Hamburg American Line."[90] However, the loss of Cuban prestige could evidently be mitigated with money because Brú conceded and agreed the passengers could disembark in Cuba, provided the government was paid $650 per person.[91]

The American Jewish Joint Distribution Committee (JDC), a group dedicated to Jewish aide, agreed to the inflated price—$150 in excess of the required bond—in order to ensure the *St. Louis*'s passengers did not have to return to Germany. The JDC sent Lawrence Berenson, a lawyer who was used to dealing with the Cuban government, with the cash required to close the deal.[92] Berenson felt he was in familiar territory; he had formerly secured one thousand visas for German Jews to land in Cuba and, more importantly, was friendly with Colonel Batista.[93]

However, when he met with President Brú and suggested a price reduction for the $650 bonds in an effort to save the JDC some money, President Brú once again ordered the *St. Louis* out of Cuban waters.[94] Evidently Brú did not want to haggle.

With the possibility of landing in Cuba no longer an option, Captain Gustav Schroeder once again turned the *St. Louis* toward Florida. He gradually sailed the ship up the coast, hoping the public exposure surrounding this humanitarian tragedy would prompt the United States to lend a helping hand. United States Treasury Secretary Henry Morgenthau, along with others, attempted to absorb the passengers into the U.S. Virgin Islands; however, this maneuver could not stand absent an act of Congress.[95]

Moreover, immigration "quotas were jealously guarded by Congress, supported by a strong, broad cross-section of Americans who were against all immigrants, not just Jews."[96] Accordingly, America's elected officials were not overly eager to render aide. Authorities are still mixed as to whether or not President Roosevelt did enough to help those aboard the *St. Louis*. As Conrad Black points out: "734 of the passengers were in quota lines for U.S. entry. Petitions were addressed to [President] Roosevelt from many groups within the United States and from the *St. Louis'* passengers, who pointed out in their plea that over 400 of their number were women and children. There were many editorials asking Roosevelt to be merciful to these unfortunates. He didn't reply to any of it."[97]

However, others suggest that Roosevelt, due to limitations of executive power, was incapable of altering the United States' immigration quota system, and as a result, could not permit those aboard the *St. Louis* to enter the United States.[98] Roosevelt's action or lack thereof, whatever it may have been, does not diminish the tragedy that surrounded the *St. Louis* saga.

With no help coming from the United States, the captain could not allow the ship to linger on the North American coast, as the onboard provisions were running low.[99] Seemingly defeated, the *St. Louis* made the long return trip across the Atlantic. Ironically, the passengers' only advocate was perhaps their most unlikely ally. Schroeder, a German and the captain of a ship sailing under the Nazi flag, promised his passengers that he would run the *St. Louis* aground off the coast of England before he would return his passengers to Germany.[100]

Ultimately, "after extensive diplomatic maneuvering and shameful rejections from many other countries," Schroeder never had to make good on his noble promise, as alternate democratic destinations were arranged for the passengers.[101] In the end, 288 of those aboard were allowed into England while the remaining passengers were absorbed into France, Belgium, and Holland, respectively.[102] Save England, all of the other nations that agreed to accept *St. Louis* refugees were hastily conquered by Hitler, and eventually the Jews living within their borders were systematically slaughtered in the Final Solution. Authorities are mixed as to exactly how many aboard the *St. Louis* met their demise upon returning to Europe; some experts suggest only approximately 450 survived the Holocaust.[103]

In fact, the United States Holocaust Museum continues to search for survivors.[104] What is not disputed, however, is the prominent role Cuba and its corrupt leaders played in the *St. Louis* tragedy. Perhaps the most revolting detail in this disaster is that the *Flander,* another ocean liner, had docked in Cuba shortly after the *St. Louis.*

On board, there were one hundred refugee passengers who held adequate visas, the same visas the JDC was willing to purchase for those on board the *St. Louis.* However, unlike the refugees on the *St. Louis,* the *Flander* passengers were admitted to Cuba without meeting any resistance.[105] This disgusting fact underscores the capricious game of Russian roulette that Cuba willingly played with the innocent lives of the Jewish people—not to mention the complicit role they assumed with the Nazis.

THE CONNECTION

"I will bless those who bless you."

—Genesis 12:3 NKJV

Within the shadows of the sad portrait painted by the SS *St. Louis* lie two illustrations regarding the fate of those who persecute the Jewish people and the promise of those who do not. Gustav Schroeder, the captain of the *St. Louis,* did not reject the children of Israel in their time of need. He could have returned his passengers to Germany as soon as they were rejected in Cuba, and arguably rebelled from his obligation to do so. Had he done this, there is little doubt that the majority, if not all of those aboard, would have perished at the hands of the Nazis. Yet, despite his allegiance to Nazi Germany, Captain Schroeder acted bravely and in the best interests of his passengers as opposed to his country. In a twist of fate, by the war's end, Schroeder's ship had sustained heavy damage and was sold for scrap.[106]

After this, the captain had no way to make ends meet, as the *St. Louis* was the last ship in his command.[107] Despite his misfortune, survivors of the *St. Louis* ensured that Schroder, in addition to his family, were taken care of.[108] In addition to this, Yad Vashem, the Holocaust museum in Israel, posthumously recognized the captain as "Righteous Among the Nations."[109] Gustav Schroeder survived because he did not reject Israel.

The Lord said, *"And I will curse him who curses you"* (Genesis 12:3 NKJV). Unlike the actions of Captain Schroeder in 1939, Cuba blatantly turned its back on the Jewish people in their time of need. Two decades later, Colonel Batista, the military powerhouse who betrayed the Jewish people during the *St. Louis* affair—despite his having the ability to save them—was overthrown by Fidel Castro.

With his rise to power, Castro ushered in a new regime of socialism and dictatorship that isolated the nation and caused its citizens to live in poverty, to live without freedom, and to flee its borders in sinking ships for another country.

We have all seen the images. Makeshift rafts and dilapidated boats overloaded with Cuban political refugees seeking a better life just ninety miles north of their island home. Sometimes the stories end well for those who risk their lives, braving the elements of sun and sea in search of freedom and the American Dream. Yet the nameless and faceless majority who never make that short journey from Cuba to Florida's shore remain captives of communism.

Perhaps they never made it because the vessel carrying them to freedom was not as strong as their will to escape Castro's tyranny at home. Regardless of the outcome, we are all familiar with the story—Cuban political refugees leaving all that they have ever known behind, in search of a life free from the Communist chains that bound them.

In 1939, the Jews sailed to Cuba in a hopeful effort to escape a country that persecuted them, only to be rebuffed by an unwilling host. Is it ironic that less than twenty years later the same country that closed its doors to the children of Israel became a nation that persecuted its own people to such a degree that its citizens are perpetually clamoring aboard vessels set for sea with that same hope in mind? Cuba allowed the children of Israel to sail to their likely deaths. Since then, countless Cubans continue to meet that same fate.

"WHY DID GOD ALLOW THIS?": GERMANY'S REJECTION

I stood in the middle of the Nazi death camp, Dachau, and was stunned at the visible signs of unspeakable horror the Jewish people had suffered at the hands of the Third Reich. They were not here because they had broken the law; they were here because at least one of their grandparents was Jewish. In the Third Reich that was all it took to guarantee your horrific death at any death camp.

Standing in the Quadrangle where the Nazis had forced the Jews to stand for hours during roll call, I looked at the remaining foundations of the sleeping quarters where Jewish people were packed in and stacked on top of each other in a compound of human suffering that defies human imagination. To my left were the ovens where human beings were burned to ash on the altars of Nazi hatred. To the right of the ovens was a blood ditch where thousands, young and old, were mercilessly slaughtered and then carried on carts to the ovens to become ashes flying through the sky.

Standing in the Dachau Quadrangle, I conceived an idea that later brought a degree of comfort and consolation to the Jewish relatives of those who had died such a horrific death there. The idea came from the prophet Ezekiel, who wrote: "I sat where they sat, and remained there astonished among them" (Ezekiel 3:15 NKJV).

It was Elijah's way of saying, "You can't know how people feel about any given tragedy or time of trouble until you feel exactly what they have felt and experienced."

As Diana and I left the death camp, we were bound for West Berlin, where I was to be the speaker for five nights at the U.S. military chapel in a week of spiritual emphasis for our military personnel.

I expressed to Diana my desire to return to Dachau at a later date and have a "lest we forget" memorial service for the Jewish people who died in the Holocaust and were related to our Jewish friends in America. We agreed we would do it.

Months later, we did exactly that. As four hundred Christians stood in formation in the Quadrangle with the Star of David on our arms and the names of the Jewish people who had died in the Holocaust attached to our clothes, we answered a roll call, stepping forward and saying, "I am here!"

Our travel troupe left Dachau for Israel, where we planted those armbands around a tree in a grove of trees with the name of the Jewish people who perished in the Holocaust on the armband. The symbolism was that they had returned to Israel to be a part of the Holy Land for all eternity.

As Diana and I left Dachau on our first visit, I took several minutes studying closely the fence the Nazis had built around the Jews in every death camp of the Third Reich. The concrete posts were square and precisely the same height, adorned with barbed wire from top to bottom.

The posts were planted in two rows exactly equidistant from each other, totally encircling the death camp. There were machine gun towers erected in the center of the "no man's land" created by the two rows of concrete posts.

It might have been possible to make it over the first barrier of barbed wire and post; none could dream of making it over the second fence before being riddled with machine gun fire.

German shepherd dogs patrolled the middle ground to make sure the marksmen in the towers knew exactly the location of anyone approaching the fence. Death and torture were art forms for the Nazis.

Little did I know that in the next few days a revelation of truth concerning this fence would explode at Checkpoint Charlie in West Berlin, where I had been invited by the U.S. military to speak in their chapel for five nights concerning the topic of the "Fight for the Family." There are many pressures on a military family that civilians never endure. I accepted the invitation and was delighted with the chapel being packed to the back walls.

The military graciously gave me a guide, a vehicle with a military driver to escort Diana and me wherever we wanted to go. We discovered that West Berlin was a beautiful city with some of the most exciting shopping opportunities Diana had ever discovered on planet Earth.

After I had spoken the five nights at the chapel, I slipped behind what was then called the Iron Curtain to speak on two different occasions. If you can believe it, I was smuggled into East Berlin as an art critic. I have the qualifications to be an art critic like a bumblebee has the potential to be a 747.

As we drove up to Checkpoint Charlie, I was captivated by the barbed-wire fence that separated West Berlin, which looked like heaven on earth compared to the barren and desolate East Berlin, the Utopia of Communism. I could understand why people risked their lives often in a desperate attempt to escape Communist oppression for the paradise of freedom and unlimited abundance in the West.

As we exited the military vehicle to visit the museum at Check Point Charlie, our guide looked at me, pointed at the fence, and asked in disgust with the Almighty, "Pastor Hagee, why did God allow the Communists to build a fence like that around the German people to cage us in like animals?"

In a flash, I saw the fence at Dachau. The fence the Communists had built around the Germans was exactly the same fence as the one at Dachau. The concrete posts were the same height, the same shape, with the arch at the top adorned with razor-sharp wire promising death to anyone who might be foolish enough to attempt escape.

There were the machine gun towers in the middle, equally spaced, with German shepherd dogs patrolling the "no man's land" in the middle. Then it hit me like a ton of bricks, and I answered the guide who was shaken to the core: "God allowed the Communists to build this fence around you, because it is exactly the same fence the Germans built around the Jews in every death camp of the Third Reich. Remember: exactly what you do to the Jews, God will do to you. God has it the same . . . down to the dog hair!"

AHMADINEJAD'S PAYDAY IS COMING! IRAN'S REJECTION

Unless President Ahmadinejad of Iran is prevented by a military pre-emptive strike, he will soon have the nuclear power to make his ma-niacal dreams of a nuclear holocaust a reality. He has threatened on international television and the world press to "wipe Israel off the map." [110]

In a television interview in June 2008, Ahmadinejad said, "Today, the time for the fall of the satanic power of the United States has come and the countdown for annihilation of the emperor of power and wealth has started." [111]

America, it's time to wake up!

We face a clear and present danger from a theocratic dictatorship that has the will and soon will have the nuclear power to destroy us. It's time to shake ourselves out of the stupor of political correctness and embrace reality. The reality is that President Ahmadinejad believes that if he starts WWIII, the Islamic messiah will appear suddenly and mysteriously.

Understand that he doesn't know *who* this messiah is or *where* he is, but he believes the moment that Iran starts this "holy war," which will engulf the entire world in chaos, his messiah will appear. This mysterious messiah will lead the "holy warriors" of radical Islam to a global Sharia, meaning that every nation on the face of the earth will come under Islamic law. Ahmadinejad believes that he has the power and the duty to bring this about.

Remember, history teaches us that those who fail to remember the mistakes of the past are doomed to repeat them. One of the most tragic events of recent history was Hitler's Holocaust against the Jewish people during World War II. There are a number of lessons that we can learn from the Holocaust, but one of the most important is this: when a maniac threatens to kill you, take him at his maniacal word.

When Hitler began his threats to kill the Jewish people, few took him seriously. That was a tragic mistake. Ahmadinejad is the new *Hitler of the Middle East*. He wants a nuclear holocaust. He wants "the Great Satan," which is America, to fall and be in submission to Islam, and he wants to destroy Israel utterly.

Will God permit this madman to attack America with nuclear weapons? I sincerely believe this will happen if Iran is permitted to obtain nuclear weapons. Iran has made a mockery of Western diplomacy and could not care less about America's proposed sanctions. Ahmadinejad and his diplomacy of deception and delay have played England and America like a harp. He wants the bomb at any cost, including a nuclear war in the Middle East.

BOLTON: "THERE IS NO DIPLOMATIC SOLUTION"

In the second chapter of this book, I shared some comments from former U.S. Ambassador to the United Nations, John Bolton, that he made to an audience at Cornerstone Church in San Antonio, Texas, as we celebrated a "Night to Honor Israel." His comments are so relevant to this topic that I want, with his permission, to share more:

> The Iranian position is they want nuclear weapons. The western position is we don't want them to have nuclear weapons. So what's the compromise? Half a nuclear weapon? You can't negotiate about a difference that profound. The fact is in the nuclear proliferation field, time almost always works on the side of the proliferator. [The proliferator in this case is Iran.] The proliferator needs time

to overcome the complex scientific and technological challenges to achieving nuclear weapons and their ballistic missile delivery systems. Time is exactly what negotiations give Iran. Time is exactly what they've gotten from nearly five years of negotiations with our European friends. Five years in which the Europeans in their best creative diplomatic way, offered the Iranians every carrot they could think of if the Iranians would give up the pursuit of nuclear weapons.

What is the net of all those negotiations? Iran is five years closer to its objective of having precisely those nuclear weapons. The fact is that there is no diplomatic solution to the Iranian nuclear weapons problem, nor will economic sanctions work.

The sanctions that apply, even though they cause economic pain to Iran, are not doing anything to deter Iran from its continued pursuit of nuclear weapons. Even our administration no longer says that the purpose of sanctions is to stop the nuclear weapons program. They say that the purpose of sanctions is to bring Iran back to the negotiating table. And even if we got them back to the negotiating table, we're right back to the problem. What are we going to say to them after we've shaken hands?

This is a fundamental problem for Israel, for the United States and indeed for the civilized world because once Iran gets nuclear weapons, the balance of power in the Middle East and globally changes forever.

The Difference between Russia and Iran

Now, I'm afraid that the Plan B that the administration has been looking at is to accept an Iranian nuclear weapons capability. We won't like it but will accept it because we believe we can contain and deter Iran as we did the Soviet Union during the Cold War. I think this is fundamentally wrong. The psychology of the leadership in Iran is very different from the leadership of Moscow during the Cold War. Say what you want about the Communists. They were atheists. They thought they were only going around once in life and they weren't about to throw it away too quickly.

The leadership in Teheran is looking forward to the day when they pass over and hopefully take as many of us with them as they can.

If Iran gets nuclear weapons, you can bet that as soon as possible thereafter, Saudi Arabia will get nuclear weapons, Egypt will, Turkey will, perhaps others in the region will also. The result will be that in a very short period of time, five to ten years, you will have half a dozen or more Middle Eastern states with a nuclear weapons capability. And if you didn't like the bipolar nuclear standoff of the Cold War, [America vs. Russia] imagine the risk of a multi-polar nuclear Middle East with many countries looking at each other, wondering who is going to strike first.

Just three and a half years ago, Israel destroyed another nuclear reactor in Syria. This nuclear reactor was being built by North Korea. North Korea? Why? Because of its long cultural ties with Syria? Of course not! We came to find out that reactor was a three-way joint venture financed by Iran because both Iran and North Korea have a vested interest in keeping their nuclear weapons programs hidden from international prying eyes. And what better way for the two of them to do it than to build it in a country where nobody is looking?

So Israel twice has attacked nuclear facilities preemptively in its own self-defense, which we believe is a legitimate right, especially for a democratic country.

Day of Decision Is Soon

We are coming to a decision point. And I don't know when it will be, but it will be soon: either the United States or Israel is going to have to make a decision to allow Iran to become a nuclear weapon state or to take preemptive military force.

It seems to me that the use of preemptive force in a very limited way to stop Iran from getting nukes is the right answer for world peace generally.

If the Iranian nuclear weapons program does come under attack, there will be a political fire storm around the world. There will be potentially grave economic consequences. I just want you to begin to think about why this decision may have to be made and to think about the implications of it for our future, for our children and our grandchildren. Because if Iran gets nuclear weapons, the world will be changed forever.

Bible prophecy, ambassadors, statesmen, and political scholars are all saying the same thing in their own way. We live in a very dangerous world and with nuclear proliferation are facing the end of days.

Think it can't happen?

Think again!

SEVEN

The Criminalization of Christianity

The criminalization of Christianity did not begin with the formation of the ACLU under the leadership of Roger Baldwin, who confessed to being a committed socialist and whose ultimate objective was the promotion of communism.[1]

The criminalization of Christianity began with the Roman Empire and their conspiracy as led by King Herod and Pilate to destroy a Jewish rabbi from Nazareth named Jesus Christ.

The plot of the Roman Empire to destroy the ministry of Jesus was simple and effective: publicly accuse Jesus of things he had never said or done in order to assassinate his character and scatter his followers, wounded by doubt. The concept of slaughter-the-shepherd-and-scatter-the-sheep was not new and is still the modus operandi of some in the liberal media.

Jesus of Nazareth was labeled a heretic, a liar, a drunkard, a demonized madman, and an insurrectionist too dangerous to live.

Before even meeting Jesus, why would Rome fear Him and twelve ordinary disciples who had no wealth, little education, no military experience, and who were virtually unknown?

Rome had Jesus on the "watch list," because He demonstrated the ability to feed five thousand people out of a boy's sack lunch. He had demonstrated the ability to heal the wounded and to raise the dead. He attracted the masses that were ready and willing to follow Him in a revolt to crush the repressive Roman Empire, if He would only give the word. However, He never did, saying, "My kingdom is not of this world."

Add to his government profile that his ministry started in Galilee, which was known as a hotbed for its antigovernment positions, and Jesus had the profile in the Homeland Security Office of the Roman Empire as a right-wing, Bible-believing, hate monger who needed to be on the "watch list," like four hundred thousand Americans are right now in Washington, DC.

He was arrested by Rome in the Garden of Gethsemane, put on trial, falsely accused, and, in a matter of hours, was brutally murdered by the Roman government at the place called Calvary as an insurrectionist too dangerous to live.

Those who present Jesus Christ as a man who was loved by everyone seriously misrepresent the message and ministry of the son of God. If he was loved by everyone, just how did he manage to get himself arrested, thrown into jail, beaten to a bloody pulp, and publicly crucified naked between two known thieves?

The truth is the government hated Jesus because of his massive influence with the public. Jesus left this postscript for those who would follow him through the centuries:

> If the world hates you, you know that it hated Me before it hated you. If you were of the world, the world would love its own. Yet because you are not of the world, but I chose you out of the world, therefore the world hates you.
>
> —John 15:18–19 NKJV

The truth is, the leaders of the New Testament church were in constant trouble with godless governments. Listen to the travelogue of suffering composed by St. Paul who wrote most of the New Testament and was given a guided tour of heaven by God Himself:

> In labors more abundant, in stripes above measure, in prisons more frequently, in deaths often. From the Jews five times I received forty stripes minus one. Three times I was beaten with rods; once I was stoned; three times I was shipwrecked; a night and a day have I been in the deep; in journeys often, in perils of water, in perils of robbers,

in *perils of* my own *countrymen,* in *perils of the Gentiles,* in *perils in the city,* in *perils in the wilderness,* in *perils in the sea,* in *perils among false brethren; in weariness and toil, in sleeplessness often, in hunger and thirst, in fastings often, in cold and nakedness—besides the other things . . . my deep concern for all* the *churches.*

—2 Corinthians 11:23–28 NKJV

St. Paul was in jail more than he was out of jail. Much of the New Testament was not written in some secluded seashore cottage with soft sea breezes stimulating the creative energies of the apostle. Much of the New Testament was written in a rat-infested jail cell with blood dripping off his back from the beatings given by sadistic Roman guards. Rome put his body in prison, but they could not capture the fire of his spirit or the passion of his unconquerable soul.

St. Paul writes, "In all these things we are more than conquerors through Him who loved us" (Romans 8:37 NKJV).

The list of Gospel jailbirds runs through the sacred Scripture concluding with John the Revelator on the isle of Patmos, labeled and slandered as an "enemy of the state" because he chose Christ over Caesar.

Martin Niemöller, a devout and passionate German Lutheran pastor trapped in the jaws of the Third Reich, was thrown into prison by Hitler and was executed. Why? Because he dared to say that Germany could not serve two masters. Either Germany would choose to serve Jesus Christ or Adolf Hitler.

The propaganda presses of the Third Reich crucified Niemöller's character and slandered his name; heaven crowned him as a champion of the cross and great was his reward the moment he stepped through gates of splendor into everlasting life.

Question: What would be your response if your pastor were thrown into jail and slandered in the media for preaching the gospel of Jesus Christ from the pulpit of your church?

Would you stand by him or leave the church? Would you be offended by the vicious slander of the media, the cruel office gossip, and the malignant lies told by people on the street who knew nothing of the truth?

Would you, like the Apostle Peter on the night that Christ was arrested by five hundred Roman soldiers from the Antonian Fortress in the Garden of Gethsemane say: "I know not the man!"

Would you be like his disciples who "returned to their nets"? They retreated to their comfort zone rather than face the conflict produced by their convictions. When you are confronted in the future about what you believe based on Bible truth, will you stand up or return to your nets? All men fall; the great ones get back up. You should never complain about what you permit. Your decisions today determine tomorrow's destiny.

As a Bible-believing Christian in America, you need to prepare yourself mentally, emotionally, and spiritually to defend your faith in court in the near future.

Think it can't happen?

Think again!

Get ready for it to happen!

WHEN CHRISTIANITY IS A CRIME

Let me address the title of this chapter, which some may consider to be too harsh: "The Criminalization of Christianity." The word *crime* is defined in Webster's New World Dictionary as "an act committed in violation of a law."

I select the title "The Criminalization of Christianity" because there are laws in place, thanks principally to the ACLU, that when violated, constitute a crime. Understand that it's not a crime according to the teachings of the Bible, but it's a crime in secularized America in the twenty-first century! We are at the point in American history where the laws of men surpass the laws of God Almighty in the courthouse. For instance, it is against the law of the Ten Commandments to commit murder. The U.S. Congress has just passed health care legislation that, in spite of the Presidential Executive Order 13535, does not change the law. As soon as Executive Order 13535 is challenged in a court of law the judge will yield to the law as it existed before the executive order and abortions will be paid for under the health care bill. The presidential executive order is not worth the paper it's written on! The government is taking your dollars and will use them to murder infants in the wombs of their mothers. Abortion is the American holocaust. Forty-three million beautiful babies butchered in America's abortion mills under the banner of "pro-choice."

Roger Baldwin, founder of the ACLU, described himself thusly: "I am for socialism, disarmament, and ultimately for abolishing the state itself as an instrument of violence and compulsion. I seek social ownership of property, the abolition of the propertied class, and sole control by those who produce wealth. Communism is the goal." [2]

"For eight decades, the ACLU has been America's leading censor, waging a largely uncontested war against America's core values, cloaking its war in the name of liberty." [3]

The result of this conflict is that Americans find themselves living in a country that, with each passing day, becomes more foreign to the positions our founders fought and died to preserve.

OUR FOUNDING FATHERS SAID WHAT?

While much has been written in recent years in an effort to deny the fact that America was founded upon the Bible, no efforts of atheist and agnostic secularists can change the facts of history. Anyone who examines the original writings, speeches, or personal correspondence of the Founding Fathers must conclude that their lives and principles were rooted and grounded in the word of God.

For the record, let's examine the statements of some of our Founding Fathers:

George Washington, the father of our nation and the first president of the United States, stated: "It is impossible to rightly govern the world without God and the Bible." [4]

John Quincy Adams, the sixth president, stated: "The first and . . . the only book deserving of universal attention is the Bible. I speak as a man of the world . . . and I say to you 'Search the Scriptures.' " [5]

Andrew Jackson, the seventh president, stated, referring to the Bible: "That book, sir, is the rock on which our Republic rests." [6]

Patrick Henry, governor of Virginia and signer of the Declaration of Independence, stated: "It cannot be emphasized too clearly and too often that this nation was founded, not by religionists, but by Christians; not by religion, but on the gospel of Jesus Christ." [7]

John Hancock, signer of the Declaration of Independence, said: "Principally and first of all, I give and recommend my soul into the hands of God that gave it: and my body I recommend to the earth . . . nothing doubting but at the general resurrection I shall receive the same again by the mercy and power of God." [8]

Henry Knox, Revolutionary War general, stated: "To the supreme head of the universe—to that great and tremendous Jehovah—Who created the universal flame of nature, worlds, and systems in number infinite . . . to this awfully sublime Being do I resign my spirit with unlimited confidence of His mercy and protection." [9]

Charles Carroll, signer of the Declaration of Independence, stated: "Without morals a republic cannot subsist any length of time; they therefore who are decrying the Christian religion, whose morality is so sublime and pure . . . are undermining the solid foundation of morals, the best security for the duration of free governments." [10]

Benjamin Rush, signer of the Declaration of Independence, declared: "My only hope of salvation is in the infinite, transcendent love of God manifested to the world by the death of His Son upon the cross. Nothing but His blood will wash away my sins. I rely exclusively upon it. Come, Lord Jesus! Come quickly!" [11]

John Hancock and John Adams shook the world with one sentence: "We recognize no sovereign but God, and no King but Jesus." [12]

THE ACLU VERSUS CHRISTIANITY

As America drifts further into the abyss of secularism, as liberal federal judges continue to overrule the will of the people in defense of godly moral standards, as the ACLU continues its high-powered and well-funded war against Christianity, the America our Founding Fathers died to birth is on the critical list with infections of political correctness, greed, apathy, immorality, and endless empowerments dragging the republic into an early grave.

The ACLU positions itself as the great defender of freedom. Occasionally they take a case that does exactly that, but the majority of their effort is to control or eliminate the freedom of millions of Americans. The ACLU has an annual budget of $45 million; its staff is stated as being three hundred in addition to sixty full-time attorneys with one thousand volunteer attorneys. This is a legal war machine and Christianity is in its crosshairs.

Bill O'Reilly, author and host of Fox News' *O'Reilly Factor*, states:

"Few Americans realize how radical the ACLU has become and the threat it poses to liberty." [13]

Dr. D. James Kennedy, PhD., founder and president of Coral Ridge Ministries and senior minister of Coral Ridge Presbyterian Church in Ft. Lauderdale, Florida, stated concerning the ACLU: "Perhaps no organization has done more to remove America from its Judeo-Christian moorings than the ACLU—whom I often call the 'Anti-Christian Litigation Union.' " [14]

The ACLU has been against America from the beginning. The objective of the ACLU is to use the judiciary, rather than the electorate, to implement its agenda.

Roger Baldwin's instruction on how to present the ACLU to the general public is expressed thusly, "Do stir away from making the organization look like a Socialist enterprise. Too many people have gotten the idea that it is nine-tenths a Socialist movement. We want to look like patriots in everything we do. We want to get a good lot of flags, talk a good deal about the Constitution and what our forefathers wanted to make of this country, and to show that we are really the folks that stand for the spirit of our institutions." [15]

The ACLU Agenda

As authors Alan Sears and Craig Osten state in their book *The ACLU vs. America:*

- All legal prohibitions on the distribution of obscene material— including *child pornography*—are unconstitutional.

- *Pornographic outlets* can locate wherever they please—whether next to churches or day-care centers or near residential neighborhoods.

- *Tax-funded libraries* should not restrict access of children to pornography on the internet.

- *Parents should have no legal recourse* when it comes to shielding their children from exposure to hard-core pornography.

- *The military* cannot enforce even the most basic codes of conduct—such as discipline of disrespectful behavior toward a superior officer.

- *The military* cannot stop open displays of homosexual behavior within its ranks.

- *Parents cannot limit their children's exposure* to, or participation in, public school classes and assemblies that violate the family's core religious and moral beliefs, except those related to Orthodox Jewish or Christian teachings.

- *Public schools cannot observe recognized religious,* historical, and cultural holidays such as Christmas, Easter, or Hanukkah, despite hundreds of years of American tradition.

- All *legislative, military, and prison chaplaincy* programs should be abolished.

- All criminal and civil laws that prohibit polygamy and *same-sex "marriage"* should be done away with.[16]

The fundamentals of freedom as guaranteed by the Constitution of the United States are being aggressively attacked in an effort to control Christians and Christianity.

Consider the freedom of speech being contested in the case of *Peterson v. Hewlett-Packard Co.,* a Christian worker who exercised his right to free speech in response to a homosexual poster the company had placed near his cubicle. He posted Bible verses to express his beliefs on the matter. He was fired.

Was he in Sweden? Canada? Try Boise, Idaho. The Ninth Circuit Court of Appeals wrote, "An employer need not accommodate an employee's religious beliefs if doing so would result in discrimination against his co-workers or deprive them of contractual or other statutory rights."[17]

Do you, as an American, have the right to practice your religious beliefs in the work place? No, according to the courts in California.

When a lesbian approached two Christian doctors in San Diego County, California, to be artificially inseminated, the doctors refused. Rather than express tolerance toward the doctors' religious convictions and their right not to participate in her plan, she sued them. And a California Appeal Court found that the two doctors were wrong to refuse. Jennifer Pizer, the lesbian's attorney, clarified her legal position on *Hannity & Colmes:* "When the doctor is in her church, she can do religion, but not in the medical office."[18]

Pastors across America are now organizing into the Coalition of Pastors to defend themselves legally in the court of law. Pastors in Pennsylvania are now seeking liability insurance to protect themselves from being prosecuted under the state's new Hate-Speech Law. That's right. They are reacting to the state's recent addition of "sexual orientation" to its hate crime laws. Of particular concern is the expansion of the term *harassment* to include "harassment by communication," which means a person can be convicted on the basis of spoken words alone.[19]

That means that if a pastor stands in his pulpit and reads Leviticus 20:13—"If a man lies with a male as he lies with a woman, both of them have committed an abomination"—he could be sent to jail for harassment by communication, which is considered hate speech by the courts in Pennsylvania.

You may not live in the state of Pennsylvania, but because courts may look to other state's laws for precedent when their state laws are silent, this Pennsylvania law has a real potential to affect you.

Under the banner of diversity, the Sixth Court of Appeals stated: "Adherence of all faiths are equally valid as religions."

That explains why U.S. Army posts have witch chaplains who have equal standing with Christian, Jewish, and Muslim chaplains.[20]

THE THREAT IS SPREADING FASTER THAN YOU CAN IMAGINE

The following laws are now enforced upon your children and grandchildren who go to public schools. Perhaps it's time for you to consider sending your child to a Christian school where your beliefs are not constantly mocked and your child is not ridiculed and humiliated for what they believe. Consider the following:

Verbal prayer offered in a school is unconstitutional even if that prayer is both voluntary and denominationally neutral. *(Engel v. Vitale, 1962; Abington v. Schempp, 1963; Commissioner of Education v. School Committee of Leyden, 1971)*

- If a student prays over lunch, it is unconstitutional for him to pray out loud. *(Reed v. Van Hoven, 1965)*

- When a student addresses an assembly of his peers, he effectively becomes a government representative; it is therefore unconstitutional for that student to engage in prayer. *(Harris v. Joint School District,* 1994)

• A city council meeting can pray, as long as they don't say the name of Jesus *(Rubin v. City of Burbank,* 1999)

• It is unconstitutional for a classroom library to contain books that deal with Christianity, or for a teacher to be seen with a personal copy of the Bible at school. *(Roberts v. Madigan,* 1990)

• It is unconstitutional for a public cemetery to have a planter in the shape of a cross, for if someone were to view that cross, it could cause "emotional distress" and thus constitute injury "in-fact." *(Warsaw v. Tehachapi,* 1990)[21]

One of the most aggressive attacks on Christian faith came from Samuel Kent, a federal judge who ruled in 1995 that if American students prayed in a public school in the name of Jesus, they would be sentenced to a six-month jail term: "And make no mistake; the court is going to have a United States Marshall in attendance at the graduation. If any student offends this Court, that student will be summarily arrested and will face up to six months incarceration in the Galveston County Jail for contempt of Court. Anyone who thinks I'm kidding about this better think again . . . anyone who violates these orders . . . is going to wish that he or she had died as a child when this Court gets through with it." [22]

If you believe children in public school are being educated on the principles of freedom that made America great, think again! Your children are not being taught what you were taught. Many are being exposed daily to a secular humanist brainwashing from the elementary grades through high school. This is evidenced by the ruling of federal judge Jennifer Coffman, nominated by President Bill Clinton in 1993, who refused to allow a California teacher to show his students the Declaration of Independence because it refers to God.

Judge Jennifer Coffman also ruled that the following documents could not be posted in public schools:

1. The Mayflower Compact, in which the colony's founders invoke "the name of God" and explain that their journey was taken,

among other reasons, "for the glory of God and advancement of the Christian faith"

2. Our national motto of "In God We Trust"

3. Excerpts from our Declaration of Independence

4. The Preamble to the Constitution of the State of Kentucky

5. A page from the Congressional Record of Wednesday, Feb. 2, 1983, vol. 12, no. 8, that declares 1983 as the "Year of the Bible" and lists the Ten Commandments

6. A proclamation by President Ronald Reagan marking 1983 the "Year of the Bible"

7. A proclamation by President Abraham Lincoln designating April 30, 1863, as a National Day of Prayer and Humiliation

8. An excerpt from President Lincoln's "Reply to Loyal Colored People of Baltimore upon Presentation of a Bible," reading, "The Bible is the best gift God has ever given to man."[23]

Pastor Ronnie Floyd, of the First Baptist Church in Springdale, Arkansas, came under fire from the Internal Revenue Service because of his July 4, 2004, sermon, when he told his congregation to "vote God, His Ways, His will, His word."

Barry Lynn, of Americans United for Separation of Church and State, is sending people to churches to videotape sermons for any "irregularities" and report them to the IRS. Lynn is joined by the so-called Mainstream Coalition, which has about a hundred volunteers monitoring churches to see whether pastors are abiding by federal laws governing political activity by nonprofit institutions."[24]

One of the masterstrokes of the ACLU is its quest to mold American law as it desires through judicial activism. The ACLU looks to force international law (at least their selective view of international law) on the American people—with complete disregard for Americans' sovereignty and the U.S. Constitution.

How does this affect you, your family, and your church? Stay tuned!

When I was recently in London, the headlines of *The Daily Telegraph*, on December 19, 2009, blared: "Churches Face Being Sued by Atheists."

As this book is being written, a law is being crafted by Harriet Har-min that will pave the way for churches to face legal action from athe-ists on a broad array of issues. Asked at a briefing of the religious press whether Michael Foster, the Minister for Equality, thought the Equality Bill going through the House of Lords would lead to legal action be-tween churches and atheists, Mr. Foster replied: "Both need to be lining up their lawyers right now."

The conservative peer Baroness O'Cathain, an evangelical Christian, told the House of Lords that "for Christian freedom" the Equality Bill was the "single most damaging bill to come before the House in my eigh-teen years as a member."

You can be sure the ACLU is watching the precedent being established in England and will be mobilizing its legal juggernaut to bring this law to America. Message? Churches get yourself the best attorney you can find and get ready to defend your faith in the courts. The other option is to become neutered and silenced by the ACLU.

PART THREE

The End of Days

EIGHT

Biblical Prophecy

W hat is biblical prophecy, why is it important, and why should we study it?

Prophecy is the history of the future. It is the study of what is to come.

Many in our contemporary humanistic culture are fascinated with fortune-telling, psychics, and astrology; and yet in this era of religious doubt and skepticism, ask those same people about biblical prophecy, and they will tell you that an individual who has an interest in Bible prophecy is either a fanatic or mentally unstable. How foolish is that! To disregard biblical prophecy is to disregard one fourth of the inerrant Word of God!

The Bible was written by approximately forty authors through the direction and inspiration of the Holy Spirit within a period of fifteen hundred years. Very few of the writers of Holy Scripture knew each other, yet the continuity and exactness within its life-changing pages is unparalleled by any other literary work. J. Vernon McGee refers to the Good Book as the "God Book," for in it, God quotes Himself twenty-five hundred times. God clearly takes credit for the contents of His book.[1]

If approximately one fourth of the Bible was prophetic at the time it was written and if God devoted that much of the written Word to prophecy, then the future, as *He* sees it, should not be ignored. It must be reiterated that biblical prophecy was not given to satisfy man's curiosity of the future, but to accomplish God's perfect will for mankind.

All Scripture is *given by inspiration of God, and* is *profitable for
doctrine, for reproof, for correction, for instruction in righteousness,
that the man of God may be complete, thoroughly equipped for every
good work.*

—*2 Timothy 3:16–17 NKJV*

Bottom line, the Bible includes prophecy; therefore God's people
should study prophecy.[2]

Can we trust the accuracy of biblical prophecy? The fact is that the
exactness of Bible prophecy can be confirmed by world history; by vali-
dating the past, we can look wisely toward the future. Peter bears out the
truth of Bible prophecy when he states:

*And so we have the prophetic word confirmed, which you do well to
heed as a light that shines in a dark place, until the day dawns and the
morning star rises in your hearts.*

—*2 Peter 1:19 NKJV*

History is Bible prophecy fulfilled. McGee precisely defined the accuracy of Bible prophecy in one sentence, "Fulfilled prophecy is one of the
infallible proofs of plenary verbal inspiration of Scripture."[3]

What about the prophetic messenger?

GUIDELINES FOR A TRUE PROPHET

Deuteronomy set the guidelines for a true prophet:

*"But the prophet who presumes to speak a word in My name,
which I have not commanded him to speak, or who speaks in
the name of other gods, that prophet shall die." And if you say in your
heart, "How shall we know the word which the LORD has
not spoken?"—when a prophet speaks in the name of the LORD,
if the thing does not happen or come to pass, that is the thing
which the LORD has not spoken; the prophet has spoken it
presumptuously; you shall not be afraid of him.*

—*Deuteronomy 18:20–22 NKJV*

Kyle M. Yates, in his book *Preaching from the Prophets,* listed the roll call of the prophets, their years and location of prophecy, and their character traits. (Note: all the years are B.C.)

The Early Group

Moses	1447 or 1225	in Egypt
Samuel	1100–	in Israel
Elijah	870–	in Israel
Joel	850–820	in Jerusalem
Jonah	800–	in Israel

The Eighth-Century Group

Amos	760–	in Israel
Hosea	745–	in Israel
Isaiah	740–698	in Jerusalem
Micah	735–	in Jerusalem

The Seventh-Century Group

Zephaniah	630–622	in Jerusalem
Jeremiah	626–585	in Jerusalem and Egypt
Nahum	625–612	in Jerusalem
Habakkuk	610–605	in Jerusalem

The Exiled Group

Obadiah	586–	in Jerusalem and Babylon
Ezekiel	592–	in Babylon
Daniel	605–530	in Babylon

The Post-Exiled Group

Haggai	520–	In Jerusalem
Zechariah	520–	In Jerusalem
Malachi	435–	In Jerusalem

The Two Main Goals of Biblical Prophecy

The study of biblical prophecy and its fulfillment reveal the two main goals of prophecy. Its foremost purpose is to reveal the divine plan of God to testify of our Redeemer, Jesus Christ (Revelations 19:10 NKJV). The second is to unveil God's will for mankind as recorded in Genesis Chapter 17:1–11 regarding Abraham's divine destiny.

God's prophets have several character traits in common:

- a prophet is not swayed by public opinion or diplomacy

- he speaks an uncompromised message

- he is loyal to his divine call

- he is humbled by the unmatched privilege of being chosen of God to be His spokesperson

- he is a man of action often causing enmity for his message

- he is often accused by his contemporaries of taking a radical stand

- he is a man of prayer

- he is pure of heart and character

- he is a loud and often lone voice against social injustice

- he is not only a preacher to his contemporaries he is also God's spokesman, revealing His will for the generations to come.[4]

To help them earn proper prophet's credentials, the Lord gave His chosen men "local" prophecies that were fulfilled within real time. Once God established men as "true prophets," based on the prophecy coming to pass, then the people would put confidence in them that what they said was in fact from God. If there came a *self-appointed* prophet who gave his own predictions, then sooner or later the law of probabilities would fail, and he would find himself with unfulfilled prognostications and a very bad reputation. If you called yourself a prophet in biblical times, you were in one of two categories; a *true prophet* or a *false prophet.*

God describes Himself as the all-knowing God who discerns the "end from the beginning."

> "*I* am *God, and* there is *none like Me, declaring the end from the beginning . . . My counsel shall stand, and I will do My pleasure."*
> —*Isaiah 46:9–10 NKJV*

To better understand prophecy and the source of prophecy, one can study the lives of some of the Bible prophets.

THE PROPHET MOSES

Consider Moses. Moses authored the first five books of the Bible, known as the Pentateuch. Deuteronomy describes this great prophet in a unique light: "But since then there has not arisen in Israel a prophet like Moses, whom the LORD knew face to face" (34:10 NKJV).

During the time of Joseph's leadership, the Jewish people flourished and grew into a "great multitude" after they arrived in Egypt from the famine-stricken land of Canaan. In time, an anti-Semitic Pharaoh grew paranoid of their potential power and attempted to limit the growth of the Israelites by oppressing them into slavery and by killing their male children. The living conditions of the Jewish people became dismal at best. Moses was a man who understood both cultures. He was born into the Jewish race and could identify with their despair and misery, and later he was adopted into the opulence of Egyptian royalty. After receiving an elite education in Egypt and enduring severe discipline in the wilderness, God chose to appoint Moses as his prophet for two main reasons: To deliver His people from captivity and to deliver His Law to man.

Moses was loved and trusted by God. He was a man who knew God and spoke to Him face to face. While the children of Israel were familiar with God's acts, they were not familiar with God Himself: "He made known his ways to Moses, his acts unto the children of Israel" (Psalms 103:7 NKJV). Moses's authorship of the Book of Deuteronomy was a direct result of his intimate knowledge of God.[5]

God chose Moses to be His "divine representative" who would deliver to this world His great system of laws, laws that have influenced nations and governments through the ages and are still, to this day, the cornerstone of our Judeo-Christian beliefs. Moses had a zealous commitment to God and was driven by a powerful trust in His divine plan and purpose for mankind. Moses was a true prophet who communed with God and was faithful to deliver His message to man. He was so in touch with the Creator that it became second nature for him to know the Divine will and to transcend that will to man.[6]

Four Major Contributions from Moses

Moses made four major contributions to our faith through his prophetic messages to the Jewish people. *First,* he established divine sovereignty by instilling in the people that Jehovah was Israel's one and only true God. *Second,* Moses set forth the concept of divine holiness in that God is righteous and demands righteousness from His people. *Third,* Moses delivered God's divine law whereby God's people could attain His favor and blessing. *Fourth,* Moses set in place the principle of God's divine love, which portrayed Jehovah God as accessible and compassionate as displayed by God's supernatural deliverance of His people.[7]

Prophecies from Moses and Their Fulfillment

The following are a few of the prophecies and their fulfillment as given through Moses.

PROPHECY: A flood to destroy the entire earth (Genesis 6:7, 17).

FULFILLMENT:

In the six hundredth year of Noah's life, in the second month, the seventeenth day of the month, on that day all the fountains of the great

deep were broken up, and the windows of heaven were opened. . . . So
He destroyed all living things which were on the face of the ground:
both man and cattle, creeping thing and bird of the air. They were
destroyed from the earth. Only Noah and those who were with him in
the ark remained alive. *And all the waters prevailed on the earth one*
hundred and fifty days.

　　　　　　　　　　　　　　　　　　—Genesis 7:11–24 NKJV

PROPHECY: God promised that the Jewish people would return to the
land (Genesis 15:26).
FULFILLMENT:

And all Israel crossed over on dry ground, until all the people had
crossed completely over the Jordan.

　　　　　　　　　　　　　　　　　　—Joshua 3:17 NKJV

PROPHECY: Egypt will recognize God as the Lord (Exodus 7:5a).
FULFILLMENT:

Then he called for Moses and Aaron by night, and said, "Rise, and go
out from among my people, both you and the children of Israel. And
go, serve the LORD as you have said."

　　　　　　　　　　　　　　　　　　—Exodus 12:31 NKJV

PROPHECY: Israel to wander in the wilderness for forty years (Numbers 14:23; 32–35).
FULFILLMENT:

So the LORD's anger was aroused against Israel, and He made them
wander in the wilderness forty years, until all the generation that had
done evil in the sight of the LORD was gone.

　　　　　　　　　　　　　　　　　　—Numbers 32:13 NKJV

PROPHECY: Israel will demand a king (Deuteronomy 17:14).
FULFILLMENT:

"No, but we will have a king over us, that we also may be like all the

*nations, and that our king may judge us and go out before us and fight
our battles."*

—1 Samuel 8:19–20 NKJV

THE PROPHET ELIJAH

Consider Elijah. Elijah is probably one of the most important men in
both biblical history and biblical prophecy. During a very dark time
in ancient Israel, God used a man who would stand against one of history's most diabolical duos: Ahab and Jezebel (1 Kings 16:29–22:40
NKJV).

He would also reintroduce spiritual purity and true worship to God's
chosen people. Elijah was not a false prophet who was willing to tickle
the ears of men for the sake of popularity as illustrated in the following
scripture:

*That this is a rebellious people, lying children, children who will not
hear the law of the LORD; who say to the seers, "Do not see," and to
the prophets, "Do not prophesy to us right things; speak to us smooth
things, prophesy deceits. Get out of the way, turn aside from the path,
cause the Holy One of Israel to cease from before us.*

—Isaiah 30:9–11 NKJV

Elijah was a true prophet who was willing to declare man's estrange-
ment from the God of Abraham, Isaac, and Jacob; he was a man who
would arouse the consciousness of a slumbering community; a man who
would openly and courageously rebuke the evildoers even if they were in
leadership and places of influence, a man who was not afraid to chastise
the religious leaders who failed to provoke the people to repentance.[8]

Elijah was my kind of man!

Not only would Elijah stand against the evils of the divided kingdoms
of the north, which were beset by apostasy, and against the southern
kingdom set apart by idolatry; but he would prevail, with God's anointing, over the false prophets of Baal (2 Kings 1:9–10 NKJV). God used
a prophet who would not compromise with godless opinions, even when

those opinions were in the majority. Anytime the church compromises with the world, it only succeeds in going further into oblivion; God's people accomplish nothing through worldly concession.

Moreover, God protected Elijah while he was on divine assignment. When 450 false prophets of Baal came against God's prophet, He sent fire from heaven, allowing the prophet Elijah to kill all 450 false prophets on Mount Carmel. Elijah was taken from the prophetic scene as quickly as he was introduced to it, for God translated him into heaven in a chariot of fire (2 Kings 2:1 NKJV), and He plans to return Elijah to earth as a witness to the Jewish people in the last days that the Messiah is coming (Revelation 11 NKJV).

While many biblical prophets speak of events that will transpire in the distant future, Elijah speaks to the needs of his contemporaries. The events of which he prophesied were fulfilled during his lifetime or shortly thereafter. The following are references to some of Elijah's prophecies and their fulfillment.

Prophecies of Elijah and Their Fulfillment

PROPHECY: No rain in the land (1 Kings 17:1).
FULFILLMENT: There was no rain for three years and six months (1 Kings 18:1, 2; Luke 4:5; James 5:17).

PROPHECY: Flour and oil to be provided for the widow of Zarephath until the end of the famine (1 Kings 17:14).
FULFILLMENT: The widow had sufficient flour and oil for the duration of the famine (1 Kings 17:15–16).

PROPHECY: Rain will come to the land (1 Kings 18:1).
FULFILLMENT: "and there was a heavy rain" as God answered Elijah's prayer on Mount Carmel (1 Kings 18:45).

PROPHECY: Ahab is to be killed and dogs to lick his blood (1 Kings 21:19).
FULFILLMENT: Ahab was killed in battle and dogs licked his blood exactly on the location God predicted (1 Kings 22:38).

PROPHECY: The end of Ahab's dynasty (1 Kings 21, 22).
FULFILLMENT: Jehu destroyed Ahab's dynasty (2 Kings 10:11, 17).

PROPHECY: Jezebel will be eaten by dogs (1 Kings 21:23).
FULFILLMENT: Jezebel was thrown to her death and was devoured by dogs who left only her skull and her hands (2 Kings 9:30–37).[9]

Elijah's Israel and America Today

Allow me to make a brief comparison of some of the conditions of Israel during Elijah's day as chronicled in 1 and 2 Kings and the current state of our nation. David became Judah's king after the death of Saul and Jonathan. Solomon succeeded his father, David, and brought many years of prosperity to his expanded kingdom. Division came when the weakness of Solomon's son, Rehoboam, divided the land in 931 B.C. into the northern nation of Israel and the southern nation of Judah. As apostasy and idol worship reigned, the economic, social, and spiritual condition of the land drastically declined.

With Ahab in power and under the control of Jezebel, the land became influenced by heathen beliefs including Baalism, which embraced the worship of nature. Jezebel was the high priestess of witchcraft and a powerful force with two goals for the land: the first was that Baal worship dominate the land and the second was to kill as many of the prophets of the God as possible.

Between anarchy, foreign invasion, severe drought, and the greed and intoxication of power—which led to the unscrupulous execution of authority over landowners—the people of Israel and Judah suffered greatly. Economic instability was rampant as God's people were enslaved by the government in order for its leaders to maintain their excessive spending. As a result of this massive assault on the nation on all fronts, the people grew spiritually lax and knew more about the gods of Baal than the God of Israel.

Sound familiar? History does repeat itself!

Lawlessness is rampant in our country with the nation's crime rate soaring to over 14 million crimes a year, which equates to an assault on one in every twenty Americans.[10] Our unsecured borders contributed to the largest massacre of human life on American soil from a foreign source since Pearl Harbor with the terrorist attack on the Twin Towers in New York, the Pentagon, and the tragic flight over Pennsylvania claiming nearly three thousand lives.[11]

Unprecedented greed has caused millions to lose their lifetime investments, jobs, and homes, with unemployment figures reaching 9.6 percent in August of 2010, the highest since 1946, and lenders took back more homes in August of 2010 since the start of the U.S. mortgage crisis. In all, lenders have repossessed over 2.3 million homes since the beginning of our current recession, with a projection of more than one million American families likely to lose their homes to foreclosures this year.[12]

The oil spill tragedy in the Gulf of Mexico, resulting in one of America's foremost environmental disasters, will devastate the growth and development of sea life as well as detrimentally impacting one of our nation's main food exports for decades to come.[13]

In 2005 the Supreme Court ruled (*Kelo vs. New London*) that it is constitutional for "local governments to force property owners to sell out and make way for private economic development" as long as the officials feel it will benefit the public. This compulsory eminent domain ruling neglects the right of the landowner and can be imposed even if the property is "not blighted or the new project's success is not guaranteed." More succinctly, though a financial exchange is required, it is still a violation of our constitutional right to own property and the blatant redistribution of land.[14]

Before the ink dries on this paper, the nation's national debt of over $14 trillion will exponentially grow to unparalleled numbers.[15] Government spending has skyrocketed to reach an unmatched number of about $4 trillion, with no end in sight. Who pays the bill? The only ones left are you, your children, and your grandchildren.[16]

And what is our spiritual condition? Noted columnist Cal Thomas commented on a recent survey of people who believe in God and the actual knowledge of their faith. The main conclusion of the study was that atheists made the highest scores on their religious knowledge. The survey also showed that the two largest branches of Christianity, Catholicism and Protestantism, were "unaware about the basic tenants of their faith." [17]

Thomas sounds the alarm:

The Bible, in both Old and New Testaments, warns about the "cares of this world" creeping in to dull our senses to the need of God in our lives. In modern times, that dullness is produced by the pursuit of pleasure and material things.

Forgetting God produces not only eternal consequences, but earthly ones as well. Moses warned about forgetting God and when ancient Israel did, she was conquered by her enemies. New Testament writers penned similar warnings.

Alexander Solzhenitsyn concluded the major reasons Russia suffered under Communism for six decades is that his people had forgotten God. Abraham Lincoln blamed the Civil War on a nation that had forgotten God "and the hand that graciously preserved us."

Ignorance is not bliss, especially when it comes to the consequences of ignoring God, His salvation, and where each of us will spend eternity.[18]

History does, in fact, repeat itself, and prophecy does hold true. The voice of the prophet Elijah still clearly rings in the ears of God's people.

"Because you have done this, and have not kept My covenant and My statutes, which I have commanded you, I will surely tear the kingdom away from you and give it to your servant."
          —1 Kings 11:11 NKJV

As stated earlier, the second purpose of prophecy is to reveal God's will in the events of history as it manifests itself in "the judgment of evil," the deliverance of judgment, and the bestowal of blessing."[19] We must study God's Word concerning prophecy to avoid His judgment. We must heed His Word to experience His deliverance and obey His Word to assure His blessing (Deuteronomy 28 NKJV).

THE PROPHET ISAIAH

Consider Isaiah. One of the reasons God appointed men to the position of prophet who would speak *His* word to *His* people was because God could not trust the unrighteous rulers to do so. Isaiah was one of His appointed prophets. Isaiah prophesied during a spiritually destitute time in Israel, for the pagan influence of the neighboring nations had played havoc on Judaism. There was no moral or religious conviction among the people, and even the self-appointed prophets were more interested in drinking wine than in the spiritual well-being of the people.

Isaiah enters the scene. He is a man who integrated into his ministry the gifts of preaching, prophesying, and counseling national leaders. Yates describes Isaiah as a "young aristocrat from a princely line who had access to the court and high standing with the people of Jerusalem." Isaiah was very well educated; he was refined and familiar with the history and culture of the surrounding nations.[20]

One of the traits I like best about Isaiah is that he was a preacher!

He was called as many of us are called. When the splendor of God's glory was supernaturally revealed to him, he examined his own unworthiness and fell repentant before the Lord crying out, "I'll go. Send Me!" (Isaiah 6:1).

The book of Isaiah is divided into three major themes: God's conviction and judgment upon Judah and Jerusalem in which His sovereign nature is revealed (Isaiah 1–35); the historical account of Hezekiah and Sennacherib giving a prophetic picture of God's deliverance during the Great Tribulation (Isaiah 36–39); consolation and hope to the exiles and the future glory of Israel with the depiction of the Suffering Servant (Isaiah 40–66).[21]

In his preaching, we can sense the Father's love and compassion for the brokenhearted, the disadvantaged, and the forgotten. Yet Isaiah does not neglect the call to repentance through his stern forewarning of impending doom and judgment upon God's people if they do not turn from their wicked ways.

However, the meaning of this prophet's name best reflects the central significance of his writings: "Yahweh is Salvation." The prophecies of Isaiah testify of our Redeemer, Jesus Christ. The most commanding distinctions of this great man of God are his "messianic prophecies," which were fulfilled for the most part in the life of Christ. Isaiah was shown by God the Father that the Messiah would willingly suffer for the sins of humanity (Isaiah 53:5) so that He could bring justice, righteousness, and redemption to a hurting world.[22] What a message! What a sacrifice! What a promise!

Isaiah is often referred to as the fifth disciple, and his book the fifth Gospel because the virgin birth of Christ, His character, His life, His ministry, His death, His resurrection, and His second coming are all presented in the book of Isaiah through the prophetic revelation of God the Father.[23]

Prophecies Concerning Christ from Isaiah

PROPHECY: A virgin will conceive and bear a son who will be called Immanuel, meaning "God with us" (Isaiah 7:14).

FULFILLMENT: Jesus, God made flesh, was born of the virgin Mary (Matthew 1:22–23; John 1:1).

PROPHECY: A servant is to wait for God to bring His children back to Himself as "signs and wonders in Israel" (Isaiah 8:17–18).

FULFILLMENT: Those who put their trust in Jesus become His children (Hebrews 2:13).

PROPHECY: A light to shine in Galilee on those who walk in darkness (Isaiah 9:1–2).

FULFILLMENT: Jesus brought light to the people of Galilee (Matthew 4:12–16).

PROPHECY: A child to be born who will sit on the throne of David and establish justice forever. A rod from the stem of Jesse (the line of David) to be filled with the Spirit of the Lord and establish righteousness on earth (Isaiah 9:6–7; 11:1–5).

FULFILLMENT: Jesus, born as a baby, will reign on the throne of David during the millennial kingdom and in heaven forevermore (Matthew 28:18; Luke 1:32, 33; 2:11; 1 Corinthians 15:24–27; Revelation 19:16).

PROPHECY: Gentiles to seek the Root of Jesse (Isaiah 10:11).

FULFILLMENT: Gentiles come to God through Jesus (Romans 15:12).

PROPHECY: God to lay in Zion a precious cornerstone as a sign for believers (Isaiah 28:16).

FULFILLMENT: Jesus is the living stone in which people must believe (1 Peter 2:4–6).

PROPHECY: A voice in the wilderness will prepare the way of the Lord (Isaiah 40:3).

FULFILLMENT: John the Baptist prepared the way of the Lord in anticipation of the coming of Jesus. (Matthew 3:1–3).

PROPHECY: A Servant chosen by God, unpretentious yet totally effective to bring justice to nations, open blind eyes, and free prisoners (Isaiah 42:1–9).

FULFILLMENT: Jesus healed the sick but desired not to be known before His appointed time; this prophecy is to be completely fulfilled during the millennial kingdom (Matthew 12:15–21).

PROPHECY: A Servant chosen to bring Israel back to God, to be a light to the nations, to restore the earth and free prisoners, yet despised by many (Isaiah 49:1–13).

FULFILLMENT: This prophecy was partially fulfilled throughout Jesus' earthly ministry as recorded in the Gospels and will be completely fulfilled during the millennial kingdom.

PROPHECY: A Servant, who is an effective teacher, to be struck, spit at, and disgraced before men (Isaiah 50:4–11).

FULFILLMENT: Jesus was beaten and spit at during His trial and crucifixion (Matthew 26:67; 27:26, 30).

PROPHECY: A Servant to sprinkle (purify) many nations (Isaiah 52:15).

FULFILLMENT: Jesus shed His blood to bring redemption to all who believe (Hebrews 12:24; 1 Peter 1:2; 1 John 1:7).

PROPHECY: A Servant to be rejected, suffer, and die for the sins of others (Isaiah 53:1–12).

FULFILLMENT: Jesus died to bring redemption to all who believe (Matthew 8:14–17; Luke 22:37; Acts 8:30–35; 1 Peter 2:21–25).

PROPHECY: A Servant appointed to proclaim good tidings, heal the brokenhearted, and set the captive free (Isaiah 61:1–3).

FULFILLMENT: Jesus announced that His ministry was to be the fulfillment of Isaiah's prophecy (Luke 4:16–21).

GOD'S MESSAGE *WILL* BE DELIVERED

Know this truth: God will make certain that His message is delivered.

Surely the Lord GOD does nothing, unless He reveals His secret to His servants the prophets.
                                                              —*Amos 3:7 NKJV*

Jeremiah complained and wanted to cease giving God's message because men mocked him when he delivered it to them. The result?

Then I said, "I will not make mention of Him, nor speak anymore in His name." But His word was in my heart like a burning fire shut up in my bones; I was weary of holding it back, and I could not.
                                                        —*Jeremiah 20:9 NKJV*

God would not allow Jeremiah to keep His message from getting to the people. Jonah tried to escape his calling and was "persuaded" within the belly of a great fish to yield to the Lord's plan (Jonah 3:1–3).

God's message will be delivered; it is up to God's people to heed the message.

HOW TO STUDY BIBLICAL PROPHECY

How should we study biblical prophecy? Most students of the Bible are intimidated by the study of prophecy. In order to fully comprehend the message of a specific prophecy, one must first know the Messenger, something of the prophet whom the Messenger appointed, the time in history that the prophecy was given, to whom it was given, and the purpose it was meant to serve.

Most credible Bible students approach the study of prophecy through the *literal method* of interpretation, which basically acknowledges the Bible to be the precise written account of God's Word.

In order to truly study prophecy:

- The student must be spiritually sensitive and reverent in regards to the Holy Scriptures, for God is the Word and the Word was God (John 1:1). The word was divinely delivered, and it must be divinely received.

- A student of prophecy must be sincere and diligent.

- Prophecy must be studied without preconceived notions or personal motives.

- The study of God's Word must be executed with pure intent, thorough commitment, and accompanied by insightful prayer.

- The student of prophecy should have some understanding of the original language of the text to fully comprehend its message.

- Above all the study of prophecy must not be convoluted with "deep" or "mystifying" meanings of Scripture. Prophecy was not meant to confuse or misdirect; the purpose of the prophet and his prophecy was to relay God's message to His people.

Prophecy is God's message given to His prophets to prepare believers for the signs of the time and the end of the age.

Prophecy accurately declares the future as God sees it. It is meant to testify of our coming Redeemer to the lost and to reveal God's divine plan for mankind. We are to read it, study it, and prepare ourselves for the world tomorrow.

NINE

We Are the Terminal Generation

Jesus of Nazareth left the Temple Mount in Jerusalem and climbed the gentle slope of the Mount of Olives, where He sat down on a large stone beneath an ancient olive tree and waited for His disciples to gather around Him. Jesus was a rabbi, and as a master teacher and prophet, He was about to reveal the future of the world to His disciples and the future church in Matthew 24, which I refer to as "the spine of prophecy."

It was in this setting that the disciples asked Jesus three critical questions concerning the future (see Matthew 24:3):

1. When will these things be?

2. What will be the sign of Your coming?

3. What is the sign of the end of the age?

The prophetic Scripture describes "the time of the end" as that era marked by four kings (see Daniel 7:17–28) on the face of the earth who will wage global war for domination and control of the planet. The four kings are:

1. *The King of the North, Russia,* will make an alliance with Iran, Turkey, Ethiopia, and Libya for the purpose of attacking Israel in a massive land invasion. This military armada will be destroyed by the hand of God, and Israel will be miraculously saved.

2. *The King of the South will be the Islamic nations* that will seek to cover the earth with the Law of Sharia.

3. *The King of the East will be China* and her eastern allies.

4. *The King of the West will be Europe and America* led by the Antichrist at the Battle of Armageddon, where they will be annihilated by the hand of God.

THE FOUR HORSEMEN OF THE APOCALYPSE

For the first time in world history, the book of Revelation, chapter six, describes four horsemen on the global stage at the same moment in time. All four of these horsemen crave one thing: world domination through the massive death and destruction of humanity.

Think it can't happen?

Think again . . . it is happening before our very eyes.

In this chapter, we will look at ten prophetic signs that clearly indicate that we are the terminal generation and that we are well on our way on the road to Armageddon. If you listen closely, you can hear the hoof beats of the four horsemen of the Apocalypse, racing toward the battle.

1. OIL

There is a very real reason why most prophetic teachings concerning the end time events occur in the Middle East. That reason is oil! This is the first prophetic sign indicating we are part of the terminal generation.

When the prophet Ezekiel revealed to the world thousands of years ago how God Almighty would orchestrate the Russian-Islamic invasion of Israel so graphically described in chapters 38 and 39 . . . he revealed the secret of the future in ten words. The ten words spoken to the invading armies of Israel were: "I will turn you around, put hooks into your jaws" (Ezekiel 38:4).

When the prophet Ezekiel speaks about the invading nations as having "hooks in your jaw," he is referring to oil. Every fisherman knows that once the razor sharp hook has been set into the jaw of the fish, the fish can be dragged without mercy through the waters under the complete control of the fishermen.

God is sovereign!

God is almighty!

God is the fisherman in Ezekiel 38 dragging the Russian-Islamic invasion coalition toward the hills of Israel to crush them, just as he crushed Pharaoh and his Egyptian army in the Red Sea before the eyes of Israel and the nations of the world. And our sovereign God will use the "bait" of oil to drag the Russian-Islamic coalition wherever He wants them to go.

Ezekiel records the future destruction of the Russian-Islamic invasion force with these words:

> *"You [the invading armies coming against Israel] will come up against My people Israel like a cloud, to cover the land. It will be in the latter days [the end of the age] that I will bring you against My land [Israel], so that the nations may know Me, when I am hallowed in you, O Gog, before their eyes."*
>
> *—Ezekiel 38:16 NKJV*

God Almighty makes it clear: "I will bring you [the Russian-Islamic coalition] against My land [Israel] so that the nations of the world may know Me."

God is warning planet earth that there is a day of reckoning coming and the death rate will stun the world. God is saying, I am going to crush the nations that have tormented the Jewish people for centuries and millennia. I will avenge the death of every Jewish person in the Holocaust; I will avenge the pogroms of Russia; I will avenge the rockets of Iran (Persia); I will avenge the harvest of death brought by every suicide bomber so that the Gentile nations of the world will know I am the only true God.

God is warning planet Earth that the day of reckoning is coming and the death rate of 84 percent of the invading armies of the Russian-Islamic coalition will stagger the earth. God Almighty, the defender of Israel, has written a Declaration of War through the pen of the prophet Ezekiel in chapters 38 and 39.

God declares in a language that is brutal and direct that he's going to avenge the death of every Jewish person who died or suffered in the Holocaust. He will avenge the death and suffering caused by the rockets furnished by Iran and launched into Israel by Hamas and Hezbollah in a reign of terror; He will avenge the harvest of death of countless suicide bombers . . . no one will escape, and His judgment will be complete. All Israel will rejoice in the supernatural demonstration of Jehovah God's power and return to the Torah of the God of Abraham, Isaac, and Jacob.

How will God orchestrate this massive drama in which He controls the nations of the earth with precise movement like pawns on a chessboard? Like a helpless fish being dragged through the water with a hook in its jaw?

Why will Russia come out of the north and enter into a covenant with Iran to attack Israel? Oil is the major reason. Oil in the latter part of the twentieth century became the ultimate weapon of war and remains so today. Oil is the new gold standard of planet Earth.

The Origin of Oil

What is the source of oil? Begin with the basic concept that God Almighty is the creator of heaven and earth. As the owner of the earth, He has the right to do exactly as His sovereign will dictates (see Genesis 1:1 and Psalm 24:1).

The billions of gallons of oil buried deeply in the bosom of the earth were planted exactly where God intended for them to be to fulfill His prophetic word millions of years before they were needed. Oil deposits result from the decomposition of plant and animal life buried ages ago. That means that forest and abundant vegetation once covered the earth until destroyed in a vast global cataclysm such as a global flood.

Geophysicist Robert Morgan believes that the earth's richest, deepest, and largest deposits of petroleum lie under the sands of countries just to the east of Israel, in the location pinpointed in the Bible as the Garden of Eden. Eden was a teaming expanse of forest and gardens with rich fertility unparalleled in human history.[1]

Satan's seduction of Adam and Eve in the Garden of Eden, leading to its destruction in the genesis of time, may have provided the oil that seduces the nations of the world to follow Russia and Iran into the Battle of Gog and Magog, and ultimately to Armageddon.

Few Americans realize the crucial role of oil in World War II. The Japanese attack on Pearl Harbor was motivated by the fact that the United States had cut off oil supplies to Japan. The military leadership of Japan estimated that Japan had enough oil to operate its machinery of war (planes, tanks, ships, trucks, etc.) for approximately eighteen months. Knowing they had little time, the Japanese decided to make a massive and decisive surprise attack on Pearl Harbor on December 7, 1941. It was America's Day of Infamy!

When the Allies invaded Europe during World War II, they immediately began to attack the refineries of the Third Reich. The ability of America to furnish an unlimited supply of oil to the war machine of the Allies turned the tide of battle and the Axis powers were defeated.

America no longer has the ability to sustain an extended war with anyone without the approval of Saudi Arabia and the oil-rich OPEC nations. Consider the following chart on the nations, their oil reserves, and their daily consumption measured in barrels per day. These charts reveal that America's Achilles' heel is indeed foreign oil. Our addiction to foreign oil is a serious threat to our national security.

Oil Reserves by Country [2]

COUNTRY COMPARISON :: OIL - PROVED RESERVES			
This entry is the stock of proved reserves of crude oil in barrels (bbl). Proved reserves are those quantities of petroleum which, by analysis of geological and engineering data, can be estimated with a high degree of confidence to be commercially recoverable from a given date forward, from known reservoirs and under current economic conditions.			
RANK	**COUNTRY**	**(BBL)**	**DATE OF INFORMATION**
1	Saudi Arabia	266,700,000,000	1 January 2009 est.
2	Canada	178,100,000,000	1 January 2009 est.
3	Iran	136,200,000,000	1 January 2010 est.
4	Iraq	115,000,000,000	1 January 2009 est.
5	Kuwait	101,500,000,000	1 January 2009 est.
6	Venezuela	99,380,000,000	1 January 2009 est.
7	United Arab Emirates	97,800,000,000	1 January 2009 est.
8	Russia	79,000,000,000	1 January 2009 est.
9	Libya	43,660,000,000	1 January 2009 est.
10	Nigeria	36,220,000,000	1 January 2009 est.
11	Kazakhstan	30,000,000,000	1 January 2009 est.
12	United States	21,320,000,000	1 January 2009 est.
13	China	15,550,000,000	1 January 2009 est.
14	Qatar	15,210,000,000	1 January 2009 est.

(NOTE: Observe that twelve of the thirteen top countries in oil reserves are hostile to the United States of America. This is a clear and present danger to our national security.)

Oil Consumption by Country[3]

COUNTRY COMPARISON :: OIL - CONSUMPTION

This entry is the total oil consumed in barrels per day (bbl/day). The discrepancy between the amount of oil produced and/or imported and the amount consumed and/or exported is due to the omission of stock changes, refinery gains, and other complicating factors.

RANK	COUNTRY	(BBL/DAY)	DATE OF INFORMATION
1	United States	19,500,000	2008 est.
2	European Union	14,390,000	2007 est.
3	China	7,999,000	2008 est.
4	Japan	4,785,000	2008 est.
5	Russia	2,800,000	2008 est.
6	India	2,670,000	2009 est.
7	Germany	2,569,000	2008 est.
8	Brazil	2,520,000	2008 est.
9	Saudi Arabia	2,380,000	2008 est.
10	Canada	2,260,000	2008 est.
11	Korea, South	2,175,000	2008 est.
12	Mexico	2,128,000	2008 est.
13	France	1,986,000	2008 est.
14	Iran	1,755,000	2008 est.

The prophet Ezekiel writes in Chapter 38:13: "Sheba, Dedan, the merchant of Tarshish, and all their young lions shall say to you, 'Have you come to take a plunder? Have you gathered your army to take booty to carry away silver and gold, to take away livestock and goods, to take away great plunder?' "

Ezekiel's "young lions" are the offspring of England, whose symbol is a lion; this would be the United States of America as an offspring of England. Ezekiel is describing in this verse the Russian-Islamic coalition coming to invade Israel and all that America will do is send a limp-wristed diplomatic protest. Does that sound familiar?

In short, America does nothing to help Israel after the church has been raptured from the earth. Ezekiel's war of Gog and Magog happens three and a half years after the rapture in the middle of Daniel's seventieth week.

Why does America send a worthless diplomatic protest to Russia and Iran? Why don't they race to defend Israel, our only friend in the Middle East and the only democratic government in that part of the world?

Could it be that the radical Islamic nations—who now control the vast majority of oil in the world and who have a seething hatred for Israel—will order America to stand down, or OPEC will shut off the U.S. supply of oil and cause the struggling American economy to collapse?

Think it can't happen?

Think again!

Do you remember the incident during the Nixon administration in 1973 when Arab nations united to launch an attack on Israel during Yom Kippur? The Arab nations told the United States to back off of its support for Israel.

We did not!

On October 17, 1973, the Arab nations conspired to reduce their oil production to punish nations that supported Israel. They used oil as a weapon of war, and oil is an even greater weapon of war today.

The result of the Arab oil embargo was long gas lines with people fist-fighting each other as they became angry and violent, waiting to get gas at service stations. The price of oil quadrupled and never went down. Billions of dollars were sucked out of America's economy and stacked in the bulging Arab treasuries.

As a sidebar, trillions of America's dollars, which have been exported to OPEC and that flow through your gas tank, are being used to poison the minds of our college and university students today. Saudi Arabia, through a series of foundations, is giving multiplied millions to universities to hire professors who are anti-American and anti-Israel to chair Middle Eastern studies. These professors are generally radical Islamic Wahhabists who poison the minds of our college and university students.

America's refusal to drill for every drop of oil under our control while developing solar, wind, nuclear, clean coal, and natural gas resources is nothing short of national insanity. Our enemies are laughing at our utter stupidity.

America's Addiction to Foreign Oil

America's addiction to foreign oil is our Achilles' heel. OPEC manipulates America to do its bidding like a mule pulling a plow. The global demand for oil has passed 86 million barrels per day and is expected to rise to 98.5 million barrels a day in 2015.[4]

Oil prices have quintupled in the past six years.[5] Notice that the United States' daily consumption of oil per day is 20,800,000 barrels. That addictive rate of consumption is greater than the next top five nations combined.

The wheels of transportation that make capitalism possible depend on oil, gas, diesel fuel, and high-octane jet fuel. If the wheel stops rolling, America's economy will shatter. The supply line stretches across the world to Saudi Arabia, Iraq, Iran, and the Middle East.

Let's connect the dots: Why will global shortage of oil be a sign that we are living in the terminal generation?

1. First, God created oil and placed it specifically in exact geographic regions, the majority of which is in Islamic nations that now hate both America and Israel.

2. The prophet Ezekiel foretells of a day when six nations will be forced to come to the Middle East by the "hook in the jaw." All of those nations are on center stage of the twenty-first century, breathing out venomous statements against Israel and America.

3. Russia must have oil to become a military superpower again. Ezekiel identifies Russia as the commander of the Russian-Islamic coalition (see Ezekiel 38:7).

   The terms "prepare yourself" and "be a guard for them" better translate as "be a commander of them."

   God makes it clear that Russia will be the leader of the Russian-Iranian Islamic coalition.

   The Russian-Iranian axis of evil has been in full operation for at least two decades. When Iran gets the nuclear bomb, made possible through the assistance of Russian scientists, World War III will happen. It will be the end of the world as we know it, when Iran becomes nuclear—and it could happen any day!

4. For the first time in world history, all the nations mentioned by Ezekiel are in place; America is falling from its position of being a global superpower by our insane addiction to political correctness and commitment to socialism, which only encourages Iran, Russia, and China. We are the terminal generation headed for the iceberg.

2. THE REBIRTH OF THE HEBREW LANGUAGE

One hundred years ago, the Hebrew language on planet earth was as dead as Julius Caesar. Yet, the prophet Zephaniah clearly declared in chapter 3, verse 9 that at the end of time the Hebrew language would be restored on the earth. Specifically, the Jewish people, who are returning to Israel from sixty-six nations speaking every language known to man, would have the ability to communicate to each other and to God in their ancient tongue . . . Hebrew.

The prophet Zephaniah writes:

> *"For then [at the time of the end] I will restore to the peoples a pure language, that they all may call on the name of the LORD, to serve Him with one accord."*
>
> *—Zephaniah 3:9 NKJV*

In my fifty-plus years of ministry, I have heard pastors and evangelists sit around the dinner table and debate which language will be spoken in the millennial reign and in heaven. Saint Paul gives a very clear answer in Acts as he gives his testimony to Agrippa.

> *"And when we had all fallen to the ground, I heard a voice speaking to me and saying in the Hebrew language, 'Saul, Saul, why are you persecuting Me? It is hard for you to kick against the goads.'"*
>
> *—Acts 26:14 NKJV*

This is Bible proof that the language spoken in heaven is Hebrew, and when Jesus Christ returns to earth "in like manner," it is obvious that He will speak Hebrew. The historical fact is that Hebrew was a dead language just one century ago.

The man called of God to give a global rebirth to the Hebrew language was Eliezer Ben-Yehuda who studied Hebrew and the Bible from the age of three. By the age of twelve, he had read large portions of the Torah, Mishna and Talmud.

His parents hoped he would become a Rabbi and sent him to a Yeshiva. There, he continued to study ancient Hebrew and was exposed to the Hebrew of the enlightenment, including secular writings. Later, he learned French, German, and Russian and was sent to Dunaburg for more education.

Reading the Hebrew language newspaper, *HaShahar,* he became acquainted with Zionism and concluded that the revival of the Hebrew language in the Land of Israel could unite all Jews worldwide. In 1881 Ben-Yehuda immigrated to Palestine, then ruled by the Ottoman Empire. He settled in Jerusalem and found a job teaching at the Alliance Israelite Universelle School. Here Ben-Yehuda set out to develop a new language that could replace Yiddish and other regional dialects as a means of every day communication between Jews who made Aliyah from various regions of the world.

Ben-Yehuda regarded Hebrew and Zionism as symbolic; "the Hebrew language can live only if we revive the nation and return it to the fatherland."[6]

By "fatherland" Ben-Yehuda meant Israel. He single-handedly revived the Hebrew language that revived the nation of Israel into a community of global immigrants who could speak to each other in perfect communication. This was prophesied by Zephaniah as one of the signs of the time of the end.

3. THE MIDDLE EAST PLAGUE: MASSIVE RADIATION BLAST

The third sign we are the terminal generation is the strange and deadly plague mentioned by the prophet Zechariah. My father's generation could not understand this prophetic passage of Scripture until the invention of the atomic bomb:

And this shall be the plague which the LORD will strike all the people
who fought against Jerusalem: their flesh shall dissolve while they stand
on their feet, their eyes shall dissolve in their sockets, and their tongues
shall dissolve in their mouths. It shall come to pass in that day that a
great panic from the LORD will be among them. Everyone will seize
the hand of his neighbor, and raise his hand against his neighbor's
hand; Judah also will fight at Jerusalem. And the wealth of all the
surrounding nations shall be gathered together: Gold, silver, and
apparel in great abundance. Such also shall be the plague on the horse
and the mule, on the camel and the donkey, and on all the cattle that
will be in those camps. So shall this plague be.

—Zechariah 14:12–15

In the Scripture, the prophet Zechariah paints a word picture of a
plague that very logically would be the result of massive radiation.

Americans who believe we are immune from a nuclear attack are deceived. President Ahmadinejad of Iran has made it very clear that the
moment Iran has nuclear capability, those weapons will be shared with
radical Islamic terrorists, who will use them on Americans in the major
cities of our nation. The persistent and continuing radical Islamic terrorist attacks in America prove they are willing to kill us; when they have
nuclear power, they will make 9/11 pale in comparison.

4. THE REBIRTH OF ISRAEL

The fourth prophetic sign that we are the terminal generation is the rebirth of the State of Israel.

The major prophets of the Old Testament all bore witness to the fact
that the Jewish people would return from their captivity to the land of
covenant given to them by Jehovah God as recorded in Genesis 17:7
saying:

And I will establish My covenant between Me and you and your
descendants after you in their generations for an everlasting covenant,
to be God to you and your descendants after you. Also I give to you and
your descendants after you the land in which you are a stranger, all the
land of Canaan, as an everlasting possession; and I will be their God.

The prophet Ezekiel made a stunning prophetic utterance in chapter 36 by prophesying:

"For I will take you [the Jewish people] from among the nations, gather you out of all countries, and bring you into your own land. . . . Then you shall dwell in the land that I gave to your fathers; you shall be My people, and I will be your God. . . . I will also enable you to dwell in the cities, and the ruins shall be rebuilt. The desolate land shall be tilled instead of lying desolate in the sight of all who pass by. So they will say, 'This land that was desolate has become like the garden of Eden; and the wasted, desolate, and ruined cities are now *fortified* and *inhabited.'"*

—Ezekiel 36:24, 28, 33–35 NKJV

This prophecy by Ezekiel was shocking because the children of Israel were in Babylonian captivity, and the dream of returning to their homes, their farms, their families, and their future seemed an absolute impossibility.

The prophet Ezekiel opens at chapter 37 by comparing the nation of Israel to a valley full of very dry bones. The dry bones indicated that the nation of Israel had been dead for almost two thousand years; but they *would* be restored. There is no doubt that Ezekiel is writing about Israel:

Then He said to me, "Son of man, these bones are the whole house of Israel. They indeed say, 'Our bones are dry, our hope is lost, and we ourselves are cut off.'"

—Ezekiel 37:11 NKJV

In the process of time, the Jewish people of the world were liberated from their captivity and returned to Israel just as the prophets had predicted.

The prophet Isaiah writes:

Who has heard such a thing? Who has seen such things? Shall the earth be made to give birth in one day? Or shall a nation be born at once?

—Isaiah 66:8 NKJV

When Jesus was seated under the branches of ancient olive trees on the Mount of Olives overlooking the city of Jerusalem, He was describing the world tomorrow for His twelve disciples. His disciples asked, "Tell us, when will these things be? And what will be the sign of Your coming and the end of the age?"

Jesus responded by saying,

"Now learn this parable from the fig tree: When its branch has already become tender and puts forth leaves, you know that summer is near. So you also, when you see all these things, know that it [His coming] is near—at the doors! Assuredly, I say to you, this generation will by no means pass away till all things take place."
—Matthew 24:32–34 NKJV

The land of Israel is a covenant land given by God to Abraham, Isaac, and Jacob and their descendants forever. Ishmael, the father of the Arabs, was not included in this covenant. The Bible makes it very clear that the Arabs and the Palestinians have no legitimate claim to this land. The Bible record of this ancient real estate transaction reads:

And Abraham said to God, "Oh that Ishmael might live before You!" Then God said: "No, Sarah your wife shall bear you a son, and you shall call his name Isaac; I will establish My covenant with him for an everlasting covenant, and with his descendants after him. And as for Ishmael, I have heard you. Behold, I have blessed him, and will make him fruitful, and will multiply him exceedingly. He shall beget twelve princes, and I will make him a great nation. But My covenant I will establish with Isaac, whom Sarah shall bear to you at this set time next year."
—Genesis 17:18–21 NKJV

This covenant land today is called "the West Bank," but it is in fact Judea and Samaria. This is the land the Palestinians want Israel to give to them—a land for which they have absolutely no legitimate or historical claim. There has never been a group of autonomous people known as the Palestinians.

This is the land about which President Obama told the Israelis there must be a "no growth" policy. This meant that a father could not build an additional room on his house to have a bedroom for his son or daughter returning home from the army. It meant what it said, absolutely no growth.

Who is the president of the United States to tell Israel what they can and cannot do? Israel is not a vassal state of the United States; they are a free and independent nation with democratically elected leaders. They are allegedly America's "best friend in the Middle East."

The president has also stated that there should be no new homes built in Jerusalem! He has no authority to tell the Jewish people what they can and cannot do in Jerusalem, the eternal and undivided capital of Israel for the past three thousand years. That would be before Obama was a community organizer in Chicago.

I believe that following the midterm elections of November 2010 the president will make a full-court press for Israel to give up their God-given land to the Palestinians as the price for peace in the Middle East. Land for peace has never worked for Israel because the enemies of Israel refuse to recognize their right to exist and the right to defend themselves from all who attack them. Israel has no partner for peace; therefore, the peace process is an act of futility until the enemies of Israel recognize there is and always shall be the State of Israel.

5. EXODUS II

The fifth prophetic sign that we are the terminal generation is Exodus II—that point in history when the Russian Jews would return to Israel in massive numbers.

During the Ronald Reagan administration, the former Soviet Union began to collapse. The door was opened for the Jews trapped behind the Iron Curtain to return to Israel. Because of the generosity of our television partners across the nation and around the world, John Hagee Ministries was able to bring twenty-three thousand Russian Jews home to Israel, by providing $17,317,000 in funding.

This is called Exodus II.

It is recorded in Scripture by the pen of the prophet Jeremiah, who writes:

"Therefore, behold, the *days are coming," says the LORD, "that they shall no longer say, 'As the LORD lives who brought up the children of Israel from the land of Egypt,' but, 'As the Lord lives who brought up and led the descendants of the house of Israel from the north country* [*Russia*] *and from all the countries where I had driven them.' And they shall dwell in their own land."*

—Jeremiah 23:7–8 NKJV

Following is a brief history of the Russian Jews returning to Israel:

A mass immigration of Jews was politically undesirable for Russia. As increasing numbers of Soviet Jews applied to immigrate to Israel in the period following the 1967 Six Day War [many were called "Refuseniks" because they were formally refused exit visas to leave Russia].

A typical excuse given by the Russian government was that persons who had been given access at some point in their careers to information vital to Soviet national security could not be allowed to leave the country. [. . .] In the years 1960–1970, only four thousand Jews were permitted to leave Russia. In the following decade, the number rose to 250,000.

In 1972 Russia imposed the so called "diploma tax" on would-be immigrants who had received higher education in the U.S.S.R. In some cases the fee was as high as twenty annual salaries. This measure was apparently designed to combat the brain drain caused by the growing immigration of Soviet Jews to the west. [. . .] In 1989 a record seventy-one thousand Soviet Jews were granted exodus. After the adoption of the Jackson-Vanik Amendment, over one million Soviet Jews immigrated to Israel.[7]

I believe the reason God permitted Ronald Reagan to crush the Soviet Union was to fulfill the prophecy of Jeremiah 23:7–8. When the Iron Curtain was ripped from top to bottom, the Jewish captives came pouring through to the Land of Israel just as God had promised thousands of years before marking the end of days.

6. JERUSALEM NO LONGER UNDER GENTILE RULE

Jerusalem is the City of God!

Jerusalem is the only city on the face of the earth that by its mere existence proves the existence of God.

Jerusalem is the city where Jeremiah and Isaiah penned the principles of righteousness that shaped the moral and spiritual destiny of the western world.

Jerusalem is the city King David captured three thousand years ago from the Jebusites, and it was declared the eternal capital of Israel forever.

Jerusalem is the place where Abraham brought Isaac, placed him upon a stone altar, and prepared to sacrifice him to prove his love to Jehovah God.

Jerusalem is the city where Jesus Christ celebrated His final Passover in the upper room with the twelve disciples; where He wept in agony for the sins of the world beneath the branches of ancient olive trees; where five hundred Roman soldiers from the Antonian Fortress arrested him after Judas betrayed Him with a kiss; where He was put on trial for His life and Pontius Pilate confessed to the mob, "I find no fault in this man."

Jerusalem is where Jesus was beaten with a Roman cat-o'-nine-tails with thirty-nine stripes as His blood poured down His emaciated back in crimson streams, splashing onto the cobblestone streets en route to the cross.

Jerusalem is where He arose on the third day that guarantees eternal life for every believer in every age and dispensation.

Jerusalem is the city that Titus and the Roman army besieged for months in A.D. 70 causing massive death through starvation among the Jewish people. Historian Josephus records that almost one million Jews died in this nightmare of suffering.

Jesus, when He was describing for His twelve disciples the signs of the times and the end of the age, described the destruction of Jerusalem saying: "But when you see Jerusalem surrounded by armies, then know that its destruction is near" (Luke 21:20).

Message? When you see the Roman army surrounding Jerusalem, leave immediately and don't come back.

Historian Josephus records that starvation became so severe that women ate their children. This is supported by the words of Jesus Christ to His disciples when He said, "But woe to those who are pregnant and to those who are nursing babies in those days. For there will be great distress within the land and wrath upon this people."

Historian Josephus states that seventy thousand Jewish men were captured and taken to Italy to build what we know to be the Roman Colosseum, where many Christians were fed to the lions for the amusement of pagan Rome. Jesus confirmed this tragedy when He said, "And they will fall by the edge of the sword, and be led away captive into all nations" (Luke 21:24a NKJV). This is the description of the beginning of the Diaspora.

The historic verse that has prophetic urgency for the immediate future is: "And Jerusalem will be trampled by Gentiles until the times of the Gentiles are fulfilled" (Luke 21:24b NKJV). The key word in this verse is *until* . . . until what? When Jerusalem is unified under Jewish control . . . then shall the end come. Jerusalem was unified under Jewish control in 1967 in the Six Day War. The time of the end is at hand.

7. DAYS OF DECEPTION

The seventh prophetic sign that we are the terminal generation is given by Jesus to his disciples on the Mount of Olives who warned:

"Take heed that no one deceives you. For many will come in My name saying, 'I am Christ,' and deceive many."
—*Matthew 24:4–5 NKJV*

Every generation has produced false messiahs with false prophets proclaiming them to be the Savior of the world.

The Romans, the Greeks, the Babylonians all produced so called gods of the earth who came on the wings of deception and brought a global harvest of death and devastation.

Adolf Hitler promised a Third Reich (*reich* is a German word meaning "kingdom") that would last a thousand years. Hundreds of thousands stood on the parade grounds, mesmerized by Germany's messiah screaming into a microphone. The frenzied throng screamed "Sieg Heil," women wept, some fainted in ecstasy, and men willingly laid down their lives for this living devil whose reign of hope left 50 million dead and

6 million Jews systematically slaughtered. This false messiah, who promised hope and change, blew his brains out and had his followers burn his body to an ash.

Benito Mussolini was Italy's messiah and was hanged upside down in mockery by the deceived and infuriated Italians.

There is one last messiah about to step onto the world stage. He will be ushered into power by a global economic meltdown. Like Hitler, he will be proclaimed the hope of the world for stability and survival. Like Hitler, he will make peace treaties he has no intention of keeping, for he will be the master of deception.

He will proclaim peace and bring a global blood bath.

He will be celebrated around the earth as living hope yet he will produce living hell.

He will bring into existence a one-world currency, a one-world government, and a one-world religion. All will be accomplished through masterful deception. His reign will endure for forty-two months before the world recognizes him to be the son of Satan—the Antichrist.

Think this can't happen?

Do you see the global economic meltdown in process?

Do you see a global dominant Islamic religion sweeping the earth?

Do you hear world leaders now proclaiming, "We need a new Caesar"?

Stop! Look! Listen!

All the pieces of the prophetic puzzle are falling rapidly into place. There is simply no denying we are living in the end of days.

8. AS IN THE DAYS OF NOAH

The eighth prophetic sign that we are the terminal generation is the statement from Jesus to His disciples:

> *"But as the days of Noah were, so also will the coming of the Son of Man be. For as in the days before the flood, they were eating and drinking, marrying and giving in marriage, until the day that Noah entered the Ark, and did not know until the flood came and took them all away, so also will the coming of the Son of Man be."*
>
> *—Matthew 24:37–39 NKJV*

It is true that "no man knows the day nor the hour" that Jesus is returning to the earth. This is a statement of a twenty-four-hour period. Jesus' illustration of Noah is an entirely different prophetic matter.

Here's why!

God told Noah that a great calamity was coming on the earth, and his mission was to build an Ark for the salvation of all who would get on board. It took Noah one hundred twenty years to build the Ark. After the Ark was built, God helped him gather the animals two-by-two placing them on the Ark. Then Noah and his family of eight were the only ones who believed the message of coming doom. Those eight got on the Ark and God shut the door.

When you are Noah on the Ark with your family and the animals with God having just shut the door, you know the only thing left is the flood. The next thing you're listening for is rain. It came and the fountains of the deep were opened and the world and all that were in it drowned in the flood.

Prophetically, we are exactly in the position of Noah on the Ark, hence the words by Jesus, "As it was in the days of Noah . . ." The message has been preached; those who believe are getting on board with Jesus Christ. We are patiently waiting for the sound of the trumpet and the rapture of the church.

The Bible says, "When you see these signs, lift up your heads and rejoice." *The ten prophetic signs have been fulfilled* . . . rejoice, the King is coming. *We are the terminal generation.*

9. EARTHQUAKES

The ninth prophetic sign that we are the terminal generation is given in Matthew 24 that states, "And there will be famines, pestilences and earthquakes in various places" (Matthew 24:7).

In the Bible, God almighty repeatedly used earthquakes to achieve His divine purposes on earth and communicate with those who chose to be spiritually hard of hearing.

The world is divided into two groups of people: those who believe and those who do not. The nonbelievers call themselves agnostics, atheists, pagans, and naturalists (naturalists believe things happen by a natural order that has nothing to do with God).

Often, when nonbelievers discover that I am a minister of the Gospel, they just can't wait to joyously announce, "Pastor Hagee, I don't believe in God!"

My answer is time-proven and battlefield tested: "What you believe has no bearing on reality." A generation of young Americans have listened to college and university professors fill their heads with the absolute nonsense that what they believe is reality.

After the smirk on their faces transforms to shock, and before they can recall the arguments they learned from their atheistic and/or agnostic professors, I continue:

"The world is round whether you believe it or not!

"The sun rises in the east whether you believe it or not!

"Fire burns whether you believe it or not!

"Poison kills whether you believe it or not!

"God controls every detail on planet earth whether you believe it or not!"

When God Almighty introduced Himself to the Jewish people in the Bible He said: "I am the Lord your God, who has brought you out of the Land of Egypt; out of the house of bondage" (Exodus 20:2 NKJV).

Why did God introduce Himself as the one who delivered Israel from Egypt and not as God the Creator? I believe God chose to introduce Himself as the one who delivered Israel from Egypt and Pharaoh because, at Creation, there was no one to see it; there was no one to testify that "God did this." Creation is taken by faith and faith alone!

However, when God led the children of Israel out of Egypt's bondage with ten consecutive, crushing plagues—leaving Egypt bankrupt, their crops destroyed, on the verge of starvation, and Pharaoh's mighty army converted to fish food—the miracles were witnessed by all of Israel and Egypt.

God didn't just send ten plagues at random! The ten plagues He sent crushed the authority of the top ten pagan gods of the Egyptians. It was the war of the gods! Jehovah God won ten to zero, and the victory was witnessed by millions who passed it verbally to generations after them. These ten plagues were a testimonial that the God of Abraham, Isaac, and Jacob absolutely controls the forces of nature, which includes storms, hurricanes, and earthquakes.

King David writes,

He calms the storm, so that its waves are still. Then they are glad
because they are quiet; so He guides them to their desired haven.
                                                    —*Psalms 107:29–30 NKJV*

The Scripture is filled with illustrations of God using earthquakes to confirm that He has "All power in heaven and on earth." In the Old Testament, when the leaders of Israel rebelled against the spiritual leadership of Moses, God gathered them before the Tent of Meeting and swallowed thousands of them alive as a testimonial to Israel, proclaiming, "Moses is My anointed servant and I am Almighty God who controls even the forces of nature."

At the crucifixion, an earthquake caused the veil of the Temple to be ripped from top to the bottom. It was God's message to Israel and the world: you no longer need a priest or preacher to pray for you; you have direct access to God forever.

At the Resurrection of Jesus Christ, there was an earthquake that dislodged the stone that sealed Jesus Christ in His tomb. That same earthquake made it possible for several citizens of Jerusalem who had been buried recently to resurrect and be seen on the streets of Jerusalem. That had to be shocking! Think about it . . . you buried Shlomo last Monday, and you see him walking on the streets of Jerusalem on Sunday morning. It's enough to shake the foundations of any atheist!

When Paul and Silas were in prison for preaching the Gospel, God Almighty sent an earthquake that shattered the jail foundation. It was the New Testaments version of the "Jailhouse Rock"! Paul and Silas walked out of the prison with the keys in one hand and a new convert in the other. God had controlled the entire great escape with an earthquake.

The Bible speaks of "signs in the sea" as evidence that we are living in the last days. An earthquake at sea is the cause of a tsunami. We have had them recently, and their power to destroy defies the imagination of man. A wall of water moving at a hundred twenty miles per hour is unbelievable . . . but we have seen the results on global television.

The greatest earthquake the world has ever seen will happen on a certain date as recorded in Revelation:

And there was a great earthquake, such a mighty and great earthquake as had not occurred since men were on the earth. . . . Then every island fled away, and the mountains were not found.
—Revelation 16:18–20 NKJV

This great earthquake is coming! When? No one knows exactly, but the same God that sent the ten plagues to liberate the Jewish people from Egyptian bondage will send it at a time of His choosing to proclaim once again to a godless generation: "I am God and there is none like Me in all the earth."

California is sitting on the San Andreas Fault, just waiting for a massive earthquake that could dump San Francisco into the Pacific Ocean. The Bible warns of a forthcoming earthquake in the City of Jerusalem that will cause the Temple Mount to split and living water to gush out of the rock and flow to the Dead Sea, where all the fish of the Mediterranean Sea will be found (Ezekiel 47:1–12; Revelation 16:18–19; Revelation 22:1–5 NKJV).

A whole book could be written about the earthquakes that have happened and will happen that—like it or not, understand it or not—are controlled by the hand of an Almighty and Sovereign God.

10. SEAS TURN TO BLOOD

John the Revelator writes of "things to come" that I believe we have recently seen on global television without being aware of what we were truly seeing. It was a mystery that was made plain in a matter of minutes. John the Revelator writes:

Then the second angel poured out his bowl on the sea, and it became as blood of a dead man; and every living creature of the sea died.
—Revelation 16:3 NKJV

You have already seen this!

I saw the images on television several times before it dawned on me what I was actually looking at. It was the first time it had happened on the face of the earth . . . and it's going to happen again—only the next time it will be worldwide.

It was the British Petroleum oil spill in the Gulf of Mexico. ...sive pipeline ruptured, pouring millions of gallons of oil into the Gulf of Mexico. Why did the president of the United States let it gush for days without using his awesome power to stop it? Remember: Everything happens for a reason.

After days of polluting the Gulf of Mexico, the massive oil spill surfaced, and a photo was taken from space of this great ecological tragedy by satellite. I looked at the photo in shock! The oil spill in the Gulf of Mexico looked exactly like blood—thick, coagulated blood, like that of a dead man. The fish, shrimp, crabs, and all living creatures were dying.[8]

Put these two things together!

The Bible says that in the future there will be a global earthquake so massive it will cause the islands of the sea to disappear and the mountains to be shaken down. It will be the greatest earthquake in the history of the world. It's coming!

That earthquake will break the pipe on every deep-water oil rig in the world. Instantly, all over the world, thousands of deep-water oil wells will be belching megamillions of gallons of crude oil into the seas of the world; what happened in the Gulf of Mexico will happen all over the earth within the same day and same hour.

All living creatures in the sea will die just as in the Gulf of Mexico!

No one will be able to stop it; just like in the Gulf of Mexico!

The seas of the earth will look like blood, and every living creature in the sea will die.

Make no mistake . . . there is an awesome and almighty God in heaven, and He is in total control. Whether you believe it or not . . . the end of days are here!

TEN

What's Going to Happen Next?

What is the next earth-shaking event in God's prophetic drama? Some are expecting the Antichrist to suddenly appear and solve the present global economic meltdown. Others are expecting the Great Tribulation—with its earthquakes, famines, wars, and endless tragedies leaving one-third of the earth's population dead.

THE GREAT RAPTURE

The truth is the next prophetic event that will shake the foundations of planet Earth is the rapture of the church. The word *rapture* is the Latin version of a phrase the Bible uses to describe the catching away of all Christians, both dead and alive, on the earth at the appointed time.

The rapture is a global event where every believer on planet Earth will be taken from the earth into heaven in the "twinkling of an eye." Simply stated: billions of people will instantly disappear and not return for seven years!

Think it can't happen?

Think again!

The Ones Who've Gone Before Us

It has already happened and has been recorded in the chronicles of eternal truth for your thoughtful consideration.

The *first* recording of a mortal man being snatched from the earth while alive was the prophet Elijah, who was taken into heaven by a whirlwind and was seen no more (see 2 Kings 2:11). Inasmuch as it is appointed for every man "once to die," Elijah will appear on the earth again during the Tribulation to bring God's message of hope to the world that the Messiah will soon appear on the earth for the second time.

Elijah and Enoch will be killed by the Antichrist on the streets of Jerusalem. Their dead bodies will lie there for the world to see for three days. On the third day, both will stand up and ascend into heaven.

The Revelation states that the whole world will see it and will be stricken with fear! How will they see it? By satellite television!

The *second* man to leave the earth and go into heaven was Enoch, as recorded in Hebrews 11:5:

> *By faith Enoch was taken away so that he did not see death,* "and was not found because God had taken him." (NKJV)

Enoch will join Elijah as messengers of Almighty God during the Tribulation. Jesus Christ made this promise to his disciples just before his crucifixion:

> *In* My Father's *house are many mansions; if* it were *not* so, *I would have told you.* . . . *I will come again and receive you unto Myself; that* where I am [*in heaven*], there *you may be also.*
> —*John 14:2–3 NKJV*

The rapture is the fulfillment of His promise to the disciples and the Church.

The *third* man to leave the earth was the Apostle Paul as recoded in 2 Corinthians 12:2–4, who was in the "third heaven," and then returned to Earth to complete his ministry.

The *fourth* man who went into heaven before his death was the Apostle John, who was called from the Isle of Patmos by Jesus who had the voice of a trumpet that said, "Come up here!" (Revelation 4:1). John ascended into heaven, where he received the Revelation of God, seeing the unspeakable things of horror that would happen on the earth during the rule of the Antichrist during the Tribulation.

Most people are confused about the sequence of past and prophetic events. I refer you to the following chart:

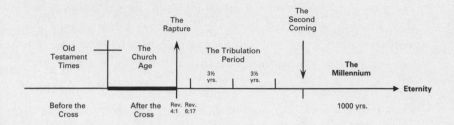

Escape from the Horrors of the Tribulation

The gospel of St. Luke records: "Watch therefore, and pray always that you may be counted worthy to escape those things that are coming upon the earth" (Luke 21:36).

St. Paul records in the book of Hebrews: "How shall we escape if we neglect so great a salvation?" (Hebrews 2:3).

The Rapture is the Great Escape! Escape from what? Escape from the horror of the Great Tribulation that will happen as soon as the church leaves the earth. Walk with me through the pages of Revelation chapters 6, 8, 9, and 16, and let me describe briefly the living hell you will escape by being part of the rapture.

These are but a few of the things that will happen during the Tribulation:

• *One-fourth of mankind will die* (see Revelation 6:8), some because of war, some because of famine, and still others by earthquakes and global disasters. Whether by death that is swift and instant or death that is lingering and excruciating, 25 percent of all people will die. Currently in 2010, the world's population is 6.5 billion. One-fourth of this amount is 1.6 billion, which is more than five times the current population of the United States. Think about it!

• *One-third of all vegetation will be burned up.* All grass, every tree, everything green will be destroyed (see Revelation 8:7).

- *The sun and moon will be darkened,* as nature goes into revolt (see Revelation 8:12).

- *The gates of hell will open and hordes of locusts, the size of horses, will come upon the earth.* These locusts will be allowed to sting men like scorpions, and the pain will last for five months. The Bible says men will beg God to let them die, but they will not die (see Revelation 9:3–6).

- *There will be a worldwide famine,* unlike anything the world has ever seen (see Revelation 18:8).

- *There will be a world war* so bloody that the blood of those killed in battle will flow for two hundred miles up to the bridle of a horse in the valley of Jezreel. This will be the Battle of Armageddon. During the Great Tribulation, one-third of all people on the earth will be killed (see Revelation 14:20).

- *Every person on Earth will be covered with great running, festering boils.* Have you ever had one boil? Imagine being covered with them, not being able to walk, lie down, or sit without pain (see Revelation 16:2–11).

- *The seven seas of the earth will be turned into blood.* Every river, every stream will become as blood. Every basin in your home will run with blood. This plague came upon the Egyptians and drove them to release the Jewish people from captivity. It's the plague that produces mind-numbing thirst from which there is no relief (see Revelation 8:8, 11:6).

- *Mighty men, kings, and men of power will gnaw their tongues in pain* and crawl into caves and beg God to kill them (see Revelation 6:15).

- *The earth will quake so severely that the islands of the sea will disappear.* Puerto Rico and Hawaii will be covered with water. Every building, every wall on earth will crumble. Millions will be trapped beneath the rubble with no one to come to their aid (see Revelation 16:18).

Now I ask you, do you want to escape the coming Tribulation? I do! And I am going to escape. When the archangel blows the trumpet and the dead in Christ rise immediately, those of us who are alive when Jesus the Messiah returns in the clouds of heaven will rise into the air in the twinkling of an eye to trade the coming hell on Earth for the wonder and majesty of heaven. We will meet the real Jesus. He is the Lion of the Tribe of Judah. He is the Lord of Glory. He is the light of the world, the Lamb of God, and the lover of my soul.

The literal, physical appearance of Jesus Christ will come soon. And soon after the church is gone, the Antichrist, the son of Satan, will appear upon the stage of the world to begin his reign of deception and terror.

BIBLE BACKUP FOR THE RAPTURE

The Bible basis for the belief in the rapture is found in the following promises of God. The provisions of God are found in His promises.

For the Lord Himself will descend from heaven with a shout, with the voice of an archangel, and with the trumpet of God. And the dead in Christ shall rise first. Then we who are alive and remain shall be caught up together with them in the clouds to meet the Lord in the air. And thus we shall always be with the Lord. Therefore comfort one another with these words.

—1 Thessalonians 4:16–18 NKJV

Then the sign of the Son of Man in heaven, and then all the tribes of the earth will mourn, and they will see the Son of man coming on the clouds of heaven with power and great glory.

—Matthew 24:30 NKJV

These words were spoken to the disciples as they watched Jesus ascend into heaven:

"Men of Galilee, why do you stand gazing into heaven? This same Jesus, who was taken up from you into heaven, will so come in like manner as you saw Him go into heaven."

—Acts 1:11 NKJV

When Will the Rapture of the Church Happen?

The absolute Bible truth is this: the rapture could happen before you finish reading this page! The preceding chapter gave ten biblically validated signs that had to be fulfilled before the rapture of the church could happen. *All* have been fulfilled! The rapture could happen at any second and as instantly as . . . the twinkling of an eye. St. Paul wrote:

> *Behold, I tell you a mystery: We shall not all sleep [in death], but we shall all be changed—in a moment,* in the twinkling of an eye. . . .
> —*1 Corinthians 15:51–52 NKJV*

The twinkling of an eye is a split second. The difference between the twinkling of an eye and the batting of the eye is the time required by the neurological response. For the eye to blink, the neurological message must go to the brain and back forcing the blink of the eye. The twinkling of an eye is the time required for the neurological message to go only to the brain. The batting of the eye takes twice as long as the twinkling of an eye.

Think of it . . . billions of people all over planet Earth will instantly disappear. *Gone!*

The trumpet of God will sound, because in Bible times, trumpets were sounded to announce the appearance of royalty.

Jesus Christ is the Prince of Peace; He is King of all kings and Lord of all lords. The day will soon come when "every knee shall bow and every tongue shall confess that he is Lord to the glory of God the Father."

The shout of the archangel is Christ's shout as He celebrates His absolute victory over the enemy of death. The resurrection morning is Christ's Super Bowl victory over death, hell, and the grave!

Jesus stood at Lazarus' tomb and shouted: "Lazarus, come forth!" and Lazarus awoke from the slumber of death to live again. Jesus shouted to the Apostle John on the Isle of Patmos, "Come up here!" and John instantly was caught up into heaven to receive the contents of the book of Revelation.

THE DAY OF RECKONING

Very soon, Jesus Christ is going to step out on the balconies of heaven and shout to his church on planet Earth, those who sleep in death, and those that are alive, "Come up here!" Instantly, in the twinkling of an eye, the dead in Christ will rise first, and we who are alive and remain shall be caught up with them in the clouds and so shall we ever be with the Lord. Are you listening for the shout? The rapture is going to happen . . . ready or not!

Instantly all over the earth billions of people will disappear. Wives who have been a living witness to their rebellious husbands will disappear from their arms into heaven while their husbands stand in total shock! They are left behind!

Automobiles will be empty on the freeway, on the streets, and abandoned in tunnels; the motors are running but the drivers are gone to mansions on high.

Homes of believers will be eternally divided in a split second. Sitting at the supper table discussing the crisis on Wall Street, suddenly the children disappear to the marriage supper of the Lamb, while the unbelieving parents are left behind.

Jumbo jets flying at forty thousand feet at 600 miles per hour with three hundred-plus passengers are in for a shock! The captain is a believer; he suddenly disappears from the cockpit, the plane crashes seconds later, and every passenger steps into eternity!

Classrooms in school will suddenly be without teachers and believing students; hospitals will be without dedicated doctors and nurses; parents will be without children; and children will be without parents. The son of God has called His triumphant church to heaven.

Phone circuits will be jammed all over the earth with sobbing people, who always intended to make things right with God who suddenly realize they are lost and left behind.

People will be standing in their front yards looking up toward the heavens, screaming, "O my God" in an effort to relieve the terror that grips their souls.

A global economic crash is guaranteed, as Bible believers who had a strong work ethic leave planet earth to the maddening designs of social architects who know not the God of Abraham, Isaac, and Jacob! Panic will grip the earth as God's "salt and light" have departed and the son of Satan waits in the wings with his plans to produce a global bloodbath for mankind!

THE FINAL SEVEN YEARS

As soon as the church of Jesus Christ is raptured into heaven in the twinkling of an eye, the wrath of God will be poured out on the earth in a series of twenty-one judgments recorded by John the Revelator as the Seven Seals, the Seven Trumpets, and the Seven Bowls.

These twenty-one global catastrophes will occur in a period of seven years; exactly one earth-shaking disaster following another, every four months.

The Seven Seals

It begins with the four horsemen who ride out on the stage of world history, in Revelation chapter 6, to deceive, to kill, and to destroy. These four horsemen represent the first four seals.

The first horse that thunders out onto the stage of world history is a white horse, which is ridden by the Antichrist. He has a bow in his hand, a crown on his head, and in his heart the passion for world domination— a one-world government that he will ruthlessly lead.

No one can buy or sell without his mark on their right hand or forehead. If you take his mark, John the Revelator states that your soul will be damned for all eternity. If you refuse his mark, the Antichrist will cut your head off. This is the first seal.

The second horse that rides out onto the stage of world history is a fiery red horse of war, and Satan gives the rider the power to take peace from the world, bringing a series of global wars that bathe the earth in blood. This is the second seal.

The third horse that rides out onto the stage of world history is blacker than a thousand midnights and his rider carries a pair of scales in his hands with which he measures food to the hungry like it is gold. This clearly indicates a world with global starvation. This is the third seal.

The fourth horse that rides out snorting and pawing the ground is a pale horse and his rider is Death and Hell. This demonic monster is given the power to kill one fourth of the world's population. This is the fourth seal.

The fifth seal is opened, and God hears the cries of those who have had their heads cut off by the Antichrist for the testimony of their faith. They are all martyrs. They are under the altar and are crying out to God for justice and vengeance.

The sixth seal is a continuation of a series of global environmental catastrophes. The sun will become black; the moon will become as blood; a great earthquake will shake the earth so violently that every mountain and island of the sea will be shaken out of its place.

Every person on earth will be filled with mind-bending terror. The wealthy, the powerful, presidents, prime ministers, senators, congressmen, and the mighty men of war will hide in caves and underground government chambers to escape the wrath of God.

The seventh seal represents thirty minutes of absolute silence in heaven. Why is there silence in heaven? God has permitted His raptured church to see the unspeakable horror that is about to be poured out on the earth, and the Bride of Christ in heaven is stunned into absolute silence.

The Seven Trumpets

Then the seven angels with the Seven Trumpets prepare to bring their judgments to those who rejected the message of God's hope and the plan of His redemption.

The first angel sounds his trumpet, and one third of all the trees and one third of all the grass on planet earth are burned up. For those of you looking for Al Gore's global warming . . . it's coming in major-league fashion.

The second angel sounds his trumpet, and a third of the sea becomes blood. As I have stated earlier in this book, I believe that the earthquakes promised in the book of Revelation will snap the deep-water oil well pipelines like a single strand of dry spaghetti. The millions of gallons of crude oil gushing into the oceans of the world will become oil slicks that look like human blood.

The third angel sounds his trumpet, and a meteor from outer space strikes the earth. According to Revelation 8:10–11 the meteor poisons the waters of the earth, causing millions to die from drinking the water.

The fourth angel sounds his trumpet, and one third of the earth is covered with darkness. When a person lives in total darkness for an extended period of time, it causes physical and psychological damage for life.

The fifth angel sounds his trumpet; he carries the key to the bottomless pit. The angel opens the bottomless pit and out of it come scorpions the size of a horse who were given the power to sting the inhabitants of earth with a paralyzing sting that will last for five agonizing months without a moment's relief.

The sixth angel sounds his trumpet, and four angels are released at an exact hour and day and month and year to kill one third of the earth's remaining population (Revelation 9:15).

The seventh angel sounds his trumpet, and there are loud voices in heaven saying, "The kingdoms of this world have become the kingdoms of our Lord and of His Christ, and He shall reign forever and ever" (Revelation 11:15 NKJV).

The Seven Bowls

Now that the Seven Seals and the Seven Trumpets with their judgments have been poured out on the earth, the survivors of earth await the seven angels with the Seven Bowls (sometimes referred to as vials) of the wrath of God, which are more severe than anything the world has seen to this point in time.

The next seven angels prepare themselves to pour their Bowls of Judgment upon planet earth.

The first angel pours out his bowl upon the earth, and every person on earth who has received the mark of the beast is covered with boils.

The second angel pours out his bowl upon the sea, and all the water of the seas of earth become as the blood of a dead man. Remember that when God was delivering the children of Israel from Egypt, He turned the Nile River to blood.

The third angel pours out his bowl, and the drinking waters, the rivers, and springs of earth turn to blood—just like what happened when God poured out upon Egypt in His deliverance of the Jewish people.

The fourth angel pours out his bowl on the sun, and the heat is so intense men are scorched with fire. Al Gore's nightmare: Act Two.

The fifth angel pours out his bowl, and the whole earth is covered with darkness—again, just as God did to Pharaoh to force him to release the Jewish people from captivity. Some who are reading this are saying to themselves, "Things like this just can't happen!" Wrong! They have already happened in Bible history; they will happen again!

The sixth angel pours out his bowl on the river Euphrates so that the waters are dried up. Then the Chinese Army of two hundred million men can march up the dry riverbed of the Euphrates to the Battle of Armageddon.

The seventh angel pours out his bowl upon the earth, and there is "a great earthquake, such a great and mighty earthquake as had not occurred since men were on the earth" (Revelation 16:18 NKJV).

Jesus Christ to Planet Earth

These twenty-one judgments are followed by the second coming of Jesus Christ to planet Earth as King of Kings and Lord of Lords. John the Revelator describes this dramatic scene in his own words:

> *Now I saw heaven opened, and behold, a white horse. And He who sat on him was called Faithful and True, and in righteousness He judges and makes war. His eyes were like a flame of fire, and on His head were many crowns. He had a name written that no one knew except Himself. He was clothed with a robe dipped in blood, and His name is called The Word of God. And the armies in heaven, clothed in fine linen, white and clean, followed Him on white horses. Now out of His mouth goes a sharp sword, that with it He should strike the nations. And He Himself will rule them with a rod of iron. He Himself treads the winepress of the fierceness and wrath of Almighty God. And He has on His robe and on His thigh a name written: KING OF KINGS AND LORD OF LORDS.*
>
> *—Revelation 19:11–16 NKJV*

Christ will destroy the armies that have come to Israel to do battle at Armageddon and will give total protection and deliverance once again to the Jewish people.

Jesus Christ will touch down on the Mount of Olives, which will split in half. He will walk across the Kedron Valley into the City of Jerusalem through the Eastern Gate. He will sit on the throne of His father, King David, on the Temple Mount and will rule the earth with a rod of iron for one thousand years of absolute peace.

After those one thousand years of the Golden Age of perfect peace, death and hell will be emptied, and all of the wicked dead will be summoned from the grave to face God Almighty at the Great White Throne Judgment. Here there will be weeping and wailing and gnashing of teeth. Why? Because every person appearing before God at the Great White Throne Judgment will know they are guilty of sin and in their life did not ask God for forgiveness. They will stand before the Judge of all judges to be sentenced to eternity in the Lake of Fire.

The earth will then be burned with fire and re-created to be like the original Garden of Eden. Then we will enter a dimension of time called Eternity where time shall be no more.

These things are exactly what will happen during the seven years immediately following the rapture of the church of Jesus Christ.

The rapture of the church could happen in the next sixty seconds! Are you ready?

You have two options: to accept Jesus Christ as Lord and Savior or to be a slave to the Antichrist, be forced to take his mark, and be damned for eternity or have your head cut off.

Think it won't happen?

Think again!

PART FOUR

The Final Days

ELEVEN

The Fourth Reich:
The Coming Antichrist

The unspeakable horrors of the Third Reich under the demonic leadership of Adolf Hitler produced the darkest page in the history of the twentieth century.

Out of demonized minds of the Nazi monsters came the nightmare of the Final Solution fathered by Adolf Eichmann, which led to the systematic slaughter of 6 million Jews, two-thirds of the Jewish population in Europe, and the death of 50 million people.

After the guns of World War II fell silent, after Berlin was pulverized by Allied artillery, after the Third Reich—which Hitler predicted would endure for one thousand years—was a wasteland of rubble,150,000 Nazis were charged with war crimes.

Thirty thousand Nazis were tried and fewer were convicted. Where did the 120,000 Nazis vanish to on planet Earth? How did they escape? Who helped them escape and find places of refuge beyond the reach of justice?

Two of the most famous Nazi criminals—Joseph Mengele, the Doctor of Death, and Martin Bormann—escaped and were never brought to trial. How could such monsters avoid and evade the judicial and intelligence systems of every government on the face of the earth?

The Simon Wiesenthal Organization investigated a secret organization labeled ODESSA, an acronym meaning, in German, the "Organisation Der Ehemaligen SS Angehörigen," which translates in English as the Organization of Former Members of the SS.

The mystery of how these tens of thousands of Nazis will forever escape detection will remain a secret known only to God Almighty. He will call all men to a day of judgment and will make every secret thing exposed.

According to the prophet Daniel, who was given a vision from God of the end of days, history will repeat itself at some point in the future with a Fourth Reich. This repeat of the future will not cover Europe alone, but will blanket the earth.

It will come to power much like Hitler came to power: on the wings of an economic crisis.

The prophet Daniel states that the leader of the coming Fourth Reich "will cause craft to prosper" (Daniel 8:25 NKJV). Daniel also writes:

> *He shall have power over the treasures of gold and silver, and over all the precious things of Egypt; also the Libyans and Ethiopians shall follow at his heels.*
>
> —*Daniel 11:43 NKJV*

John the Revelator records concerning the Antichrist's determination to control absolutely every financial transaction on planet Earth with the words:

> *He [the Antichrist] causes all, both small and great, rich and poor, free and slave, to receive a mark on their right hand or on their foreheads, and that no one may buy or sell except one who has the mark or the name of the beast, or the number of his name. Here is wisdom. Let him who has understanding calculate the number of the beast, for it is the number of a man; his number is 666.*
>
> —*Revelation 13:16–18 NKJV*

SEVEN REASONS FOR THE MARK

There are seven reasons that the Antichrist will place a mark on those he controls.

1. The mark is open rebellion against the law of God, which states: "You shall not make any cuttings . . . nor tattoo any marks on you: I am the Lord" (Leviticus 19:28 NKJV).

Your body is the temple of the Holy Spirit and when you decorate it with graffiti, it angers the Lord!

2. The mark extends favors to those who support the One World Government, such as food, medicine, and the right to buy and sell (see Revelation 13:16).

3. The mark identifies and eliminates all opposition to the One World Government.

4. The mark tracks and controls all commerce.

5. The mark forces people to stop worshipping God. When you take the mark of the beast, you lose your soul. The book of Revelation records:

> *"If anyone worships the beast and his image, and receives his mark on his forehead or on his hand, he himself shall also drink of the wine of the wrath of God, which is poured out full strength into the cup of His indignation. He shall be tormented with fire and brimstone in the presence of the holy angels and in the presence of the Lamb [of God]."*
> —*Revelation 14:9–10 NKJV*

The point is this: the moment you take the mark of the beast, you no longer look to God Almighty as your source and savior; you are officially recognizing the Antichrist as your provider.

6. The mark forces people to worship the Antichrist. When you take the mark of the beast, the only one left to worship is the Antichrist. When you reject truth, all that's left is a lie. Your first step away from light is your first step toward the kingdom of darkness.

7. The mark permanently ties people to the kingdom of the Antichrist with absolute control of their lives and their souls.

If you miss the rapture of the Church, you have two alternatives. One is to be beheaded for your refusal to reject Jesus Christ as savior. The other is to receive the mark of the beast and lose your soul for all eternity.

I believe the coming global economic czar, the Antichrist, is now standing in the wings of history, waiting for the economies of the world, now deeply in debt, to crash! He will step onto the stage of world history much like Hitler, as the economic messiah. World rulers will applaud his coming; they will demand his coronation as the new Caesar of the world. You will read this phrase in the print media in the near future: "A global leader for a global problem." Watch for it!

COMPARING HOW HITLER AND
THE ANTICHRIST CAME TO POWER

Let's compare the process by which Adolf Hitler came to power and the process by which the prophet Daniel says the Antichrist will soon come to power.

1. Adolf Hitler came to power through the economic crisis created by the Versailles Treaty. This treaty was the womb of World War II. History proves that poorly written treaties are the breeding ground for the next war.

The Treaty of Versailles placed the German people in financial crisis and demanded payment of reparations created by World War I to England and America. This enormous debt, created by the treaty, led to hyperinflation in Germany where the ink on the German mark was more valuable than the money.

Inflation became so severe that people walked into stores with a handful of money to buy a single loaf of bread. Wealthy Germans drove their Mercedes into the countryside and traded them for sacks of potatoes.

Into this chaos came Adolf Hitler and the Nazis. Hitler pledged to revive the German economy by rebuilding the national infrastructure and building a car for the common people. Thus the autobahns were born, as the Volkswagen means "car of the people." Hitler endeared himself to the German people by defying America and England in refusing to repay the onerous war debt required by the Treaty of Versailles. His defiance made him an instant hero to the disheartened German people.

In like manner, the coming Antichrist, leader of the Fourth Reich, will come to the world stage to resolve an economic crisis—not for one nation, but for the nations of the world. Excessive global debt will cause a global economic meltdown accelerated by the rapture of the church when billions of people suddenly disappear.

The leaders of the world will call for and even demand that there be a global economic czar to save the world from an economic catastrophe. That man, like Hitler, will come out of Europe and will be the Antichrist.

2. Hitler made his debut upon the stage of the world with hypnotic charm, charisma, and arrogance. Men cheered his speeches with thunderous applause and mesmerized women wept and some even fainted in extreme ecstasy.

The prophet Daniel presents the coming Antichrist, leader of the coming global Fourth Reich, to be extremely arrogant and demonically anointed as an orator.

> "... *shall do according to his own will: he shall exalt and magnify himself above every god,* ... *for he shall exalt himself above* them *all.*
> —*Daniel 11:36–37 NKJV*

Revelation 13:5–6 states:

> *And he* [*the Antichrist*] *was given a mouth speaking great things and blasphemies* ... *then he opened his mouth in blasphemy against God, to blaspheme His name, His tabernacle, and those who dwell in heaven (NKJV).*

The Antichrist will have the arrogance to challenge the right of God Almighty to rule the very earth He created and to which He has complete ownership.

3. Adolf Hitler and the SS were absolutely committed to and controlled by the powers of the occult. The book *The Twisted Cross* reveals historical evidence demonstrating the demonic mind-set and practices of the leaders of the Third Reich. The SS were Hells Angels in long black leather coats!

Just so, the prophet Daniel states that the coming Antichrist, leader of the Fourth Reich, will "understand dark sentences" (Daniel 8:23 NKJV).

In Scripture, there are two kingdoms: the kingdom of light and the kingdom of darkness. Satan is referred to as the Prince of Darkness. The word *prince* means one who has authority in a specific kingdom. Hence, Satan and his chief son, the Antichrist, have authority in the kingdom of darkness ruled by the occult. When the church, which is God's salt and light, is taken from the world, the Prince of Darkness will be in absolute control of planet earth.

Simply stated, the coming Antichrist will be anointed by Satan himself to rule the world with demonic deception, total economic control, and brutality that numbs the mind. The Bible says, "His power shall be mighty, but not by his own power" (Daniel 8:24 NKJV).

The Antichrist will rule the world with the full authority and anointing of Satan himself. Satan and his legions are coming!

Even a casual observer will be aware of the cultic explosion now taking place in Western civilization. The Harry Potter book series is nothing less than Witchcraft 101 and is the most celebrated publication in the history of literature other than the Bible. Children in every country have been exposed to blood curses, witches, and the occult in a positive light. Satan is preparing the youth of the world for the appearance of his messiah, the Antichrist, to rule the world with demonic power!

Cultic movies magnify the demonic power of hell's legions. Books and magazines exalting the power of witchcraft have a large and enthusiastic audience in the Western world.

4. As Hitler came out of Europe, so will the Antichrist come out of the revived Roman Empire. The Antichrist will come from the European Union or a country or confederation that was once part of the Roman Empire. The Roman Empire stretched from Ireland to Egypt and included Turkey, Iran, and Iraq.

In Daniel's vision, the "little horn" sprouted among the other ten, which we know are ten divisions of the final world government, as confirmed by Daniel's vision of the ten toes of Nebuchadnezzar's image (see Daniel 2:31–35 and 7:8). In his rise to power, the Antichrist will weave his hypnotic spell, first over one nation in the ten-kingdom federation, then over all ten. He will conquer three of the ten nations and then take control over all of them. He will then turn his ravenous eye toward the apple of God's eye: Israel. His masterwork of deception will be the Seven-

Year Peace Accord, which Israel will accept (see Daniel 9:27 and Revelation 17:17).

I believe that in the future, global, political, and economic power will shift from America back to Europe. In the final analysis, Israel's salvation will not come from America or Europe; it will come from heaven by the awesome power of the God of Abraham, Isaac, and Jacob.

5. As Hitler did, the Antichrist will come as a man of peace. When England's Prime Minister, Chamberlain, went to Hitler seeking peace for England as the Nazi war machine crushed Poland and France, Hitler gave Chamberlain a written document pledging peace between Germany and England. Chamberlain flew back to England in triumph, joyously disembarked from his plane waving the document Hitler had given proclaiming "peace in our times." But it was a farce, a colossal deception. Hitler never intended to keep the peace; he did exactly what the prophet Daniel said the Antichrist would do in the future:

> *He will destroy wondrously with peace.*
> —*Daniel 8:25 NKJV*

> *"Then he shall confirm a covenant [Peace Treaty] with many for one week [seven years]; but in the middle of the week [three and half years after the treaty is signed] he shall bring an end to sacrifice and offering."*
> —*Daniel 9:27 NKJV*

The Antichrist will guarantee peace for Israel and the Middle East and sign a seven-year peace treaty but will break the treaty in three and a half years, according to the prophet Daniel.

If you've ever been to Israel, you'll note that their history of betrayal and persecution makes its people extremely cautious about trusting anyone with their safety other than themselves. In fact, this history is part of the great need for the Jewish people to have their own homeland. They can trust their government because their government is truly their own. You can even say that the nation of Israel is an incarnation of their desire as expressed in the solemn utterance "Never again."

Never again a pogrom; never again a persecution; never again an exile; never again a holocaust. So just imagine what it would take for them to entrust their security to another. This gives you an idea both of the coming change of attitude in Israel and of the incredible power of the Antichrist to deceive.

In the months ahead, it is a distinct possibility that Iran will go nuclear and a person out of the European Union will have the political power and presence to guarantee Israel's security. The Jewish people could be granted the right to rebuild the Temple on the Temple Mount and to initiate daily sacrifices as inducement. We know this because the Antichrist will stop the daily sacrifices and offerings at the midpoint of the Tribulation, and sacrifices have to have been started again in order for the Antichrist to stop them. Another clue that the Temple will be rebuilt is that the Antichrist will take over the Temple, an event that occurs at the midpoint of the Tribulation:

> *He will [the Antichrist] oppose and exalt himself over everything that is called God or is worshipped, so that he sets himself up in God's Temple, proclaiming himself to be God.*
> *—2 Thessalonians 2:4 NKJV*

Again, a temple must have been built in order for the Antichrist to seize and defile it, as he will.

The rebuilding of the Temple constitutes an enormous political and religious problem, for the place the Bible decrees for the location of the Temple is currently occupied by the Dome of the Rock.

The Dome of the Rock is located on the Temple Mount, or Mount Moriah, the third holiest place in the world for Muslims.

If you doubt that the Jewish people would ever attempt something so spectacular, you need to know that some Jewish people are already planning for it, working to make all the necessary preparations for the construction and operation of the third Temple (the first being Solomon's temple and the second being Herod's temple). One of the organizations working toward this end is called the Temple Foundation. I have personally seen their work, and they have created authentic Temple vessels and priestly garments according to biblical specifications.

This is an ongoing process, and to date, over sixty sacred objects have been re-created from gold, silver, and copper. These vessels are not models or replicas, but they are actually made according to all the complicated requirements of biblical law. If the Holy Temple were to be rebuilt immediately, the divine service could be resumed utilizing these vessels.

Only the destruction of the great mosques in Mecca and Medina could have a more explosive effect on Muslims. And no greater blow could be inflicted on the Muslims than Israel to be given the privilege of building the third Temple on the Dome of the Rock. But even as international forces guarantee the security of Israel in their decision to rebuild the Temple, the Islamic nations will prepare for war. The "King of the North" will lead them toward Israel in the Battle of Ezekiel 38–39.

6. As Hitler was a man committed to the force of military power, so will the Antichrist be committed to military power. Revelation 6:2 describes the vision of John on Patmos as the Antichrist rides out on the stage on World History.

And I looked, and behold, a white horse. He who sat on it had a bow; and a crown was given to him, and he went out conquering and to conquer (NKJV).

John again describes the beast saying:

Now the beast which I saw was like a leopard, his feet were like the feet of a bear, and his mouth like the mouth of a lion. The dragon [Satan] gave him his power, his throne, and great authority.
—Revelation 13:2 NKJV

Daniel reports:

But in their place he shall honor a god of fortresses.
—Daniel 11:38 NKJV

7. As Hitler had a hatred for the Jewish people, so will the Antichrist determine to destroy the Jewish people. God will prevent it by the Jewish people fleeing to Petra, where God will supernaturally provide for them for three and half years, just as He provided for the children of Israel in the wilderness, following Moses from Egypt to the promised land.

With Satan and his angels cast down to Earth to join forces with the Antichrist and the False Prophet, the powers of hell will be unfurled on the earth as never before in human history. The Prince of Darkness will attack everything that reminds him of the God of heaven. He will attack both Christians and Jews.

Satan will target the beloved of God, because attacking them is the only way he can retaliate against God. Unable to prevail against God militarily, Satan will seek revenge against Him by targeting the righteous. The Antichrist will be motivated by revenge against the Jewish people who attempted to snuff out his life. All of this will happen at about the same time that the image of the Antichrist is erected in the Temple. God's warning to the seed of Abraham in that day is clear and urgent. Jesus said,

> *"Therefore when you see the* 'abomination of desolation,' *spoken of by Daniel the prophet, standing in the holy place (whoever reads, let him understand),"* *then let those who are in Judea flee to the mountains. Let him who is on the housetop not go down to take anything out of his house. And let him who is in the field not go back to get his clothes. But woe to those who are pregnant and to those who are nursing babies in those days! . . . and unless those days were shortened, no flesh would be saved; but for the elect's sake* [the Jewish people] *those days will be shortened.*
>
> —*Matthew 24:15–22 NKJV*

God will prepare a special place of refuge for the Jewish people in the desert. Those who follow the words of Jesus and flee to the desert will be supernaturally cared for by the hand of God throughout the last three and a half years of the Tribulation (see Revelation 12:6).

The desert area of divine protection is identified as Edom, Moab, and Ammon—modern-day Jordan (see Daniel 11:41). Undoubtedly, the place of refuge will be Petra. I have been there, and it is the most massive natural fortress in that part of the world. It is here that the Jewish people will receive the same supernatural care the children of Israel received as they journeyed from Egypt to the promised land. Manna from heaven for food and water from a rock, if necessary, will meet their every need. Israel and the Jewish people will survive and prosper in the Tribulation.

8. *Just as Hitler was subject to an assassination attempt, so will the Antichrist be wounded in the head and recover miraculously, emulating the death and resurrection of Jesus Christ.* People around the world will worship him as God! John the Revelator gives a full and graphic description of the assassination attempt.

> And I saw *one of his heads as it had been mortally wounded, and his deadly wound was healed. And all the world marveled and followed the beast. So they worshipped the dragon* [*Satan*] *who gave authority to the beast . . . saying, "Who* is *like the beast? Who is able to make war with him?"*
>
> —*Revelation 13:3–4 NKJV*

When the Antichrist seizes the Temple and ends the daily sacrifices, he will enrage the Jewish people.

The location of the Temple is still the same . . . smack in the middle on the third most holy spot in Islam. The Antichrist's actions will enrage the Jewish people, sparking white-hot fury in the very core of their being by the most appalling insults to the true God and the Temple, which is set apart to the holiness of His name. They will be motivated by two outraging factors:

1. They will already be disgusted by the Antichrist's failure to honor his Seven-Year Treaty to come to their aide when Russia and the Islamic coalition invaded them.

2. Israel's heart will already be softening toward the Most High God because of His miraculous intervention to defeat the Russian-Iranian Islamic coalition. Now motivated by a combination of fury and zeal, a lone assassin will attempt to assassinate the Antichrist . . . and he will succeed.

To Hell and Back

With the Antichrist lulled into a sense of complacency by both his arrogance and the ease of his victories, his security breaks down. An assassin will exploit the opportunity and strike a lethal blow to the head of the Antichrist, a wound so grievous that those attending to him believe he is dead (see Revelation 13:3).

I believe that upon his death, the Antichrist will descend directly into hell. I believe this is at least part of the reason why the Antichrist is depicted in the book of Revelation as being he who ascends from the Abyss to prevaricate and plunder.

Just as Satan took Jesus up into a mountain, showing Him all the kingdoms of the world and offering them as a reward, I believe that Satan may take the Antichrist into the depths of hell and offer him the kingdoms of the world.

While Jesus refused to bow to Satan, the Antichrist will gladly bow to Satan and worship him. In return for this worship, Satan reanimates the Antichrist, infusing him to the very core of his being with demonic rage and ruthlessness. John makes it clear,

> *The dragon [Satan] gave him his power, his throne, and great*
> *authority.*
>
> *—Revelation 13:2 NKJV*

The Antichrist will capture the imagination and confidence of the world through his miraculous recovery. To the satanically blinded world of the Tribulation, the Antichrist's healing will look exactly like the death and resurrection of Jesus Christ . . . except in this instance, they will see it happen with their own eyes on CNN.

9. As statues of Hitler were planted throughout the Third Reich, so will the Antichrist set up a statue of himself in the city of Jerusalem and demand that the nations of the world worship him. John the Revelator says of the Antichrist,

> *All who dwell on the earth will worship him, whose names have not*
> *been written in the Book of Life of the Lamb slain from the foundation*
> *of the world.*
>
> *—Revelation 13:8 NKJV*

It is difficult to imagine a world filled with Satan worshippers, but that's exactly what will happen when the church, the salt and light of God, leave planet Earth. The Antichrist is Satan's son . . . and the world is worshipping him openly and enthusiastically.

The Antichrist will introduce idolatrous worship inside the Holy Temple on the Temple Mount and set himself up as God:

> *Then he shall confirm a covenant [Peace Treaty] with many for one week [seven years]; but in the middle of the week [three and half years after the treaty is signed] he will bring an end to sacrifice and offering. And on the wing of abominations shall be one who makes desolate, even until the consummation, which is determined, is poured out on the desolate."*
>
> *—Daniel 9:27 NKJV*

> *He will oppose and will exalt himself over everything that is called God or is worshipped, so that he sets himself up in God's temple, proclaiming himself to be God.*
>
> *—2 Thessalonians 4 NIV*

10. As Hitler's reign of terror lasted seven years, from Kristallnacht on November 10, 1938, until 1945, so will the Antichrist have complete domination of the earth for seven years.

This world domination of the Antichrist begins with the signing of the Seven-Year Peace Accord with Israel and lasts until the second coming of Jesus Christ, which will be exactly two thousand five hundred twenty days later. A prophetic year is three hundred sixty days in duration. This number times seven gives you the exact date of the second coming of the son of God.

11. As Hitler captured France, Poland, and Czechoslovakia, just so will the coming Antichrist conquer three nations and then establish ten groups of nations as he becomes the new Caesar of the world.

The prophet Daniel teaches that the Antichrist will come up among the ten horns (nations) and uproot three of them (see Daniel 7:7–8, 23–25). The Antichrist will take over the power of three nations—either through seduction or assassination—and the other seven nations will surrender to him quickly. He is then the head of the world government. He is the world's new Caesar!

The New World Order

Our world has been moving to a New World Order for centuries. The United Nations now wants a world constitution, a world currency, a world income tax, a world military power, and a world global ethic, which is another way of saying a One World Religion.

Think it can't happen?

Think again!

Here is a concept of how the ten regions of the New World Order might appear.

Region 1: The United States and Canada

Region 2: The European Union

Region 3: Japan

Region 4: Australia, New Zealand, South Africa, and the Pacific Islands

Region 5: Eastern Europe

Region 6: Latin America: Mexico, Central America, and South America

Region 7: North Africa and the Middle East

Region 8: Central Africa

Region 9: South and Southeast Asia

Region 10: Central Asia[1]

Never in world history has one government completely ruled the world, but the Antichrist will "devour the whole earth" (Daniel 7:23 NKJV). He will rule over them by their consent and with absolute and total authority (see Daniel 11:36). His personality will be marked by great intelligence, persuasiveness, subtlety, deception, and pomposity.

Daniel says his mouth "speaks pompous words" (Daniel 7:8 NKJV), and he is a "master of intrigue" (Daniel 8:23 NIV). He will be the world's most prominent, powerful, and popular personality in the beginning of his deceptive reign.

There's nothing new about a new world order. Satan has been scheming to institute one ever since Nimrod proposed to build a mighty tower on the plains of Shinar. The purpose of what we know as the Tower of Babel was to defy God's authority on Earth—to cast God out of the earth and institute the government of man. The Bible records the first New World Order thusly:

> Now the whole earth had one language and one speech. And it came to pass, as they journeyed from the east, that they found a plain in the land of Shinar, and they dwelt there. . . . And they said, "Come, let us build ourselves a city, and a tower whose top is in the heavens; let us make a name for ourselves, lest we be scattered abroad over the face of the whole earth."
>
> —*Genesis 11:1–2, 4 NKJV*

God Almighty endured the arrogance of man for a limited time, then He scattered them across the earth.

After World War I, "the war to end all wars," President Woodrow Wilson crafted the League of Nations to uphold peace through a One World Government. Adolf Hitler told the German people he would bring "a new order" to Europe. He did, dragging Europe into the bowels of a living hell and turning the streets crimson with rivers of human blood.

The Communists of the former Soviet Union pledged to institute a new world order and erected an atheistic empire that has now collapsed like a house of cards. Now the United Nations wants to establish a new world order!

What does that mean? Brock Chisholm, former director of the United Nations World Health Organization, said, "To achieve world government, it is necessary to remove from the minds of men their individualism, loyalties to their families, national patriotism, and religion."

12. Hitler and his Third Reich were destroyed by the righteous might of the U.S. military and their allies. Just so will the coming

Antichrist be destroyed "without hand." John the Revelator describes the end of the Antichrist and the False Prophet in Revelation 19:20–21 saying:

> *Then the beast was captured, and with him the false-prophet who worked signs in his presence, by which he deceived those who received the mark of the beast and those who worshipped his image. These two were cast alive into the lake of fire burning with brimstone. And the rest were killed with the sword which proceeded from the mouth of Him who sat on the horse (NKJV).*

This means that the Antichrist and the False Prophet will be destroyed, not by men and military power, but by the mighty right hand of God's own son, who will crush them as the enemies of righteousness and of the Jewish people.

It's ironic that Hitler ordered his body to be burned with fire as a forerunner of Satan's son, who will receive exactly the same treatment in the future by the hand of God.

HIS NAME EQUALS 666

John the Revelator writes,

> *Here is wisdom. Let him who has understanding calculate the number of the beast, for it is the number of a man; his number is 666.*
> *—Revelation 13:18 NKJV*

The Antichrist's number of 666 represents the satanic trinity: Satan, the Antichrist, and the False Prophet, who will lead the worldwide cult that worships the son of Satan. The number 666 could also be a reference to the worldwide idolatry attempted by Nebuchadnezzar when he erected a statue of himself and commanded all the world to worship it or face death (see Daniel 3). You might say that 666 was stamped upon the very image of Nebuchadnezzar, since the image was sixty cubits high and six cubits wide.

In Revelation 13 the focal point is the rise of the man, the Antichrist, and 666 is said to be "the number of a man." In light of this emphasis, there is another explanation of the cryptic number "666." Certainly some of John's readers were familiar with the method of calculating a name by the use of numbers, a practice known to the Jews as Gematria (or Gimetria). The Greeks also practiced it, but not as seriously as the Jewish people did.

The transition from number to letter or from letter to number was possible because most ancient languages did not have independent symbols for numbers as we do. Rather, the letters of the alphabet were also used to designate numbers in the way that Roman numerals use letters to designate numbers. It was a simple matter for members of the early church to convert a number into a name or a name into a number.

In Revelation 13:18, John made it possible for the world to positively identify the Antichrist. This cryptic puzzle is not intended to point a finger at some unknown person. It is, however, intended to confirm to the world someone already suspected as being the Antichrist. And in the idolatry of the end time, "the number of a man" is fully developed and the result is 666.

This information about how to identify the Antichrist is of no practical value to the church, since we will be watching from the balconies of heaven by the time he is revealed. But for those of you who are reading this book after the church has been taken in the rapture, and for those of you who come to trust Christ during the Tribulation, you will have the ability to confirm which personality rising out of a European Federation is the devil incarnate, the son of Satan.

Do you think a society that produced Adolf Hitler could never come to America? Do you realize that we have already begun walking down that road?

Hitler returned Christmas and Easter into pagan holidays.[2] Presently, in America, the word "Christmas" is now being referred to as a "midwinter celebration." Children in school are criticized for using the word "Christmas" and are required to use a secular word in its place.

Hitler's Third Reich hung signs the length and breadth of the land saying, "Jews unwelcomed."[3] In his book, *The Case for Israel*, celebrated attorney Alan Dershowitz demonstrates how that some of America's foremost universities are openly anti-Semitic and refuse to allow pro-Israel speakers to address the students at their campuses.

Nazi Propaganda Minister Joseph Goebbels said, "Someday Europe will perish of the Jewish disease."[4] The Jewish people were people of faith, whom the demonized Hitler hated.

In 1996, evolutionist Richard Dawkins was named Humanist of the Year. In his acceptance speech, he compared the threat of AIDS and "mad cow disease" to the threat posed by faith. According to Dawkins, faith is "one of the world's great evils, comparable to the small pox virus but harder to eradicate."

America is now in an all-out culture war for the soul of this nation. There will be a winner and a loser. To the winner go our children, our grandchildren, and the fate of the nation.

During the Third Reich, crosses of Christ in the German class-rooms were replaced with pictures of Hitler.[5] In America, no Christian crosses are allowed in public schools. Christian symbols are now considered off limits. CNSNews.com, on April 15, 2009, reported that the White House requested that Georgetown University cover its monogram "IHS"—symbolizing the name of Jesus Christ—because it was inscribed on a pediment on the stage where President Obama spoke at the university.

How dramatically different from President George Washington, father of our nation, who said, "It is impossible to rightly govern the world without God and the Bible."[6]

Abraham Lincoln, who is recognized by historians as the greatest president in the history of the United States said, speaking of the Bible, "All the Good Savior gave to the world was communicated through this Bible."[7]

Listen to these words from two of our Founding Fathers who had no shame in the proclamation of their faith: "We recognize no Sovereign but God and no king but Jesus."[8] These are the words of John Hancock and John Adams.

Pity! The good savior's name is covered up at Georgetown University to prevent unbelievers from being offended. The Bible says, "But whoever denies me before men, him I will also deny you before my Father who is in heaven (Matthew 10:33 NKJV).

In the Third Reich, block wardens who monitored their neighbors, waiters who reported on their patrons, workers who made note of employer violations, and children who reported on their parents were a reality.[9] "Thought police" in West Virginia and elsewhere have been trained to do the very same things—listen in and report any speech "violations" to law enforcement officials.

Samuel Kent, a federal judge, ruled in 1995 that if American students prayed in the name of Jesus, they would be sentenced to a six-month jail term. Now you can take Jesus' name in vain. You can soak his cross in urine for your art project as practice for when you are funded by the National Endowment for the Arts. But you had better not pray, or you're going to jail.

Samuel Kent is not from China or the former Soviet Union. He is from the United States of America. He is just trying to make America resemble the former Soviet Union.[10]

TWELVE

Armageddon: The Final Battle for Planet Earth

Armageddon is the mother of all battles that will determine who rules and reigns on planet Earth. It is not one battle; it is a desperate three-and-a-half-year campaign by the King of the North (Russia), the King of the South (Islamic nations), the King of the East (China), and the King of the West (led by the Antichrist and the European Union).

In the final battle, John the Revelator describes scenes of absolute horror that stagger the human mind. So many will be slaughtered in this final fight that human blood will flow for two hundred miles up to the horses' bridles. Unbelievable!

> So the angel thrust his sickle into the earth and gathered the vine of the earth, and threw it into the great winepress of the wrath of God. And the winepress was trampled outside the city, blood came out of the winepress, up to the horses' bridles, for one thousand six hundred furlongs.
>
> —*Revelation 14:19–20*

One thousand six hundred furlongs is two hundred miles.

Armageddon is the great finale of the Prince of Darkness to rule and reign planet Earth. This battle between good and evil, light and darkness, began with the war in the heavenlies before the book of Genesis was ever written.

This supernatural war was brought to Earth in the Garden of Eden.

Adam and Eve fell to the seductive powers of the serpent and the forces of evil. They were driven out of the garden by angels with flaming swords to live under the curse God spoke into existence all the days of their lives.

God Almighty then sought for Himself a special people who would serve Him only, who would turn from evil, who would bring the Torah of God to mankind, who would bear the torch of truth for generations to come. He chose Abraham who, in time, produced the Jewish people.

God gave Abraham and his seed a royal land grant called the Promised Land by an everlasting covenant (see Genesis 17:7–8) that remains in effect until this day. Out of Abraham's loins came the nation of Israel, the apple of God's eye, and the target of the legions of the Prince of Darkness. The battle of light verses darkness that started in the Garden of Eden continued to rage.

The history of Israel in the Old Testament is the history of Satan's agenda to wipe the chosen people off the face of the earth. The Jewish people would produce the patriarchs: Abraham, Isaac, and Jacob. The Jewish people produced the prophets and the first family of Christianity: Mary, Joseph, and Jesus. The Jewish people produced the twelve disciples, the Apostle Paul, and, of utmost importance in world history, the Word of God. God's promise to Abraham was kept: "And in you all the families of the earth shall be blessed" (Genesis 12:3).

Coming out of Egypt, the Jewish people were attacked by the Amalekites, whose objective was extermination. The seed of Abraham during the reign of the Persian Empire was threatened with the first holocaust plot through the evil mind of Haman. God spared the chosen people through the courage of a Jewish beauty named Esther and the fasting and prayer of the nation of Israel.

In the time of Christ, the iron fist of the Roman Empire ruled the Jewish people. In 70 A.D., Titus attacked the city of Jerusalem, destroyed Herod's temple, and, according to the historian Josephus, killed approximately 1 million Jews. Seventy thousand Jewish men were taken as slaves back to Rome to build the coliseum, where Christians would later be fed to the lions for Rome's amusement. Other Jews would be sold into slavery throughout the Mediterranean basin, beginning what history calls the Diaspora: the dispersal of the Jews.

Sixty years later, in 130 A.D., Rome sent Hadrian to slaughter once again the Jews of Jerusalem. Within three hundred years of the death of

Jesus Christ, who taught the foundational truth of "Love thy neighbor as thyself," people who called themselves Christians were killing Jews in the name of God. Then came the Crusaders who slaughtered tens of thousands of Jewish people, because they refused to convert to Christianity.

Following the Crusades came the Spanish Inquisition, the brutality of which, under the banner of the cross of Christ, would make you sick to your stomach.

Following the Spanish Inquisition came the living hell and horror of Adolf Hitler and the Holocaust in the twentieth century. The evil seed of anti-Semitism produced a harvest of hatred.

Why?

In my judgment, because the Jewish people from the beginning of time have been the source of divine light, and the Prince of Darkness has fought them relentlessly. Every Christian on earth is indebted to the Jewish people for the monumental sacrifices they have paid from the beginning of time to bring light and truth to "those that sat in darkness" (see Luke 2:32). Jesus said in John 4:22, "Salvation is of the Jews."

What does that mean?

That means if you take away the Jewish contribution to the world, there would be no Christianity. Judaism does not need Christianity to explain its existence; on the other hand, Christianity cannot explain its existence without Judaism.

What does this have to do with the Battle of Armageddon? Armageddon is the final battle between light and darkness and takes place on the exact piece of real estate God gave to Abraham and the Jewish people forever. The Jewish people, who were given the light of truth, are once again being attacked by the disciples of the Prince of Darkness. World history has come full circle; it's ending where it began.

Armageddon is the Hebrew word that means the *mountain of Megeddo,* which lies east of Mount Carmel in the northern part of Israel. This battlefield is a great extended plain stretching from the Mediterranean Sea eastward across the northern part of Israel.

For the first time in world history and for the right motives, the armies of the world are in perfect position to fulfill their prophetic destiny. Russia, the king of the north, has a "hook in their jaw" and God is dragging them along with the Iranian Islamic coalition toward the hills of Israel (see Ezekiel 38:5–6). God is bringing the nations of the

world to crush them as grapes of wrath in His winepress. King David
writes:

> *Behold, He who keeps Israel shall neither slumber nor sleep.*
> *—Psalm 121:4 NKJV*

After watching the Jews of the Holocaust walk into the gas chambers,
after seeing the "apple of His eye" thrown into ovens and their ashes
dumped by the tons into the rivers of Europe, after seeing the "land of
milk and honey" run red with Jewish blood in five major wars for freedom and endless suicide bombers slaughter the innocent, God stands up
and shouts to the nations of the world, ENOUGH! "MY FURY SHALL
COME UP IN MY FACE" (see Ezekiel 38:18).[1]

GOD RELEASES HIS WRATH AGAINST ISRAEL'S ENEMIES: ENOUGH IS ENOUGH!

God shatters His longstanding silence.

> *"'Surely in that day there shall be a great earthquake in the land of*
> *Israel, so that the fish of the sea, the birds of the heavens, the beasts of*
> *the field, all creeping things that creep on the earth, and all men who*
> *are on the face of the earth shall shake at My presence. The mountains*
> *shall be thrown down, the steep places shall fall, and every wall shall*
> *fall to the ground.' "I will call for a sword against Gog throughout all*
> *My mountains," says the LORD. "Every man's sword will be against*
> *his brother. And I will bring him to judgment with pestilence and*
> *bloodshed; I will rain down on him, on his troops, and on the many*
> *peoples who are with him, flooding rain, great hailstones, fire, and*
> *brimstone. Thus I will magnify Myself and sanctify Myself, and I will*
> *be known in the eyes of many nations. Then they shall know that I am*
> *the LORD."*
> *—Ezekiel 38:19–23 NKJV*

Here comes the judge of all the earth and He is HOT! God releases
His supernatural wrath against Israel's enemies with lethal results.

First, God will shake the Middle East with a mighty earthquake that will neutralize every tank and every foot soldier instantly. Many will doubtless be buried alive.

Second, God will cause mass confusion to come upon every invading army on the hills of Israel. The invading armies will turn their weapons on each other, which is called, in modern combat, "death by friendly fire."

This combat technique God used when He commanded Gideon to blow the trumpets and break the pitchers. The Philistines became divinely confused and turned their swords on each other. Gideon won a great military victory without one casualty; what God has done He will do again in the Middle East when Iran and Russia invade Israel.

Third, the prophet Ezekiel states that God "will rain down . . . on his troops (those who are invading Israel), and on many peoples who are with him . . . great hailstones, fire, and brimstone" (Ezekiel 38:22 NKJV).

Ezekiel's graphic account in chapter 39 makes clear just how thorough and disastrous the defeat of Russia, Iran, Ethiopia, Libya, Turkey, and the massive Islamic coalition that will invade the land of Israel in the future (see Ezekiel 38:5–6).

Ezekiel opens chapter 39 by stating: "I am against thee, O Gog." When what is left of the world living in the Tribulation looks at the millions of bloated bodies in the warm Israeli sun, this statement will go down in history as one of the greatest understatements of all time.

In this passage God does not tell us how many died; He tells us how many are left: only a "sixth part" (Ezekiel 39:2 KJV). That means that the casualty rate for this battle will be 84 percent, unheard of in modern warfare.

The narrative of the aftermath of the war continues. Ezekiel says that the bloated bodies of the enemies of Israel will be a banquet for buzzards. The beast of the field will have a feast unlike anything since dogs ate the body of Jezebel (see Ezekiel 39:5–7, 11–16).

The dead bodies of the invaders will be strewn in the fields in the mountains of Israel, and the burial detail will take seven months and will involve all the people of Israel. Ezekiel hints very strongly that even tourists will be asked to look for stray bodies to mark the spot for burial details. *Hamon-Gog* is a Hebrew word for "the multitude of Gog," which is to become the name of this vast cemetery for the invaders of Israel (see Ezekiel 39:17–20).

But not only is there tremendous carnage, the weapons left by these devastated forces provide fuel for Israel for seven years—in other words, beyond the Tribulation and into the Millennium (see Ezekiel 39:9–10).[2]

GOD MAGNIFIES HIMSELF

Why does God allow the nations to make war upon Israel? First of all: for the glory of God. Ezekiel makes it very clear that the world will know that the God of Abraham, Isaac, and Jacob is God Almighty.

Ezekiel declares:

> *"Thus I will magnify Myself and sanctify Myself, and I will be known in the eyes of many nations. Then they shall know that I* am *the LORD."*
>
> *—38:23 NKJV*

The earth is full of many gods but who is the Almighty God? When the God of Abraham, Isaac, and Jacob finishes mopping up the enemies of Israel on the mountains of Israel (note that Jerusalem and the cities of Israel are saved), there will be no doubt that Jehovah God is the Almighty God.[3]

> *"It will be in the latter days that I will bring you against My land, so that the nations may know Me, when I am hallowed in you, O Gog, before their eyes."*
>
> *—Ezekiel 38:16 NKJV*

The drama of Ezekiel 38–39 and the crushing defeat of Russia, the king of the north, and the Islamic coalition, the king of the south, is a demonstration of God's power not seen in the defense of Israel since Pharaoh and his army were drowned in the Red Sea. Those nations that are bragging about wiping Israel off the map are only predicting their own future.

All Israel Shall Be Saved

A second reason for this great display of God's awesome power is to testify to His beloved Jewish people that He alone is their God. Through their miraculous deliverance, the hearts of the Jewish people will be turned to the God of Abraham, Isaac, and Jacob and "all Israel will be saved" (Romans 11:26 NKJV).

> *"So the house of Israel shall know that I* am *the LORD their God from that day forward. The Gentiles shall know that the house of Israel went into captivity for their iniquity; because they were unfaithful to Me, therefore I hid My face from them. I gave them into the hand of their enemies, and they all fell by the sword. According to their uncleanness and according to their transgressions I have dealt with them, and hidden My face from them."*
>
> *Therefore thus says the Lord GOD: "Now I will bring back the captives of Jacob, and have mercy on the whole house of Israel; and I will be jealous for My holy name—after they have borne their shame, and all their unfaithfulness in which they were unfaithful to Me, when they dwelt safely in their* own *land and no one made* them *afraid. When I have brought them back from the peoples and gathered them out of their enemies' lands, and I am hallowed in them in the sight of many nations, then they shall know that I* am *the LORD their God, who sent them into captivity among the nations, but also brought them back into their land, and left none of them captive any longer. And I will not hide My face from them anymore; for I shall have poured out My Spirit on the house of Israel," says the Lord GOD.*
>
> *—Ezekiel 39:22–29 NKJV*

Note carefully that the Jewish people at this point in time do not recognize Jesus as the Messiah. The Bible is very clear that this will happen at the end of the Tribulation, when the Jewish people . . .

> *"will look on Me whom they pierced. Yes, they will mourn for Him as one mourns for* his *only son, and grieve for Him as one grieves for a firstborn."*
>
> *—Zechariah 12:10 NKJV*

That is the day, the Scripture declares, when "all Israel will be saved" (Romans 11:26).

Because of this colossal battle on the soil of Israel, the Jewish people will abandon their disastrous relationship with the Antichrist and begin turning toward the Most High God.

The question is, where was the Antichrist? Didn't he guarantee peace and safety for Israel in the Seven-Year Peace Treaty? The Jewish people recognize that the Antichrist did not resist the Russian-Islamic coalition, that the Antichrist is another false messiah who is, at this point, wounded in the head and presumed dead.

Upon his miraculous recovery, most of the world will worship him, but as the son of Prince of Darkness, he will turn on the children of Light (the Jewish people) with a vengeance. They will take refuge in Jordan at the natural fortress known as Petra. There they will be divinely protected and provided for by God Himself for three and a half years until the battle is over.

NEWS FROM THE EAST

China, the king of the east, needs the oil of the Persian Gulf, just as did Russia. China will gather an army of two hundred million men and march them down the dry riverbed of the Euphrates River toward Israel. In Revelation 16:12, we read,

The sixth angel poured out his bowl on the great river Euphrates, and the water was dried up, so that the way of the kings of the east might be prepared (NKJV).

The Antichrist, who intended to pursue the Jewish people to Petra, stops in his tracks when he hears news from the east that troubles him deeply and forces him to change course instantly.

But news from the east . . . shall trouble him; therefore he shall go out with great fury to destroy and annihilate many. And he shall plant the tents of his palace between the seas and the glorious holy mountain; yet he shall come to his end, and no one will help him.
—Daniel 11:44–45 NKJV

Given these facts, describing the Antichrist as "troubled" is without doubt an understatement. He will fight with the forces of China and those Asian countries that come with them who are called in Scripture the kings of the east, for world supremacy.

The Antichrist has three additional allies of his own that are supremely powerful: Satan; the False Prophet, with his ability to call fire down from heaven; and the image of the Beast, which has the power to destroy those who refuse to obey the Antichrist. This grand finale is the mother of all battles.

The Antichrist is the commander of a large military force in Israel and is across the Mediterranean Sea from his supply bases. Daniel writes that the Antichrist will "plant the tabernacle of his palace between the seas in the glorious holy mountain" (Daniel 11:45).

The glorious holy mountain is Jerusalem. "Between the seas" is obviously between the Dead Sea and the Mediterranean Sea. Here the Antichrist, the leader of the European Union, decides he is going to meet this 200 million-strong marching army by setting himself up in the mountains of Judea where there will be some natural defenses.

To conclude this Armageddon campaign, we turn to Revelation chapter 19, where planet earth will have another invasion. This invasion is not from the king of the north; it's not from the king of the south; it's not from the king of the east or west . . . it's from the King of kings and Lord of lords. It's from Jesus Christ, the son of David, who has come for the second time to claim His throne on the Temple Mount to begin the Golden Age of Peace that will last for one thousand years.

ISRAEL'S ENEMIES ANNIHILATED

The second coming of Jesus Christ to the battle of Armageddon is one of the towering historical moments in world history. It is also the most staggering defeat that any military coalition has ever suffered. There will be no survivors! No one can improve on John's majestic description of this event in Revelation 19:

I saw heaven standing open and there before me was a white horse, whose rider is called Faithful and True. With justice he judges and

makes war. His eyes are like blazing fire, and on his head are many
crowns. He has a name written on him that no one knows but he
himself. He is dressed in a robe dipped in blood, and his name is the
Word of God. The armies of heaven were following him, riding on
white horses and dressed in fine linen, white and clean. Coming out
of his mouth is a sharp sword with which to strike down the nations.

"He will rule them with an iron scepter." He treads the winepress of
the fury of the wrath of God Almighty. On his robe and on his thigh
he has this name written: KING OF KINGS AND LORD OF
LORDS.

And I saw an angel standing in the sun, who cried in a loud voice
to all the birds flying in midair, "Come, gather together for the great
supper of God, so that you may eat the flesh of kings, generals, and the
mighty, of horses and their riders, and the flesh of all people, free and
slave, small and great."

Then I saw the beast [the Antichrist] and the kings of the earth
and their armies gathered together to wage war against the rider on
the horse and his army [Jesus, His angels, and the saints raptured to
heaven at the very beginning of the Tribulation]. But the beast was
captured, and with it the false prophet who had performed the signs
on his behalf. With these signs he had deluded those who had received
the mark of the beast and worshipped its image. The two of them were
thrown alive into the fiery lake of burning sulfur. The rest were killed
with the sword coming out of the mouth of the rider on the horse, and
all the birds gorged themselves on their flesh.

—verses 11–21 NIV

Think of it! There are 200 millions soldiers fighting for the kings of
the east led by China. There has to be that many soldiers fighting for
the kings of the west, which would be the European Union and what's
left of America. The battle begins, and the invasion from heaven happens. There are only two survivors—the beast and the False Prophet
who are thrown into the lake of fire. The hand of God kills every other
soldier, general, king, and mighty man. Their bodies are eaten by
buzzards.

"I WILL CURSE HIM WHO CURSES YOU"

The armies of the world will be defeated, but the Jewish people—the object of God's loyal covenant love—will totally be protected.

One of the most commonly ignored biblical principles is this: What men and nations do to Israel, God repays them exactly and in the same manner. Where is Pharaoh and his mighty army that pursued the Jewish people at the Sea of Reeds? Pharaoh told the Egyptian midwives to drown Jewish male children; God repaid Pharaoh by drowning him and his army in the Red Sea.

Where are the Babylonians?

Where are the Greeks?

Where are the Romans and their mighty empire?

Where is the Ottoman Empire?

All are buried in the boneyard of human history because they forgot the Bible principle God made to Abraham and the Jewish people when he said,

> *I will bless those who bless you, and I will curse him who curses you.*
> —*Genesis 12:3 NKJV*

The Antichrist will track down, torment, and attempt to destroy Israel; in return, God will track down, torment, and annihilate him and his forces from the face of the earth. The true Messiah will come, bringing the armies of heaven with Him, and the Antichrist and his forces will be demolished.[4]

Remember, what you do to the Jewish people will be done to you. Two-thirds of the Jews of Europe were killed by Adolf Hitler in the Holocaust while the world was silent. During the Tribulation, one-third of the population of earth will be destroyed. There is a payday someday!

For the righteous there is hope in the living God!

For those who reject the Torah of God, there is the Great Tribulation, the last seven years on earth that will be a living hell. Which do you choose?

PART FIVE

Hope for a Troubled Nation

THIRTEEN

Hope for the Troubled Heart

After reading several hundred pages of gut-wrenching facts concerning the reality of our past and the dire threat to America's future, this question must be asked: "Is there hope for America?"

Absolutely!

Hope for the future is the anchor of the soul, the call to action, and the motivation to achievement.

Every farmer who plants a seed joins in partnership with God for the future. If the farmer plants no seed, he has no right to expect anything in his future but hunger and starvation. If he plants a small amount of seed, he can hope for a limited harvest and some hardship. If he plants abundant seed, he has the right to hope for a barn-bursting harvest and blessings he cannot contain.

This book is a call to action for the American people to storm the voting booths on every election day and vote out of public office all whose policies call for America to slip into the sewer of socialism. Hope is born in action!

If it were not for hope, the heart would break. Lost hope is the undertaker's best friend. Hope is God's gift to those who take action. Take action to control your life or someone else will.

The prophet Jeremiah writes,

For I know the plans I have for you, declares the LORD, plans to prosper you for good and not to harm you, plans to give you a hope and a future.

—*Jeremiah 29:11 NIV*

King David put his pen to parchment declaring the source of all hope: "Hope thou in God" (Psalms 42:5 NKJV). If you depend on the government and other people to provide for you, you will live your life going from one disappointment to a greater disappointment. God is your source, not Washington, DC.

St. Paul writes, "Now abideth faith, hope and charity"— "charity" is in fact love (1 Corinthians 13:13 NKJV).

This hope *we have as an anchor of the soul, both sure and steadfast, and which enters the* Presence *behind the veil.*
> —*Hebrews 6:19 NKJV*

Hope sees the invisible and achieves the impossible. As long as there is life, there is hope.

A number of years ago, in a mental institution outside Boston, a young girl known as "Little Annie" was locked in a dungeon. The dungeon was the only place, said the doctors, for those who were hopelessly insane. In Little Annie's case, they saw no hope for her, so she was consigned to a living death in a small cage that received little light and less hope. During Annie's confinement, an elderly nurse was nearing retirement. She felt there was hope for all of God's children, so she started taking her lunch into the dungeon and eating outside Little Annie's cage. She felt perhaps she should communicate some love and hope to the little girl.

In many ways, Little Annie was like an animal. On occasions she would violently attack the person who came into her cage. At other times, she would completely ignore them. When the elderly nurse started visiting her, Little Annie gave no indication that she was even aware of her presence.

One day, the elderly nurse brought some brownies to the dungeon and left them outside the cage. Little Annie gave no hint that she knew they were there, but when the nurse returned the next day, the brownies were gone. From that time on, the nurse would bring brownies when she made her Thursday visit.

Soon after, the doctors in the institution noticed a change was taking place. After a period of time, they decided to move Little Annie upstairs. Finally, the day came when the "hopeless case" was told she could return home. But Little Annie did not wish to leave. She chose to stay, to help others.

It was she who cared for, taught, and nurtured Helen Keller, for Little Annie's name was Annie Sullivan. Hope had achieved the impossible.[1] Hope is the source of all joy!

There is hope for anyone who can look in a mirror and laugh at what they see. Hope is not found in a bottle; hope is not found in a prescription; hope is not found in an erotic sexual affair; hope is not found in illegal drugs that dull the mind in an effort to reach some magical Shangri-la. "Be joyful in hope" (Romans 12:12 NKJV) and recognize that all true hope comes from God (see Psalm 42:5).

Hope produces the confidence you need to achieve your dreams and reach your destiny. Take away hope, and life—with all of its fascinating opportunities—is reduced to a dull existence.

A man in his middle years was on a Caribbean cruise. On the first day out he noticed an attractive woman about his age who smiled at him in a friendly way as he passed her on the deck, which pleased him. That night he managed to get seated at the same table with her for dinner.

As the conversation developed, he commented that he had seen her on the deck that day and he had appreciated her friendly smile. When she heard this, she smiled and commented, "Well, the reason I smiled was that I was immediately struck by your strong resemblance to my third husband."

At this he pricked up his ears and said, "Oh, how many times have you been married?"

She looked down at her plate, smiled demurely, and answered, "Twice."[2]

LIFE WITHOUT HOPE

Without hope, life becomes bleak, drab, joyless, a burden, and a never-ending pain. People without hope sink into depression and despair, and life becomes meaningless.

Recently, the Associated Press carried the story of four teenagers who locked themselves in a car and committed suicide by carbon monoxide poisoning. They left a note written on a brown paper bag asking to be buried together.

Why would four young people from an affluent neighborhood, living in the wealthiest nation on earth, choose to kill themselves? Why is the suicide rate among America's teenagers running off the charts? The answer is they have lost their hope for the future.

I repeat, lost hope is the undertaker's best friend. Many people no longer hope for the best; they just hope to avoid the worst. You will not succeed in life without hope.

There is hope for a brighter tomorrow!

There is hope for your dreams to come true!

There is hope that will never fail you, provided that hope is in God. King David puts his pen to parchment and declared for all the world to read, "Hope thou in God!" (Psalm 42:5 NKJV).

Hope in God is not wishful thinking; it's alive!

Hope in God is real, it's eternal, it's powerful, and it's available for the asking.

For our heart shall rejoice in Him, Because we have trusted in His holy name. Let Your mercy, O Lord, be upon us, Just as we hope in You.
—Psalms 33:21–22

Hope in God will make you laugh and sing again, and it will lift you up from the depths of despair and depression and motivate you to try again.

THE GOD OF HOPE

Now may the God of hope fill you with all joy and peace in believing, that you may abound in hope by the power of the Holy Spirit.
—Romans 15:13 NKJV

Hope in God is faith looking at the promises of the Lord, knowing with absolute assurance that what God has done in the past He can do for you today.

Allow me to tell you a true story of a newspaper reporter and his wife who had "the impossible dream" of having a child.

I was preaching in Pennsylvania, and just before the first service was to begin in the three-night crusade, I was approached by a young and handsome newspaper reporter. He wanted to do a story on the Pennsylvania crusade, which had attracted thousands of people who packed the arena.

I gave him the interview and asked him in closing, "Are you a Christian?" He looked at me for a long moment and then confessed, "I am an atheist."

I smiled and responded, "Why would your newspaper send an atheist to cover a Christian event?" He responded, "This crusade has attracted thousands of people and it's news. I'm a newsman who reports the news."

"But why are you an atheist?" I probed.

"I am an atheist because I can't see God do anything in the lives of people." He was very polite but very direct, which I appreciated.

"What is it in your life you would like for God to do for you? What is your impossible dream?" He hesitated for a long moment, took a deep breath and said: "My wife and I have been married for fifteen years and would love to have a child. We have not been successful in becoming pregnant. The doctor says it's not going to happen. It's a dream that will never come true."

I told him to bring his wife to the crusade the next night and I would pray for her to conceive a child. He quickly told me, "I don't believe in things like that!"

I responded, "I am not depending on your faith; I'm depending on my faith in what I know God can do . . . even for an atheist." He was stunned. Only after he was totally convinced I truly wanted to pray for his wife did he finally agree to come to the crusade the next night.

The following evening, thirty minutes before the crusade service was about to begin, the reporter and his attractive wife appeared backstage. I took them into a room and explained that God had all power in heaven and on earth and that she would have a child as a direct result of this prayer. She smiled and shyly said, "I hope so."

I responded, "That's all it takes . . . hope!"

I anointed her with oil and prayed that God would cause her to conceive a child with her husband. After the prayer, both of them disappeared into the audience, and I did not see them again until two years later.

I was speaking in Roanoke, Virginia, and was sitting in the green-room of the coliseum waiting for the service to begin. The security guard knocked on the door and said, "Pastor, there's a man from the press who wants to see you."

Thinking it was a local newspaper reporter I said, "No, it's too near service time." The security guard left and knocked on the door a second time five minutes later and said, "This newspaper reporter is the man and wife you prayed for in Pennsylvania to have a baby. I think you want to see them."

"Indeed I do!"

In the door came a beaming husband and wife pushing a baby carriage filled with two beautiful identical twin girls. The mother looked at me and said, "We are big believers now! Our hope is in God and the promises of His Word." With hope in God, they had achieved their impossible dream . . . just as you can.

Atheists, agnostics, and pseudo-intellectuals oppose hope because they see it as escapism from reality. One of the most brilliant thinkers in world history wrote these words: "The world through wisdom did not know God."[3]

Brilliant minds may know some things yet not know the best things. Men may treasure rags and throw away priceless pearls.

A man may know all about rocks and his heart be as hard as a rock. A man may know about the tides of the sea and his life resemble the words of the prophet Isaiah:

> *The wicked* are *like the troubled sea, when it cannot rest, whose waters cast up mire and dirt.*
>
> —*Isaiah 57:20 NKJV*

A man may know all about the light of a million stars, the light of the moon when it hangs in the sky like a sickle and yet not know the God of heaven who is the Father of Lights.

What shall it profit a man if he is the world's greatest investor and does not know the Pearl of Great Price?

What shall it profit a man if he is a great doctor and does not know the Great Physician?

What shall it profit a man if he is the greatest farmer in the world and does not know the Lord of the Harvest?

What shall it profit a man if he is the world's most renowned florist and does not know the Rose of Sharon or the Lily of the Valley?

What shall it profit a man if he is an accomplished geologist and does not know the Rock of Ages?

What shall it profit a man if he is a wise judge and does not know the Righteous Judge?

What shall it profit a man if he is a respected scholar and does not know the Incarnate Truth?

What shall it profit a man if he is the wisest man on earth and yet lives without hope?

Our hope is based on the Word of God.

Our hope is steadfast, sure, and unshakable.

Our hope gives us a song in the night.

Our hope looks at the coming storm and shouts with joy, "The anchor holds." Hope sees the invisible, hope feels the intangible, and achieves the impossible.

HOPE AGAINST ALL ODDS

Some of the most celebrated lives in the world overcame physical challenges against all odds to live lives of greatness recognized around the world.

Helen Keller was both blind and deaf, yet she graduated from college with honors.

Glenn Cunningham was burnt over 90 percent of his body in a schoolhouse fire and his doctors said the massive scars would prevent him from walking again! Wrong! Glenn Cunningham set a world record running the mile; he became a world champion.

Alexander the Great conquered much of the known world yet suffered with epilepsy.

Michael Jordan—arguably the greatest basketball player to walk on the court, whose heroic exploits will be told and retold for a hundred years—was cut from the basketball team when he was in ninth grade.

Beethoven, whose musical compositions have inspired the world, became deaf!

Itzhak Perlman, a Jewish violinist whose musical skill has hushed the angels in heaven, contracted polio at the age of four. Against all odds he pressed on, mastered the violin, and sits in a chair while the world listens in absolute amazement.

COTTON PATCH ECONOMICS 101

One day we worry about going to the poorhouse, and the next day we buy a new car. There are a lot of hot arguments over cold cash.

My father was the pastor of a small church in a small town in southeast Texas. I was born toward the end of the Great Depression and before World War II.

Money was extremely tight. Then, as now, the poor complained about the money they couldn't get, and the rich complained about the money they couldn't keep.

My mother, who was the vortex of my universe, had a solution to all financial problems: Work! Mother was a Bible school graduate and a fabulous Bible teacher. Her mantra was "The Bible teaches work-fare . . . not welfare." Go to work!

In keeping with her mantra, when I was eight years old, my mother took me to the fields of a cotton farmer who attended our church. For the benefit of our young readers, cotton-picking machines in those days were called people. I was about to become one of those people.

When we arrived at the cotton fields, I was given a sixteen-foot cotton sack, pointed down a thousand-foot cotton row, and told to keep picking until I got to the end.

As I looked down that cotton row, it seemed to touch the horizon on the other end. I asked the farmer, "How do you get to the end of this row?"

He said something that stayed with me for the rest of my life . . . "Head down, hiney up! Don't stop until you get to the end of the row."

I was paid one dollar per hundred pounds. That summer I became a born-again tightwad. Every dime I spent, I calculated how long it took me to earn it in that blazing hot East Texas cotton patch.

I learned some valuable lessons in that cotton patch that have benefited me for a lifetime. I challenge you to try them in your life; they have been tested and proven in the battlefield of time.

Lesson One: *If you have a financial problem, work your way out of it!*
Stop blaming other people and circumstances, and stop looking to the government or your rich relatives to bail you out.

God gave you two ends to accomplish your divine destiny: A head with which to think and a behind upon which to sit. Heads, we win; tails, we lose. Nothing will work in your life until you do! You can't spend your way to wealth. Debts are the only thing you can acquire without money.

Grab your cotton sack and start picking! Financial success is at the end of the row.

Lesson Two: *Decide what you want your money to do.*
At the end of the cotton-picking season, I put my last "cotton-picking money" in a cigar box. Why a cigar box? Because a piggy bank cost money and a cigar box was free!

As I stared at my fortune in the cigar box with pure lust and pleasure, my economics professor, aka mother, asked me, "What are you going to do with that money?" My mother was not given to idle conversation. If she asked you a question, she was not looking for information. She had the answer before she started talking. I stalled for time to think of an intelligent response to her question.

"I really don't know!" I offered.

"Let's think about that," she said. "You've been dragging that sixteen-foot cotton sack for weeks, and you don't have a plan for spending your money?"

Mother could see through me like an MRI X-ray. She knew I had an exact plan for every dime of that money. As I stared into the contents of the cigar box, my newly acquired fortune, Mom opened up her Cotton Patch Economics 101 lecture with, "That money represents your life!"

"What do you mean?"

"I mean you gave your summer to earn that money, and when you spend money for which you gave the time of your life to earn, you should be able to put your hands on what it produced. Make this money—and every dime you earn for the rest of your life—count for something."

That Saturday Mom and I drove to the downtown metroplex of Goose Creek, Texas, and purchased blue jeans, sports shirts, and tennis shoes. It was a shopping trip I did not enjoy, but I certainly learned a lesson of a lifetime.

I brought these practical and beneficial purchases home, laid them out on the bed, and my mother said, "That's what you accomplished this summer with your money. Son, always remember to make your money produce something tangible and make it work for you."

So I ask you, as the reader, what do you want your money to do for you?

1. Pay off debt?

2. Save for desired goals?

3. Go toward your retirement?

4. Give you the trip of a lifetime to Europe or to Israel?

5. Contribute to your children's college fund?

6. Save for your needs as a family, such as a better car (not necessarily a new car, because a significant percentage of value is lost the moment you drive a new car off the lot)?

Take a pad and pen to review what your money is or is not doing for you. Are you working for it, or is it working for you?

Lesson 3: *Your attitude toward money reveals your attitude toward God.*
Before mother and I went on the shopping trip to Goose Creek, we had a heart-to-heart conversation about the "t" word . . . tithing.

Before we left for shopping, Mother sat me down as I held the cigar box and told me that 10 percent of everything I earned belonged to God. It did not sit well with me. As an eight-year-old child, *tithing* was just a word . . . but it was about to become an experience.

"Why should I tithe?" I heard myself screaming. "I worked for that money. That money belongs to me!"

"Wrong! The first ten percent of everything you make belongs to God. God gave you the health and strength to earn that money. The life you have is God's gift to you; what you do with your life is your gift to God."

I wasn't going to go down without swinging. "Where does it say that in the Bible?" In my house, if you had a Bible verse to back it up, you could do anything.

Mother was a walking Bible. She looked at me and said: "I can quote it or I can read it."

I was now playing hardball. "I want to see it in print."

Mother found her Bible and opened it to Malachi chapter 3, verses 8–11, which reads:

"Will a man rob God? Yet you have robbed Me! But you say, 'In what way have we robbed You?' In tithes and offerings. You are cursed with a curse, for you have robbed Me, even this whole nation. Bring all the tithes into the storehouse, that there may be food in My house, and try Me now in this," says the LORD of hosts, "If I will not open for you the windows of heaven and pour out for you such blessing that there will not be room enough to receive it. And I will rebuke the devourer for your sakes, so that he will not destroy the fruit of your ground, nor shall the vine fail to bear fruit for you in the field," says the LORD of hosts. (NKJV)

I am now seventy years of age and for sixty-two years, I have tithed to God the first fruits of every dime I have ever made. I can testify to the financial reality that God has "opened the windows of heaven and blessed me with blessings for which there is not enough room to store."

If you don't tithe, you are in rebellion to God and will live every day of your life under a financial curse (see Malachi 8:9).

It's your choice! Every time the offering pan passes in your church, you are determining your financial future. If you give abundantly, you will receive abundantly. If you give sparingly, you will receive sparingly. If you give nothing you will never prosper.

Givers gain!

GIVE UP EVERY IDEA OF QUITTING

A mother, wishing to encourage her young son's progress at the piano, bought tickets for a Paderewski performance. When the night arrived, they found their seats near the front of the concert hall and eyed the majestic Steinway waiting on stage. Soon the mother found a friend to talk to, and the boy slipped away. When eight o'clock arrived, the spotlights came on, the audience quieted, and only then did they notice the boy up on the bench, innocently picking out "Twinkle, Twinkle, Little Star."

His mother gasped, but before she could retrieve her son, the master appeared on the stage and quickly moved to the keyboard. He whispered to the boy, "Don't quit—keep playing." Leaning over, Paderewski reached down with his left hand and began filling in a bass part. Soon his right arm reached around the other side, encircling the child, to add a running obbligato. Together, the old master and the young novice held the crowd mesmerized. In our lives, unpolished though we may be, it is the Master who surrounds us and whispers in our ear, time and again, "Don't quit—keep playing."[4]

FOURTEEN

Hope for America

A merican history is being rewritten in an effort to destroy the portrait of our founding fathers as being men of faith, hope, and charity.

What were our founding fathers really like? What did they truly believe? What were the foundations they established for America with their blood, sweat, and tears? "If the foundations be destroyed, what can the righteous do?"

Can America survive?

Yes we can—if we the people take action and return to our spiritual and moral foundations established by the founding fathers of America. If we do not take action, America's best days are behind us. Our children and grandchildren will become economic slaves to a socialist state because our generation failed to control its spending and get its financial house in order.

HOPE OF OUR FOUNDING FATHERS

What did our founding forefathers truly believe? Consider the following:

John Adams, the second president of the United States, said: "The general principles upon which the Fathers achieved independence were the general principles of Christianity . . . and I avow that I believed and now believe that those general principles of Christianity are as eternal and immutable as the existence and attributes of God."[1]

Samuel Adams, signer of the Declaration of Independence, said: "He who made all men hath made the truths necessary to human happiness obvious to all . . . our Forefathers opened the Bible to all."[2]

The Declaration of Independence recognized the existence and belief in an almighty and sovereign God saying: "We hold these truths to be self evident, that we are endowed by our Creator with certain inalienable rights that among these are life, liberty and the pursuit of happiness."

The founders made it clear to all Americans for generations to come that "Life, liberty and the pursuit of happiness" do not come from the government . . . they are gifts of a sovereign God.

The founding fathers were a core group of fifty-five men who met at the Constitutional Convention and laid the moral and spiritual foundations of America.

History records that in this delegation of fifty-five men, twenty-eight were Episcopalians, eight Presbyterians, seven Congregationalists, two Lutherans, two Dutch Reform, two Methodists, two Roman Catholics, three Deists, and one unknown. While all were not Christians, 93 percent of its members were members of Christian churches and all proclaimed the Bible to be the foundation of America.[3]

What positive action can we as Americans take to bring about a rebirth of hope for the future of our nation, our children, and our grandchildren? Be inspired by the writing below, which reveals the courage, commitment, and sacrifice of the men who signed the Declaration of Independence:

Have you ever wondered what happened to those fifty-six men who signed the Declaration of Independence?

Five signers were captured by the British as traitors and tortured before they died. Twelve had their homes ransacked and burned. Two lost their sons in the Revolutionary Army, another had two sons captured. Nine fought and died from wounds or the hardships of the Revolutionary War.

What kind of men were they? Twenty-four were lawyers and jurists. Eleven were merchants, nine were farmers and large plantation owners, men of means, well educated. But they signed the Declaration of Independence knowing full well that they pledged their lives, their fortunes and their sacred honor.

Carter Braxton of Virgina, a wealthy planter and trader, saw his ships swept from seas by the British navy. He sold his home and properties to pay his debts and died in rags.

Thomas McKean was so hounded by the British that he was forced to move his family almost constantly. He served in the Congress without pay, and his family was kept in hiding. His possessions were taken from him, and poverty was his reward.

Vandals or soldiers or both looted the properties of Ellery, Clymer, Hall, Walton, Gwinnett, Heyward, Ruttledge, and Middleton.

At the Battle of Yorktown, Thomas Nelson Jr. noted that the British General Cornwallis, had taken over the Nelson home for his headquarters. The owner quietly urged General George Washington to open fire, which was done. The home was destroyed, and Nelson died bankrupt.

Francis Lewis had his home and properties destroyed. The enemy jailed his wife and she died within a few months.

John Hart was driven from his wife's bedside as she was dying. Their thirteen children fled for their lives. His fields and gristmill were laid waste. For more than a year he lived in forests and caves, returning home after the war to find his wife dead, his children vanished. A few weeks later he died from exhaustion and a broken heart.

Morris and Livingston suffered similar fates. Such were the stories and sacrifices of the American Revolution. These were not wild-eyed, rabble-rousing ruffians. These were soft-spoken men of means and education. They had security, but they valued liberty more.

Standing tall, straight and unwavering, they pledged: "For the support of this declaration, with a firm reliance on the protection of the Divine Providence, we mutually pledge to each other, our lives, our fortunes, and our sacred honor."

They gave us a free and independent America, with hope we can keep it.[4]

HOPE AND THE BLACK-ROBED REGIMENT

Another group of patriots who gave hope for a free nation to be birthed were the "Black-Robed Regiment."

So numerous were the fighting pastors that the Tories began referring to them as "the black regiment," blaming them for much of the resurging hope of the colonial troops.

One of the most colorful examples is what happened in a staid Lutheran church in the Shenandoah Valley of Virgina one Sunday morning in 1775. The thirty-year-old pastor Peter Muhlenberg delivered a rousing sermon on the text "for everything there is a season, and a time for every matter under heaven" (Ecclesiastes 3:1 NKJV).

Reaching the end of his sermon he said a solemn prayer and continued to speak. "In the language of the Holy Writ, there is a time for all things. There is a time to preach and a time to fight." He paused and then threw off his black pulpit robe to reveal the uniform of a colonel in the Continental Army. "And now is the time to fight!" he thundered, followed by his cry, "Roll the drums for recruits!"

The drums rolled, and that same afternoon he marched off at the head of a column of three hundred men. His regiment was to earn fame as the 8th Virginia, and Muhlenberg was to distinguish himself in a number of battles, rising to the rank of brigadier general in charge of Washington's first light infantry brigade.[5]

AMERICA'S ANSWER: PRAYER

What did our founding forefathers do in every hour of national crisis? The answer is . . . THEY PRAYED! Those who know and understand world and American history know that the concerted prayers of the righteous have turned the tide of history repeatedly.

When General George Washington knelt in the snows of Valley Forge to pray to the God of Abraham, Isaac, and Jacob, America was on the verge of being defeated. In the first two battles with the British army, the American farmers—poorly trained and poorly equipped—turned and ran from the battlefield.

In December of 1776, General Washington knew he needed a major breakthrough in this battle for the birth of America's freedom. Following his prayer, he made the dramatic decision to cross the Delaware River in the middle of the winter when the Hessian troops (German mercenaries fighting with the British) were camped awaiting spring.

The Hessians were shocked they were being attacked, and Washington's bold and unprecedented tactic produced a brilliant victory for America. Within weeks, Washington was commanding many thousands of volunteers who believed victory over the world's greatest army, Great

Britain, was possible. Victory did come after eight years of blood and sacrifice.

Fast forward to the Civil War when America was ripped asunder by the bitterness and rancor of slavery. Father fought against son, and brothers fought against each other, and their blood ran down a common stream in Gettysburg where 51,000 men were killed in three days. The Civil War was the most destructive war in the history of America. Every man who fell was an American.

Abraham Lincoln, a committed, Bible-believing Christian, knew America was being torn apart and called for a national day of fasting and prayer for the Congress and for all Americans.

Can you imagine someone in Washington today calling Americans for a day of fasting and prayer?

Americans responded to President Lincoln's call for a national day of fasting and prayer. Shortly thereafter, the Civil War ended with General Robert E. Lee giving a gracious surrender at Appomattox. The long and bitter war was over.

In Bible history, when Haman, the Old Testament Hitler, conspired to exterminate the Jews of Persia (modern-day Iran), Esther called for three days of fasting and prayer for God to save the Jewish people from this monstrous holocaust. God answered the prayers of the Jewish people. They were spared, and Haman, as well as his sons, hung on the gallows they had built to hang the Jews.

It's time for all Bible-believing Americans to pray for our nation to change course. To pray for a return to righteousness.

The word of instruction from God is clearly written in 2 Chronicles:

If My people who are called by My name will humble themselves, and pray and seek My face, and turn from their wicked ways, then will I hear from heaven, and will forgive their sin and heal their land.
—2 Chronicles 7:14 NKJV

There is hope for America when we take the positive action of prayer. God is still on His throne, and He will hear us and heal our land.

Prayer Proclamation for America

Father, God of Abraham, Isaac, and Jacob . . .
Your word declares that if we, your people,
who are called by your name, will humble ourselves and pray and
seek your face and turn from our wicked ways,
then will we hear from heaven and
You will forgive our sin and will heal our land.

—2 Chronicles 7:14

We bow before your throne and humbly ask your forgiveness for
the sin of idolatry!
Your word demands; "Thou shalt have no other gods before me,"
and yet we have, under the banner of pluralism and hedonism,
embraced and worshipped the gods of this world.
Take us back to the God of Abraham, Isaac, and Jacob!

—Exodus 20:30

Through moral and spiritual compromise and complacency,
we have allowed our nation to conform to the ways of the world
by turning away from our spiritual roots found in Your Word.

—Romans 12:2

Our silence has produced a secular nation
and all nations that forget you, shall be forsaken.
We ask that you hear our cry, for we need you
in these desperate times, to lead us out of our politically correct fog
of constant confusion and take us back to Your moral clarity.

—Psalm 9:17

O Lord our God, King of the Universe,
we confess that America cannot survive without Your presence.
Your statutes founded this blessed land and we look to You,
Father God, to preserve it, for "blessed is the nation whose God is
the Lord."

—Psalm 33:12

As commanded in Scripture,
we pray for all who are in authority who govern our nation;
may their decisions be led by the perfect compass
of your Holy Word, which clearly discerns right from wrong.

—1 Timothy 2:1–3

O Lord Our God, You have promised to raise up
righteous leaders into high places and to
remove those who have displayed unrighteous authority.

We earnestly pray that you will once again
exalt the righteous and expose the deeds of the ungodly.

—Proverbs 14:33–35

America must have spiritual renewal for moral survival!
In this season of prayer, we unite in humble, heartfelt hope
and ask that you forgive us and deliver us
from the folly of our transgressions.
Guide and sustain our nation as we turn from our sin
and return to you, the God of our Fathers.

—Psalm 51:1–17

The time has come to declare our trust in you to heal our land.

—2 Samuel 22:2–4; Psalm 5:11–12;
Psalm 57:1–3

We pledge to exercise our God-given rights of
"life, liberty and the pursuit of happiness" in voting for
future leaders from the county courthouse
to the White House who obey and honor Your Word.

—Deuteronomy 28:1–14; Psalm 119:44–
48; Psalm 5:11

We pledge to vote the Bible in selecting
those that will govern our country.

—Deuteronomy 16:18–20

Blessed are You, O Lord our God,
for you are good and your mercy endures forever.
We petition heaven with our united prayers as we seek
your blessing,
your peace and your protection for America.

—1 Chronicles 16:34; Numbers
6:22–26; Romans 15:13; Psalm 5:11

May the Lord, our God, be with us,
as He was with our forefathers;
may He not leave us or forsake us;
so that He may incline our hearts to Himself,
To walk in all his ways . . . that all peoples of the earth
may know that the Lord is God and that there is no other.

—Kings 8:57–60

Notes

CHAPTER ONE: ANATOMY OF DISASTER!
1 Gary Bauer, American Values, November 18, 2009.
2 FOXNews.com, November 18, 2009, as given during a one-on-one interview with FOX News' Major Garrett and the president.
3 Jeffery Flier, Op-Ed, *Wall Street Journal*, October 18, 2009.
4 Congressional Budget Office, Director's Blog, January 31, 2008, "Technological Change and the Growth of Health Care Spending," http://cboblog.cbo.gov.
5 Amanda Carpenter, *Washington Post*, September 28, 2009.
6 Daily Alert, daily newsletter prepared by The Jerusalem Center for Public Affairs for the Conference of Presidents of Major American-Jewish Organizations. dailyalert@list-dailyalert.org, September 10, 2009.
7 Paul Williams, "American Hirojima," World Net Daily, September 3, 2005.
8 Ibid.
9 Joseph Farah, "Iran Plans to Knock Out U.S. with One Nuclear Bomb," World Net Daily—G2 Bulletin, April 25, 2005.

CHAPTER TWO: IRAN IS READY FOR WAR!
1 "How the CIA Got It Wrong on Iran's Nukes," *Wall Street Journal*, Edward Jay Epstein, July 29, 2010.
2 James Risen, *State of War* (New York: Free Press, 2006).
3 U.S. Rep. Elton Gallegly, as printed in the *Jewish Journal*, July 26, 2010, "Iranian Sanctions Impact Depends on Waivers, Timing."

4 *USA Today,* August 13, 2010, as reported by the Associated Press.

5 Ibid.

6 Bloomberg Report, "Russia Opening Iran Nuclear Plant Helps Bid to Be Power Broker," Yuriy Humber and Lucian Kim, August 20, 2010.

7 Ibid.

8 Ibid.

9 Ibid.

10 Fox News, August 17, 2010.

11 Ibid.

12 Rowan Scarborough, "Bombers, Missiles Could End Iran Nukes," *Washington Times,* August 2, 2010.

13 William J. Broad and David E. Sanger, "Report Says Iran Has Data to Make a Nuclear Bomb," *New York Times,* October 3, 2009.

14 William J. Broad and David E. Sanger, "How Many Other Secret Nuclear Facilities Does Iran Have?" *New York Times,* September 30, 2009.

15 James Blitz, Daniel Dombey and Najmeh Bozorgmehr, "Iran 'Has Secret Nuclear Arms Plan,'" *Financial Times-UK,* September 29, 2009.

16 David E. Sanger and William J. Broad, "Atomic Agency Is Pressed on Iran Records," *New York Times,* August 26, 2009.

17 Matthias Kuntzel, "Ahmadinejad's Demons—A Child of the Revolution Takes Over, *The New Republic,* April 24, 2006.

18 Farhad Khosrokhavar, *Suicide Bombers: Allah's New Martyrs* (London: Pluto Press, 2005), p. 76.

19 Barry Rubin, *Paved with Good Intentions: The American Experience in Iran* (New York: Penguin Books, 1981), p. 303.

20 Martin Gilbert, *Churchill and the Jews* (New York: Henry Holt, Parliamentary Debates, April 13, 1933), p. 100.

21 Louis Weber, publisher, *The Holocaust Chronicle* (Publications International, Ltd.), p. 33.

22 Ibid., p. 36.

23 Ibid., p. 34.

24 Howard LaFranchi, "Iran's Ahmadinejad: US Used 9/11 to Prolong World Domination," *Christian Science Monitor,* September 23, 2010.

25 Alia Abrahim and Joel Greenburg, *Washington Post,* October 14, 2010.

26 Ben Dror Yemini, *First Gaza, Then the World*; War Propaganda Crimes; Moral Criminals; originally published in Hebrew, January 3, 2009 (*Maariv*); Steven Simpson, October 11, 2010 (Canada Free Press).

27 M. Sadeq Nazmi-Afshar, *The Origins of the Aryan People.* Iran Chamber Society: History of Iran. www.iranchamber.com/history/articles.

28 *Iranian National Socialist Movement (a History)* Part 2. Iranpolitics club.net/history/nazis2.

29 Mitchell Bard, *The Mufti and the Fuhrer; the Nazi/Islam Connection,* August 1, 2006. www.jewishvirtuallibrary.com/jsource/History.

30 Ibid.

31 Ibid.

32 Herman Rauschning, *Hitler Speaks* (Whitefish, MT: Kessinger Publishing, 2006), p. 234.

33 Qur'an 9:33, M.M. Ali; see also 48:28 and 61:9.

34 Don Richardson, *Secrets of the Koran* (Regal Books, 2008), p. 160.

35 Qur'an, Ishaq: 240.

36 Louis Weber, publisher, *The Holocaust Chronicle* (Publications International, Ltd.), p. 154.

37 USAToday.com, May 14, 2008.

38 Ben Dror Yemini, "First Gaza, Then the World," Smashingtruth .com, November 15, 2009.

39 Ibid.

40 Bruce Bawer, *While Europe Slept* (New York: Doubleday, 2006), p. 16.

41 Ibid., p. 103.

42 Ibid., p. 124.

43 Fern Oppenheim, "Monitoring Palestinian Incitement Is Not Enough," *Jerusalem Post,* April 11, 2010.

44 Dore Gold, "Saudi Arabia's Dubious Denials of Involvement in International Terrorism," October 1, 2003 (Jerusalem Center for Public Affairs), p. 12.

45 http://www.infoplease.com/ipa/A0001454.html#ixzz14VennoQL.

46 Ibid.

47 Sean Hannity, "Frightening Film on U.S. Terrorism Training Camps," Fox News, February 17, 2009.

48 Fred O. Williams, "Muslim TV Mogul Muzzammil Hassan's Alleged Beheading of Wife, Aasiya Hassan, May Be 'Honor Killing,' " *Buffalo News,* February 17, 2009.

49 FoxNews.com, "Westernized Woman Allegedly Hit by Dad's Car Dies," November 3, 2009.

50 Daniel Pipes, "The Danger Within: Militant Islam in America," *Commentary,* November 2001.

51 Support of this family statistic may be found at *All Experts Encyclopedia,* s.v. "Osama bin Laden," http://experts.about.com/e/o/os/Osama_bin_Laden.htm (October 3, 2006).

52 See Answers.com, s.v. "Osama bin Laden," http://www.answers.com/topic/osama-bin-laden (October 3, 2006).

53 Gary Bauer, "9/11 Plotters May Walk," American Values, November 13, 2009.

54 Ibid.

55 Ibid.

56 Ibid.

57 Joshua Rhett Miller, "New York–Based Muslim's Website Calls for God to 'Kill the Jews,' " October 13, 2009, Fox News.

58 Ibid.

59 Ibid.

60 Ibid.

61 Gary Bauer, "Jihad at Fort Hood," American Values, November 6, 2009.

62 Ibid.

63 Tarek Fatah, "The Significance of Hasan's Attire," *Ottawa Citizen-Canada,* Daily Alert, November 11, 2009.

64 Gary Bauer, "Jihad at Fort Hood," November 6, 2009.

65 Ibid.

66 Ibid.

67 Ibid.

68 Nick Allen, "Fort Hood Gunmen: Infidels Should Have Their Throats Cut," Telegraph-UK, November 8, 2009, www.telegraph.co.uk/news/worldnews/northamerica/usa.

69 Dana Priest, "Fort Hood Suspect Warned of Threats Within the Ranks," *Washington Post,* November 9, 2009.

CHAPTER THREE: IRAN'S PLAN OF ATTACK
1 Elaine Sciolino, "Showdown at UN? Iran Seems Calm," *New York Times,* March 14, 2006.
2 Dore Gold, *The Rise of Nuclear Iran* (Washington, D.C.: Regnery Publishing, 2009), pp. 11–12.
3 Alireza Jafarzadah, "The Islamic Revolutionary Guards Corps Use Universities for Research to Build the Bombs," Statement to National Press Club, Washington, D.C., March 20, 2006.
4 Therese Delpech, *Iran and the Bomb: The Abdication of International Responsibility* (New York: Columbia University Press, 2003), p. 113.
5 Con Coughlin, "Defiant Iran Begins Nuclear Production for 'Five Bombs,' " *Daily Telegraph,* September 13, 2004.
6 Philip Sherwell, "How We Duped the West, by Iran's Nuclear Negotiator," *Daily Telegraph,* April 3, 2006.
7 Ibid.
8 Michael Rubin, "Diplomacy by Itself Won't Work with Iran," *Investors Business Daily,* February 13, 2009, reproduced by Middle East Forum, February 14, 2009.
9 Dore Gold, "Iran's Nuclear Aspirations Threaten the World," *Los Angeles Times,* August 6, 2009.
10 Ibid.
11 Amir Taheri is the source of this famous Khomeini quote, the veracity of which was contested by Shaul Bakhash and Andrew Sullivan. Taheri has countered saying that the quote can be found in several editions of Khomeini's collected speeches like *Messages and Speeches of Imam Khomeini* (Tehran: Nur Research and Publication Institute, 1981). In subsequent editions, Taheri explains the quotation in question was removed, as Iran tried to mobilize nationalistic sentiment during the Iran-Iraq War. For the details on the debate, see Norman Podhoretz, "A Response to Andrew Sullivan," *Commentary Magazine—Contentions,* November 19, 2007.
12 Barry Rubin, *Paved with Good Intentions, The American Experience and Iran* (New York: Penguin Books, 1981), p. 303.

13 Mehdi Khaliji, *Apocalyptic Politics: On the Rationality of Iranian Policy* (Washington, D.C.: Washington Institute for Near East Policy, 2008), p. 26.

14 "Paper: French FM in Memoir—Ahmadinejad Tells European FMs in 2005 Meeting, 'After the Chaos We Can See the Greatness of Allah,' " he MEMRI Blog, February 2, 2007 (Source: al-Sharq al-Awsat, London, February 2, 2007).

15 Y. Mansdorf and A. Savyon, "Escalation in the Positions of Iranian President Mahmoud Ahmadinejad—A Special Report," MEMRI Inquiry and Analysis Series, No. 389, September 17, 2007.

16 Fox News, "Iran to 'Blow Up the Heart of Israel' If Attacked!" October 10, 2009.

17 Kevin Johnson, "Alleged Terror Threat Seen as 'Most Serious' Since 9/11 Attacks," *USA Today*, September 25–27, 2009.

18 Ibid.

19 Ibid.

CHAPTER FOUR: THE DAY AFTER THE BOMB

1 Ryan Mauro, "Paul Williams Details 'American Hiroshima,' " World Net Daily, September 3, 2005, accessed at http://www .wnDCom/news/article.asp?ARTICLE_ID=46127 on September 30, 2005.

2 Ibid.

3 Andrea Elliott, "Americans Recruited to Join al-Qaeda Linked Somali Terrorist," Daily Alert, November 24, 2009.

4 Basic facts of the blast radius, radiation factors, and basic procedures for self-preservation in a nuclear blast are taken in part from "The Day After: Action Following a Nuclear Blast in a U.S. City," *Washington Quarterly*, autumn 2007.

CHAPTER FIVE: DEATH OF THE DOLLAR

1 Thomas Jefferson to John Wayles Epps, 1813. ME 13:169; available at: http://etext.virginia.edu/jefferson/quotations/jeff1340.htm (accessed July 22, 2010).

2 EMAC's Stock Watch available at http://emac.blogs.fox business .com by Elizabeth MacDonald (accessed on October 12, 2010).

3 Ibid.

4   Ibid.
5   Ibid.
6   Ibid.
7   Ibid.
8   Ibid.
9   "U.S. is 'Practically Owned by China: Analysts-CNBC'," September 27, 2010, by Antonia Orprita, CNBC.com.
10 "China's Switch from Dollar Reserves to Gold," Energy and Capital.com by Jim Amrheim, June 21, 2010.
11 Ibid.
12 Ibid.
13 Ibid.
14 Ibid.
15 Bloomberg News by Artyom Danielyan and Emma O'Brien, September 8, 2010.
16 Dr. Jerome Corsi's Alert, World Net Daily, "420 Banks Demand One World Government," http://thesop.org/story/20101013/420-banks-demand-1world-currency.html (accessed October 13, 2010).
17 Ibid.
18 Ibid.
19 Craig Karmin, *Biography of the Dollar: How the Mighty Buck Conquered the World and Why It's Under Siege* (New York: Crown Business, 2008), pp. 100–101.
20 Menzie Chinn and Jeffrey Krankel, "Why the Euro Will Rival the Dollar," *International Finance* 11:1 (2008): 50.
21 Karmin, *Biography of the Dollar,* pp. 34, 101.
22 William Greider, *Secrets of the Temple: How the Federal Reserve Runs the Country* (New York: Simon & Schuster, 1987), pp. 254–255; Karmin, *Biography of the Dollar,* pp. 105–108.
23 John Steele Gordon, *Hamilton's Blessing: The Extraordinary Life and Times of Our National Debt* (New York: Walker and Company, 1997), p. 71; James Turk and John Rubino, *The Coming Collapse of the Dollar and How to Profit from It* (New York: Doubleday, 2004), pp. 47–49; Greider, *Secrets of the Temple,* pp. 228, 246–247.
24 Karmin, *Biography of the Dollar,* pp. 110–117; Greider, *Secrets of the Temple,* pp. 282–283; Turk and Rubino, *Coming Collapse of the Dollar,* pp. 53–55.

25 Turk and Rubino, *Coming Collapse of the Dollar,* pp. 56–57.

26 Karmin, *Biography of the Dollar,* pp. 118–119; Greider, *Secrets of the Temple,* 336; Austin Pryor, "A Dollar in Danger Leads Many to Gold," *Sound Mind Investing,* August 2009.

27 Greider, *Secrets of the Temple,* pp. 315–318, 324–325.

28 Karmin, *Biography of the Dollar,* pp. 120–124; Turk and Rubino, *Coming Collapse of the Dollar,* 57; Pryor, "A Dollar in Danger."

29 Greider, *Secrets of the Temple,* pp. 335–338; Karmin, *Biography of the Dollar,* pp. 125–127; Turk and Rubino, *Coming Collapse of the Dollar,* 58; Pryor, "A Dollar in Danger."

30 Greider, *Secrets of the Temple,* pp. 339–340; Turk and Rubino, *Coming Collapse of the Dollar,* pp. 171–172; Karmin, *Biography of the Dollar,* pp. 129–134; Pryor, "A Dollar in Danger."

31 Karmin, *Biography of the Dollar,* pp. 136–139, 144–146.

32 Robert J. Shiller, *The Subprime Solution: How Today's Global Financial Crisis Happened, and What to Do About It* (Princeton: Princeton University Press, 2008).

33 Karmin, *Biography of the Dollar,* pp. 146–147, 253.

34 Nelson D. Schwartz, "In Dollar's Fall, Upside for U.S. Exports," *New York Times,* October 19, 2009.

35 Article I, Section 8.

36 Quoted in Gordon, *Hamilton's Blessing,* p. vii.

37 Gordon, *Hamilton's Blessing,* pp. 61–65.

38 Ibid., pp. 80–81, 90.

39 Ibid., pp. 81–102.

40 Greider, *Secrets of the Temple,* pp. 284–285; Gordon, *Hamilton's Blessing,* pp. 103–107.

41 Gordon, *Hamilton's Blessing,* pp. 121–131.

42 Ibid., pp. 126–127, 132–134.

43 Ibid., pp. 134–136.

44 Data computed from the Office of Management and Budget, *Budget of the United States Government, Historical Tables.* www.whitehouse.gov/omb/budget/fy2009/his.pdf, table 1.1, pp. 21–27.

45 Martin Crutsinger, "Deficit Hits a Record $1.42 Trillion," Associated Press, October 17, 2009.

46 Jonathan Rauch, "The Government in 2008: 40 Years of Stability," *National Journal,* November 7, 2009.

47 Pryor, "A Dollar in Danger."

48 U.S. Office of Management and Budget, *Budget of the United States Government, Historical Tables.*

49 David M. Smick, *The World Is Curved: Hidden Dangers to the Global Economy* (New York: Portfolio Press, 2008), pp. 225–226.

50 *The Federal Government's Financial Health: A Citizen's Guide to the 2008 Financial Report of the U.S. Government,* pp. 7–8.

51 "Mountain of Debt," Associated Press, July 4, 2009.

52 Jeb Hensarling and Paul Ryan, "Why No One Expects a Strong Recovery," *New York Times,* November 20, 2009; Robert J. Barro and Charles J. Redlick, "Stimulus Spending Doesn't Work," *Wall Street Journal,* October 1, 2009; Tony Perkins, "Washington Update," Family Research Council, November 19, 2009; Heritage Foundation, "The Pelosi Blueprint for Government-Run Health Care," *Morning Bell,* October 30, 2009.

53 "Are Health Care Reform Cost Estimates Reliable?" Joint Economic Committee, July 31, 2009; Mortimer B. Zuckerman, "The 'Reform' That Ate America," *U.S. News & World Report,* December 2009; John M. Broder, "Climate Deal Likely to Bear Big Price Tag," *New York Times,* December 9, 2009. Original Dirksen quote, using billions instead of trillions of dollars, in Gordon, *Hamilton's Blessing,* p. vii.

54 Mortimer B. Zuckerman, "U.S. No Longer the Great Job Creation Machine," *U.S. News Weekly,* December 4, 2009; James Pethokoukis, "12 Reasons Unemployment Is Going to (at Least) 12 Percent," *Reuters Blogs,* November 11, 2009; Heritage Foundation, "The Road to Recovery Begins with the End of Obamacare," *Morning Bell,* December 3, 2009; George Melloan, "Why 'Stimulus' Will Mean Inflation," *Wall Street Journal,* February 6, 2009.

55 Sara Lepro, "Falling Dollar a Boost for Gold," Associated Press, October 7, 2009.

56 Turk and Rubino, *Coming Collapse of the Dollar,* pp. 29–31.

57 Ibid., p. 31.

58 Karmin, *Biography of the Dollar,* pp. 200–205.

59 Ibid., pp. 209–209, 223–225.

60 Joseph E. Stiglitz, "Death Cometh for the Greenback," *The National Interest,* November/December 2009; Karmin, *Biography of the Dollar,* pp. 231–240.

61   David Barboza, "China Urges New Money Reserve to Replace Dollar," *New York Times,* March 24, 2009; Breitbart.com, "Medvedev Sees Single Currency Dream in G8 Coin Gift," July 10, 2009; Malcolm Moore, "China Criticizes Dollar," *Telegraph,* July 10, 2009; Robert Fisk, "The Demise of the Dollar," *The Independent,* October 6, 2009; Jack Healy and Keith Bradsher, "Stocks and Gold Gain as Investors Shun the Dollar," *New York Times,* October 7, 2009; Eamon Javers, "Whodunit?: Sneak Attack on U.S. Dollar," Politico.com, October 8, 2009; Allen Sykora and Matt Whittaker, "Dethroning the Dollar: What If?" *Wall Street Journal,* March 30, 2009; Edmund Conway, "UN Wants New Global Currency to Replace Dollar," *Telegraph,* September 7, 2009; Turk and Rubino, *Coming Collapse of the Dollar,* pp. 195–198.

62   Helene Cooper, Michael Wines, and David E. Sanger, "China's Role as Lender Alters Obama's Visit," *New York Times,* November 15, 2009; Robert Kagan and Dan Blumenthal, " 'Strategic Reassurance' That Isn't," *Washington Post,* November 10, 2009; David M. Smick, *World Is Curved,* pp. 97–102, 115–116.

63   John Maggs, "It's Worse Than You Think," *National Journal,* November 7, 2009; Lawrence Kadish, "Taking the National Debt Seriously," *Wall Street Journal,* October 11, 2009; Paul Kennedy, "The Dollar's Fate," *New York Times,* August 29, 2009; Edmund Conway, "Is This the Death of the Dollar?" *Telegraph,* June 20, 2009; Niall Ferguson, "An Empire at Risk," *Newsweek,* December 7, 2009.

64   Robert L. Heilbroner, *The Worldly Philosophers: The Lives, Times and Ideas of the Great Economic Thinkers,* 5th ed. (New York: Simon & Schuster, 1980), pp. 290–292; Karmin, *Biography of the Dollar,* p. 243; Gordon, *Hamilton's Blessing,* p. 55.

65   John Maynard Keynes, *The Economic Consequences of the Peace* (London: MacMillan and Co., 1920), pp. 220–221.

CHAPTER SIX: THE REJECTION OF ISRAEL

1   The Declaration of Independence.

2   The inscription on the Statue of Liberty in New York Harbor given to America by France.

3   www.revolutionarywararchives.org/salomon.html.

4 Peter Wiernik, *History of the Jews in America* (New York: Jewish Press Publishing, 1912), p. 95.

5 Andrew McCarthy, *The Grand Jihad: How Islam and the Left Sabotage America* (New York: Encounter Books, 2010).

6 Mark Hemingway, "337 House Members Sign Letter Criticizing Obama's Israel Policy," *Washington Examiner,* March 28, 2010.

7 "Obama Hates Israel Because He Hates America," GrasstopsUSA .com Exclusive Commentary by Don Feder, June 15, 2010, p. 4.

8 The account of the children of Israel was taken from the books of Genesis and Exodus (NKJV).

9 Aish HaTorah, *Discovery* (Jerusalem: Arachim, 1995), p. 79.

10 Carmelo Lisciotto, "The First Nuremberg Trial." Holocaust Education & Archive Research Team. http://www.holocaustresearch project.org/trials/nurnbergtrial.html.

11 Ibid.

12 Ibid.

13 Ibid.

14 "The Nuremberg Laws," Jewish Virtual Library: A division of the American-Israeli Cooperative Enterprise, 2009, http://www.jewish virtuallibrary.org/jsource/Holocaust/nurlaws.html.

15 Carmelo Lisciotto, "The First Nuremberg Trial," Holocaust Education & Archive Research Team, http://www.holocaustresearch project.org/trials/nurnbergtrial.html.

16 "Nuremberg Trials Project," Harvard Law School Library, http:// nuremberg.law.harvard.edu/php/docs_swi.php?DI=1&text=nur_ 13tr; Scmidt, Dana, Adams. "Army Investigates Suicide of Goering as Mystery Grows," *New York Times,* October 17, 1946.

17 Ibid.

18 Ibid.

19 Dana Adams Schmidt, "Goering Note Said to Explain Suicide," *New York Times,* October 19, 1949; Carmelo Lisciotto, "The First Nuremberg Trial," Holocaust Education & Archive Research Team, http://www.holocaustresearchproject.org/trials/nurnberg trial.html.

20 Carmelo Lisciotto, "The First Nuremberg Trial."

21 Ibid.

22 "Last Laugh," *Newsweek,* October 28, 1946.

23   "The 13 Steps," *Newsweek,* October 28, 1946.

24   "Army Investigates Suicide of Goering as Mystery Grows," *New York Times,* October 17, 1946.

25   Ibid.

26   Ibid.

27   Christopher Lehmann-Haupt, "Books of the Times," *New York Times,* November 4, 1985.

28   Donald E. Wilkes Jr., "The Trial of the Century—And of All Time, Part Two" *Flagpole,* July 17, 2002, http://www.lawsch.uga.edu/academics/profiles/dwilkes_more/his34_trial2.html.

29   Personal interview with Rabbi Ariyeh Scheinberg; and "Ask the Rabbi" *Topic: Haman's Sons, Different Size Letters,* Ohr Shomayach. http://ohr.edu/ask_db/ask_main.php/228/Q5/.

30   Ibid.

31   Ibid.

32   Ibid.

33   Ibid.

34   Aish HaTorah, *Discovery* (Jerusalem: Arachim, 1995), p. 79 (referencing the Zohar—Vayikra 316).

35   Ibid., Aish HaTorah, *Discovery* (Jerusalem: Arachim, 1995) (referencing the Zohar—Vayikra 316).

36   "Chol HaMoed." National Jewish Outreach Program. http:www.njop.org/html/SukCH.html.

37   Aish HaTorah, *Discovery* (Jerusalem: Arachim, 1995), p. 78.

38   Personal interview with Rabbi Ariyeh Scheinberg.

39   Ibid.

40   Ibid.

41   E. W. Bullinger, *Number in Scripture: Its Supernatural Design and Spiritual Significance* (London: Eyre & Spottiswoode, 1921), available at http://philologos.org/_eb-nis.

42   Ibid., Genesis 14:4 (NKJV).

43   E. W. Bullinger, *Number in Scripture: Its Supernatural Design and Spiritual Significance* (London: Eyre & Spottiswoode, 1921), available at http://philologos.org/_eb-nis.

44   Aish HaTorah, *Discovery* (Jerusalem: Arachim, 1995), p. 78 (referencing *Mysteries of the Bible* a documentary produced by MultiMedia Entertainment, Inc., and A&E Networks).

45 "The 13 Steps," *Newsweek*, October 28, 1946; Aish HaTorah, *Discovery* (Jerusalem: Arachim, 1995), p. 79.

46 Abraham Sutton, *Pathways to the Torah* (Jerusalem: Arachim, 1987), at 54.40.

47 Melanie Phillips, *Londonistan* (New York: Encounter Books, 2006), p. xx.

48 Ibid., p. 189.

49 Paul Sperry, "The Pentagon Breaks the Islam Taboo," FrontPage Magazine.com, December 14, 2005.

50 Herbert Karliner, (first-person account) "Passenger Stories." The St. Louis Project. http://thestlouisproject.com/p=48.

51 Ibid.

52 Ibid.

53 Ibid.

54 Ibid.

55 *The SS St. Louis Project* (video available at http://thestlouisproject .com).

56 Conrad Black, *Franklin Delano Roosevelt: Champion of Freedom* (New York: Public Affairs, 2003), p. 490.

57 Ibid.

58 Ibid.

59 Ibid.

60 Jennifer Rosenberg, "The Tragedy of the SS St. Louis," 2009, The American-Israeli Cooperative Enterprise, http://jewishvirtual library.org/jsource/Holocaust/stlouis/html (1).

61 Robert N. Rosen, *Saving the Jews: Franklin D. Roosevelt and the Holocaust* (New York: Thunder's Mouth Press, 2006), p. 91.

62 Rosenberg, p. 1.

63 Rosen, p. 91

64 Ibid.

65 Rosenberg, p. 3.

66 Ibid.

67 Ibid, p. 4.

68 Ibid.

69 Rosen, p. 92; Black p. 404.

70 Rosen, p. 92.

71 Ibid.

72   Ibid.

73   Black, p. 493.

74   Rosenberg, p. 1.

75   "The Voyage of the *St. Louis*," HERMES, Columbia Business School, fall 2004, www.4gsb.columbia.edu/hermes/article/70794/The+Voyage+of+the+St-+Louis#.

76   Rosenberg, p. 2.

77   Black, p. 493.

78   Rosenberg, p. 3; Black, p. 493.

79   Ibid.

80   Rosenberg, p. 3.

81   Black, p. 494.

82   Ibid.

83   Rosen, p. 93.

84   Rosenberg, p. 7.

85   Ibid.

86   Ibid.

87   Ibid.

88   Jeff King, "Let Us Weep for Zion," *Charisma*. July 31, 2001, http://charismamag.com/index.php/features2/319-gods-love-for-israel/1271-let-us-weep-for-zion.

89   Black, p. 494.

90   Rosen, p. 95.

91   Ibid.

92   Rosen, p. 94

93   Ibid.

94   Ibid.

95   Black, p. 494.

96   William J. Vanden Huevel, "America and the Holocaust," *American Heritage* July/Aug. 1999, vol. 50, no. 4, http://americanheritage.com/articles/magazine/ah/1999/4/1999_4_34_print.shtml.

97   Black, p. 494.

98   Ibid., p. 3.

99   Vanden, p. 4.

100 "Gustav Schroeder." The Righteous Among The Nations. Yad Vashem   http://www1.yadvashem.org/righteous_new/germany_schroeder_print.html.

101   Black, p. 494.

102   Rosen, p. 103.

103   Rosen, p. 103; Marilyn Henry, "Voyage of the Damned," *Jerusalem Post,* July 20, 1998, http://holocaustforgotten.com/voyageofthe damned.htm.

104   http://www.ushmm.org/museum/exhibit/online/stlouis/search/bot new.htm

105   Black, p. 495.

106   Bernie M. Farber, "Voyage of the SS *St. Louis:* Journey Toward a Better Future," *Toronto Star,* May 27, 2008, http://www.thestar .com/printarticle/431217.

107   Ibid.

108   Ibid.

109   "Gustav Schroeder." The Righteous Among the Nations Yad Vashem   http://www1.yadvashem.org/righteous_new/germany_ schroeder_print.html.

110   Aljazeera.net, "Ahmadinejad: Wipe Israel Off Map," October 26, 2005.

111   Kenneth R. Timmerman, "U.S. Intel: Iran Plans Nuclear Strike on U.S., NewsMax.com, July 29, 2008.

CHAPTER SEVEN: THE CRIMINALIZATION OF CHRISTIANITY

1   Peggy Lamson, *Roger Baldwin, Founder of the American Civil Liberties Union: A Portrait* (Boston: Houghton Mifflin, 1976), p. 192.

2   Ibid., p. 192

3   Alan Sears and Craig Osten, *The ACLU vs. America* (Nashville: Broadman and Holman, 2005), p. 2.

4   *American Patriot's Bible,* ed. Dr. Richard Lee (Nashville: Thomas Nelson, 2009), pp. 1–12 .

5   Ibid.

6   Ibid.

7   Ibid.

8   Ibid.

9   Ibid.

10   Ibid.

11   Ibid.

12   Ibid.

13   Sears and Osten, *The ACLU vs. America,* p. 1.
14   Ibid., p. 1
15   Ibid., p. 16
16   Ibid., p. 3
17   Janet L. Folger, *The Criminalization of Christianity* (Portland, OR: Multnomah Publishers, 2005), p. 20.
18   Ibid., p. 23.
19   Ibid., p. 27.
20   Ibid., p. 25.
21   Ibid., pp. 101–103.
22   Ibid., p. 107.
23   Ibid., p. 156.
24   Ibid., p. 162.

CHAPTER EIGHT: BIBLICAL PROPHECY

1   J. Vernon McGee, *Thru the Bible, Proverbs thru Malachi* (Nashville: Thomas Nelson, 1984), p. x.
2   Ralph M. Riggs, *The Path of Prophecy* (Springfield, Mo.: Gospel Publishing House, 1937), p. 24.
3   McGee, *Thru the Bible, Proverbs thru Malachi,* p. 184.
4   Kyle M. Yates, *Preaching from the Prophets* (Nashville: Broadman Press, 1953), pp. 4–5.
5   McGee, *Thru the Bible, Proverbs thru Malachi,* p. 533.
6   Yates, *Preaching from the Prophets,* pp. 11–15.
7   Costen J. Harrell, *The Prophets of Israel* (n.p.: Cokesbury Press, 1933), p. 32.
8   Arthur W. Pink, *The Life of Elijah* (Grand Rapids, Mich.: Zondervan, 1968), p. 16.
9   John C. Hagee, *Prophecy Study Bible* (Nashville: Thomas Nelson, 1997), p. 397.
10   "Crime Trends by Population Group," www.fbi.gov, 2009.
11   Special 2001/9/11 memorial, www.cnn.com.
12   www.usatoday.com, September 16, 2010.
13   www.thedailygreen.com, September 21, 2010.
14   Charles Lane, *Washington Post,* June 24, 2005.
15   www.usdebtclock.org.
16   Ibid.

17 U.S. Religious Knowledge Survey, September 18, 2010, The Pew Forum on Religion and Public Life.

18 Cal Thomas, FoxNews.com, published September 28, 2010.

19 Hagee, *Prophecy Study Bible,* p. xii.

20 Yates, *Preaching from the Prophets,* p. 86.

21 Ibid., p. 89; McGee, *Thru the Bible, Proverbs thru Malachi,* p. 187.

22 Hagee, *Prophecy Study Bible,* p. 836.

23 McGee, *Thru the Bible, Proverbs thru Malachi,* p. 186.

CHAPTER NINE: WE ARE THE TERMINAL GENERATION

1 Robert J. Morgan, *My All in All* (Nashville: B and H Publishing, 2008).

2 CIA World Facebook, accurate as of January 1, 2009.

3 CIA World Facebook, accurate as of January 1, 2009.

4 Fareed Zakaria, "Why We Can't Quit," *Newsweek,* March 24, 2008.

5 Ibid.

6 http://en.wikipedia.org/wiki/Eliezer_Ben-Yehuda.

7 http://en.wikipedia.org/wiki/Russian_Jews#Mass_emigration.

8 www.boston.com/bigpicture/2010/05/disaster_unfolds.

CHAPTER ELEVEN: THE FOURTH REICH:
THE COMING ANTICHRIST

1 Damond R. Duck and Larry Richards, *The Book of Revelation* (Nashville: Thomas Nelson, 2006), p. 186.

2 Janet L. Folger, *The Criminalization of Christianity* (Portland, OR: Multnomah Publishers, 2005), pp. 163–166.

3 Ibid.

4 Ibid.

5 Ibid.

6 Walker P. Whitman, *A Christian History of the American Republic: A Textbook for Secondary Schools* (Boston: Green Leaf Press, 1939, 1948), p. 42.; Henry Halley, *Halley's Bible Handbook* (Grand Rapids, MI: Zondervan, 1927, 1965), p. 18; Gary DeMar, *America's Christian History: The Untold Story* (Atlanta, Ga.: American Vision, Publishers, 1993), p. 58.

7 *The American Patriot's Bible,* ed. Dr. Richard Lee (Nashville: Thomas Nelson, 2009).

8 Ibid.
9 *The Criminalization of Christianity,* pp. 163–166.
10 Ibid., p. 107.

CHAPTER TWELVE: ARMAGEDDON:
THE FINAL BATTLE FOR PLANET EARTH
  1 John C. Hagee, *Beginning of the End* (Nashville: Thomas Nelson, 1996), p. 153.
  2 Ibid., pp. 155–156.
  3 Ibid., p. 157.
  4 Ibid., p. 180.

CHAPTER THIRTEEN: HOPE FOR THE TROUBLED HEART
  1 James S. Hewett, ed., *Illustrations Unlimited* (Wheaton, Ill.: Tyndale House, 1988), pp. 289–290.
  2 Ibid., p .290.
  3 Ibid., p. 237.
  4 Hewett, ed., *Illustrations Unlimited,* p. 237.

CHAPTER FOURTEEN: HOPE FOR AMERICA
  1 Dr. Richard G. Lee, ed., *The American Patriot's Bible* (Nashville: Thomas Nelson, 2009), pp. i–10.
  2 Ibid., pp. i–10.
  3 Ibid., pp. i–11.
  4 James S. Hewett, ed., *Illustrations Unlimited* (Wheaton, Ill.: Tyndale House, 1988), pp. 398–399.
  5 Peter Marshall and David Manuel, *The Light and the Glory* (Grand Rapids, Mich.: Revell, 2009), pp. 367–368.

Reading Group Guide

This reading group guide for **_Can America Survive?_** by John Hagee includes an introduction, discussion questions, and ideas for enhancing your book club. The suggested questions are intended to help your reading group find new and interesting angles and topics for your discussion. We hope that these ideas will enrich your conversation and increase your enjoyment of the book.

INTRODUCTION

As an outspoken, conservative Christian leader, Pastor John Hagee heats up the debate about the intersection of American politics, Iran's nuclear capabilities, Israel's heritage, and the end of the world as we know it. Using biblical prophecy as his inspiration, Hagee issues a wake-up call to his readers, urging them to pay attention to the warning signs around us that the end of days may soon be at hand.

DISCUSSION QUESTIONS

1. In the opening pages of *Can America Survive?* Pastor John Hagee compares our country's complacency to that of travelers on the *Titanic,* who believed their ship "unsinkable," despite its having struck an iceberg (p. 4). Given the impact of the terrorist attacks of 9/11 and a series of widely publicized incidents that reveal our country is at risk, what accounts for our country's false sense of security? Do you agree?

2. "The only thing that can prevent the imminent nuclear attack on America, Europe, and Israel is to prevent Iran from becoming a nuclear nation. . . . America's government does not presently have the will to face down Iran with the military option." What are the international implications of a nuclear-armed Iran?

3. Pastor Hagee blames a culture of "political correctness" for the murderous rampage against soldiers at Fort Hood, Texas, which many believe was the work of a U.S. Army officer, Major Nidal M. Hasan, a radical Muslim. How might political correctness have abetted this heinous crime?

4. "The Islamic terrorist cells that have the ability to make and set off nuclear dirty bombs are not coming—they are already here. They are trained! They are ready! They are willing! *You* and your family are the targets!" (p. 68). How do you respond to Pastor Hagee's warnings? What steps have you taken or will you take to protect yourself and your country?

5. "The three major entitlement programs—Social Security, Medicare, and Medicaid—will consume 100 percent of the federal budget within the next sixty years, crowding out all other budget categories, including interest payments and national security." If you were president of the United States, what steps would you take to prevent

the economic and social crises our nation is facing? When the obligations of domestic programs threaten to overtake a nation's ability to defend itself, how should it proceed?

6. What does the dollar's potential loss of dominance to other currencies mean to the country's status as an economic and military superpower? How concerned are you about this possibility and why?

7. "An assessment of Hebrew Scripture in the book of Esther reveals signs that foreshadow the hanging of Hitler's Nazis at Nuremburg . . ." (p. 124). To what extent do you agree with Pastor Hagee's interpretations of Scripture? Which correlations made by Hagee between Scripture and contemporary history seem especially persuasive? Which, if any, seem more tenuous to you?

8. "America has rejected the truth of God's word. We have rejected God Himself, and all we have left is the secular humanist lie." In what ways has America as a nation departed from its Judeo-Christian foundations? Given that America was established by its founders as a democracy and not a theocracy, to what extent is this evolution in keeping with its formation?

ENHANCE YOUR BOOK CLUB

1. You've already read Pastor John Hagee's book. Now watch Pastor Hagee preach a sermon from the sanctuary of Cornerstone Church in San Antonio, Texas. Your book club can enjoy a sermon virtually, by visiting the website of Cornerstone Church and accessing a live webcast of a Sunday morning service. Live webcasts are available at 11 a.m. and 6:30 p.m. CST. Just visit: http://www.jhm.org/ME2/Default.asp and follow links to "Live Webcast."

2. Throughout *Can America Survive?* Pastor John Hagee revisits the biblical prophets who anticipate future events. Who were they? Have you ever experienced prophetic moments in your life, where something significant that occurred seemed to have been predicted days, months, or even years earlier? Write down some of the experiences you've had and the people you've encountered and share with your book club.

3. What do you already know about Iran that isn't reported in the evening news? Would you like to learn more about a country that may soon possess nuclear weapons? The CIA website offers a detailed compendium of information about the country's history, geography, government, economy, communications, transportation, and military. Visit: https://www.cia.gov/library/publications/the-world-factbook/geos/ir.html to read more.